Broken America

Broken America

David Cooper

iUniverse, Inc.
New York Lincoln Shanghai

Broken America

iUniverse books may be ordered through booksellers or by contacting:

iUniverse
2021 Pine Lake Road, Suite 100
Lincoln, NE 68512
www.iuniverse.com
1-800-Authors (1-800-288-4677)

ISBN-13: 978-0-595-37774-9 (pbk)
ISBN-13: 978-0-595-82150-1 (ebk)
ISBN-10: 0-595-37774-2 (pbk)
ISBN-10: 0-595-82150-2 (ebk)

Printed in the United States of America

Contents

1

Introduction

Broken America began as a few simple essays meant to be passed to a few close friends through e-mail discussions. As it became clear both my conservative Republican and liberal democratic friends wanted the same things for this country, but had very different ideas about where the country was and where the country was going, frustration set in. All my friends, conservative and liberal, lean towards the middle of their respective parties, as does most of the country. I have conservative friends who are pro-choice and liberal friends who hold gun permits. Why then is there this deep split, not just among my friends, but in the country as a whole?

The Program on International Policy Attitudes (PIPA) studies public opinion on international issues and is a joint program of the Center on Policy Attitudes (COPA) and the Center for International and Security Studies at the University of Maryland. The results of PIPA's studies over the last few years are astonishing. For instance, 70% of people who voted for George W. Bush in 2004 believed weapons of mass destruction had been found in Iraq, Saddam Hussein participated in the attacks of September 11th and Iraq actively supported al-Qaeda, none of which are true. These same people said they would not have supported the Iraq invasion if these things were not true. [1]

A whopping 94% of respondents to another PIPA study said the U.S. should limit its greenhouse gasses at least as much as other countries do on average and 44% said more than other countries do. This is consistent with the statement above that I believe people, whether Republican, Democrat or Independent, share a lot of common ground regarding where we as a country should be focused. The problem is 68% of these same respondents believe the U.S. is doing this. 73% of the respondents said the U.S. should participate in the Kyoto agreement to reduce global warming and almost half believe the president shares their view. [2] Not true. One of the first things Bush did in 2001 was to pull the U.S. out of the Kyoto agreement even though the U.S. had signed it in 2000. Only

52% of the respondents believe there is scientific consensus on global warming. The White House has consistently altered scientific data on this and many other issues, for ideological and political reasons, to create the belief there is not enough data to take action. [3]

In another study, PIPA found the vast majority of people believed the U.S. spends too much on foreign aid. When asked how much of the federal budget goes to foreign aid the average answer from the respondents was 20%, the high was 24%. When asked what is the appropriate amount of the federal budget which should be spent on foreign aid the average answer was 10% with the high being 14%. The percent of the federal budget actually spent on foreign aid is less than 1%. [4] People who believe that we spend too much on foreign aid, at the same time believe we should spend ten times what we are actually spending. As a percent of GDP the Millennium Development Goals call for the developed countries of the world to give seven tenths of one percent, of GDP which the U.S. agreed to in 2000. 77% of respondents approved with democrats being only slightly higher than Republicans. The majority of respondents believed the U.S. already meets this goal; in reality the U.S. spends less on the war on poverty (as a percent of GDP) than any other developed nation. Again, most people in this country do share a common ground. They just don't know it.

Yet another PIPA study found 70% of respondents oppose giving large corporate farms government subsidies and 74% approved giving small farmer's subsidies. What three quarters of the people, both democrat and Republican, believe should be policy is exactly opposite of what the government does. 80% of government subsidies go to large agri-business corporate farms and not just during bad years, but on a regular annual basis. Only 19% of respondents understood the effects of U.S. farm subsidies on poor farmers in poor countries. (Farm subsidies and their effect on not only tax payers but poor countries are discussed in detail in chapter eight).

The above studies suggest that the reason for the divide in this country is because the majority of people believe things that are not true. The next logical question, therefore, is why do people believe things that are not true?

According to the Pew Research Center, nearly 40% of Americans regularly get their news from the cable news networks with the majority of those tuning into Fox News (25%). [5] Fox is nothing but a mouthpiece for the conservative agenda. While there is no problem with that in and of itself, it becomes a problem when many of the claims made by the O'Reilly's, and Hannity's, and others on Fox, routinely distort, misrepresent and fabricate information. Media Matters for America is a non-profit research and information center dedicated to monitoring, analyzing, and correcting conservative misinformation in the U.S. media [6] and has found it to be a full time job reporting these inaccuracies. They also report the inaccuracies they find on CNN, MSNBC, the networks and on radio and in print, which include publications like the *Washington Post* and the *New York Times*, considered to be two of the most liberal publications in America.

The Pew Research study found 40% of Americans get their news from talk radio which is dominated 90% by conservative talk shows. Newspaper readership is declining with only 6% reading a newspaper other than their local paper.

Due to the deregulation of the industry, there are roughly ten mega-corporations that control over 90% of all mass media television networks, radio networks, newspapers, and magazines; [7] virtually everything we see, hear and read. In 1980 the number was 50. While General Electric, for instance, which is one of the big ten who owns NBC, they don't own all the local affiliates. There is a subgroup, if you will, that own an ever increasing share of the local outlets. One such corporation is Sinclair Broadcasting, owner of the largest chain of local stations in the nation that reaches 24% of all U.S. television households, and owns 62 local stations. During the presidential campaign of 2004 they ordered all of their ABC affiliates not to air the April 30th edition of *Nightline* because of Ted Koppel's intention to read the names of more than 500 soldiers killed in Iraq saying the episode was "motivated by a political agenda." However a few months later they ordered all of their 62 affiliates to preempt regular prime time programming to air a documentary that accused presidential candidate John Kerry of betraying American POW's during the Vietnam War. They also had no problems airing the controversial Swift Boat ads during the same time period. Not surprisingly, 98% of Sinclair's political contributions went to the GOP.

The importance of getting not only information, but accurate, unregulated, impartial news and information cannot be underestimated. It is the only way to hold our elected officials accountable. Without an educated electorate democracy doesn't stand a chance. Our Founding Fathers recognized this over 200 years ago when they charged us, the people, with maintaining the democracy they created for us. The media in this country is increasingly providing more and more infotainment and less and less information, creating a culture where we are the most entertained people on the planet but the least informed with regards to the actions of the government. The breakdown of our "mainstream" media does not relieve us of our obligation to question and to inform ourselves and does not give us an excuse to disconnect from the process. (The dissemination of information and our media is discussed in chapter 14).

The following pages are an attempt to make sense of the issues that have divided this country more than we've seen since the Vietnam War. To do this, I've spent the last year following the November 2004 elections pouring over thousands of pages of reports, memo's, statements, press conferences, etc. in an attempt to sort it out in my own mind. Many of these issues (not all), both domestic and foreign, have been covered in the "mainstream" media; however, there doesn't seem to be the follow-up they deserve. This isn't to say there are not individuals in the mainstream doing some good reporting; however, stories that don't meet some corporate or political agenda often fade from the front pages before they've had a chance to be fully explored, replaced by the story de jour. The Michael Jackson distraction, if you will.

It is beyond the scope of this book to examine every single issue affecting us today, so I have covered the one's that seem, to me at least, to be the most important. Many, I believe, should be on the front page of every major newspaper in the country, but aren't.

I have kept three things in mind throughout the writing of this book:

1.   What has this administration said

2.   What have they actually done, and

3.   Who has benefited.

I've tried wherever possible to use the words of the players themselves by quoting their memos, reports, and public statements. The one source not used is internet blogs. While the internet is becoming the last source of unfettered information, and there are many great blogs doing ever increasing amounts of "citizen reporting," (and I regularly visit many of them) anyone can post anything on a blog. Because people post everything from fact to opinion stated as fact, it can be an overwhelming task to verify a lot of the information posted on blogs, therefore it was preferable to use the words of the president and the people in and around his administration themselves.

At the end of *Broken America* is a list of publications and websites not owned by any of the big ten corporations listed above. These publications and websites not only use their own professional staff writers but utilize the services of contributing writers and columnists who are experts in taxes, foreign and domestic policies, economics, Social Security and Medicare and every other aspect of politics imaginable. No matter what the source, whether it's the official White House website or Fox news or government agency reports or one of the above publications or websites not owned by the big ten, all sources of quotes, reports, transcripts of speeches and news conferences etc. are listed in the end notes so the reader can access them and read them in their entirety.

I'm not suggesting people pour over thousands of documents, but it is not unreasonable to expect the average person to read a book by an administration insider like Paul O'Neill or Richard Clarke for example. Instead of watching CNN or Fox exclusively try *The News Hour* on PBS, funded by viewers not the big ten, once in a while. If we don't engage in the political process more than a couple of months every four years, we're going to find ourselves in a place the vast majority of us don't want to be.

I should note here; I am not a journalist or a political analyst; I have never taken a journalism class or a poli-sci class, but that should not, and it does not, preclude me or anyone else in this country from having a voice in our political debates, in fact it is the John Q. and Jane Q. Public's of this country who need to exert their influence to affect the changes needed.

As stated in the first paragraph *Broken America* began as a discussion among friends, both Republican and democrat, that forced me to dig for the answer to questions which were not being discussed in the "mainstream" media. The education continued throughout the writing of this book. I went where the facts took me, to a realization our democracy is in crisis and the underlying facts are not filtering down to the average hardworking, decent, middle class people that make up the backbone of this country. This is partly our fault for letting our guard down and allowing an extreme group to insert themselves into and manipulate our political process. They have done this with the help of an historical mistake (chapter five) and by leveraging staggering amounts of dollars.

We will either become overwhelmed by the entities currently holding the power and disconnect from the process at which time we will no longer be in control of our government which was originally established for the people by the people by our Founding Fathers, or we will heed the warnings of the Founders and re-assert ourselves as the owners of our government. The choice, or the consequence, is ours.

2

How did we end up here?

*"I'm tired of hearing it said that democracy doesn't work. Of course it doesn't work.
We are supposed to work it."*
Alexander Woollcott

The 2004 presidential election is over. It seems Bush has won a second term. The news programs are attributing the victory to the fact the Republicans were able to motivate their base to turn out in larger numbers than the Democrat's. They cite the exit polls in which 22% of those polled said moral values were their reason for voting (more than the economy, jobs, terrorism, or the war in Iraq). Only 4% said education. This theory started with the right wing talk show hosts Bill O'Reilly, Sean Hannity, Bob Novak, Rush Limbaugh and some others. As they tend to do, they said it over and over and over, until it bounced out of their echo chamber and into the mainstream media where it has become the official "reason" for Bush's victory. And most of the country will accept it. What has not gotten covered is the fact that our election process has been corrupted.

First, we need to go back to 1996. Chuck Hagel had a 1 million to 5 million dollar financial stake in The McCarthy Group, a private merchant banking company in Omaha Nebraska. A company called Election Systems & Software (ES&S) is a subsidiary of McCarthy Group. ES&S at that time made nearly half of all the voting machines in the U.S. and all those used in Nebraska. ES&S prior to 1996 was known as American Information Systems Inc. (AIS). Hagel was the Chairman for AIS until 1995. He was also president of McCarthy & Co. until the beginning of 1996. [1] Shortly after ES&S successfully negotiated with Nebraska to provide all the voting machines to the state, Hagel resigned and announced his candidacy for Senator of Nebraska. In his first ever run for political office, the voting machines his former company sold to the state showed he won overwhelmingly. He won almost all demographic groups including many largely black communities that had never before voted Republican. He was the first Republican in 24 years to win a Senate seat in Nebraska. [2] Six years later, in 2002, Hagel ran again against Democrat Charlie Matulka. He won the biggest landslide in Nebraska history with 83% of the vote. 80% of the vote was counted on ES&S machines.

This also happened in Georgia in 2002. Heavily favored in the polls, incumbent Democrat and Vietnam War hero Max Cleland, who lost an arm and both legs in Vietnam, was defeated by Saxby Chambliss on electronic voting machines that provided no paper trail. Chambliss sat out the Vietnam War on a medical deferment and ran on a platform that suggested Max Cleland was not patriotic enough to serve in the Senate. The victories of Chambliss and Hagel sealed Republican control of the Senate.

Matulka said, "This story is going to be bigger than Watergate ever was." [3] In a January 30, 2003 interview he said, "I suspect they're getting ready to do this all across the Country. God help us if Bush gets his touch screens all across the country, these corporations are taking over America, and they just about have control of our voting machines."

This is important because Hagel's Senate run in 1996 and 2002, the debacle of the 2000 presidential election and the 2002 midterms (in which there are many cases of vote fraud), were the beginning of conflict of interests and a criminal takeover of our voting process.

In Texas in 2002 another strange thing happened. Republican Senator Jeff Wentworth won with exactly 18,181 votes. Republican Carter Casteel won her state House seat with exactly 18,181 votes, and conservative Judge Danny Scheel won his seat with exactly 18,181 votes, all in Comal County.

In Alabama in 2002 initial returns from across the state showed incumbent Democratic Governor Don Siegelman won the governor's race with 19,070 votes. [4] Later Baldwin County election officials recounted and reduced Siegelman's tally to 12,736 giving the election to the Republican challenger, Bob Riley, blaming a "program glitch" in the software. "The governor claimed results were changed after poll watchers left," said Fox news. It was later learned the "glitch" was discovered by Republican National Committee regional director Kelley McCullough who "logged onto the county's municipal website and confirmed Siegelman had actually only received 12,736 votes, not the 19,070 the AP projected for him...If it hadn't been for one woman, the Republican National Committee's regional director Kelley McCullough, things might have gone terribly wrong for [Republican Gubernatorial candidate] Riley." [5]

Some more examples: After the election fiasco in 2000 the Help America Vote Act (HAVA) was passed. It called for the president to appoint, with the advice of the Senate, members to "the Election Assistance Commission Standards Board" to establish standards and oversee compliance of the law by voting machine companies. Its intent was to fix the problems of the 2000 elections. At the last minute the portion of the bill which required voter verified paper trail's was lobbied out, paving the way for the paperless machines we used in 2002 and again in 2004.

In 2003 Representatives Rush Holt (D-NJ) and Robert Wexler (D-FL) introduced legislation which would require all states to have a voter verified paper trail by the November 2004 elections, the Voter Confidence and Increased Accessibility Act of 2003 (H.R. 2239). It attracted more than 140 co-sponsors, more than half the House of Representatives. Republican leaders in the House, Tom DeLay and Denny Hastert, have kept this legislation from coming to a vote insuring there will be no possible audit of the votes of at least one third of the 2004 electorate. "I don't doubt that if this legislation came out and members of Congress heard the concern and the outrage that people have, this legislation would move and it would become law" Holt said. As of this writing it still has not seen the light of day. [6]

Jump ahead to 2004. We voted in arguably the most important election in at least two generations and it's turning out to be worse than the 2000 elections. In Franklin County, in Columbus, Ohio at the Gahanna precinct Bush received 4,258 votes to Kerry's 260. One would think this must be a very conservative little community. Maybe so, but the problem is the records show only 638 voters cast ballots in that precinct. [7]

In Warren County, Ohio officials locked down the county administration building on election night and blocked anyone from observing the vote count. The reason officials used: The threat of terrorism. Warren County Emergency Services Director Frank Young said he acted on information received from the U.S. Department of Homeland Security. *Cincinnati Enquirer* Attorney Jack Greiner said, "this is a process that should be done in complete transparency and it wasn't." WCPO-TV (Channel 9) News director said, "Frankly, we consider that a red herring, something that's put up when you don't know what else to put up to keep us out." [8] This is also against the law in Ohio.

In Cuyahoga County, Ohio, 30 precincts had more votes than there were registered voters. One precinct, Highland Hill Vil has 760 registered voters. There were 8,822 votes cast. That's a difference of 1,160.70%. In Woodmere Vil there are 558 registered voters. There were 8,854 votes cast. That's a difference of 1,586.74%. All totaled the difference adds up to 97,484 more votes cast than there are registered voters. And that's just in one county. [9]

During the 2000 presidential campaign, Florida's Secretary of State, Katherine Harris had the states voter rolls "scrubbed" so ineligible voters would not be able to vote. The job was given to a company called Choicepoint/DBT, whose board was made up of prominent Republicans. This was the first time any state had ever handed over regulation of its voter rolls to a private corporation. DBT produced a list of 58,000 names to be "scrubbed." With no regard for accuracy, Harris ordered the names to be removed. The Co-Chair of the Bush campaign in Florida ended up disenfranchising thousands of otherwise eligible voters, mostly black, who have historically voted democrat in the state of Florida. [10] If only 10% of the names on that list were on there in error, that's 5,800. Bush won Florida by only 537 votes. On November 26th, 2000 Katherine Harris, then Florida's Republican Secretary of State and Co Chair of Bush's campaign in Florida, certified the election and declared Bush the winner in Florida, effectively giving him the presidency. Katherine Harris is now Congresswoman Harris.

During the 2004 election cycle, CNN requested the Florida voter rolls presumably to see if history was repeating itself. They were denied. In early June 2004 CNN sued the state of Florida to obtain the voter rolls. Gov. Jeb Bush fought the law suit. CNN eventually won and when they obtained the rolls they discovered the improprieties of 2000 were in fact repeating. Thousands of black voters had been "purged" from the rolls, but interestingly only a handful of Hispanic voters had been removed. Hispanic voters historically tend to vote Republican, at least in Florida. This is disturbingly reminiscent of the racist tactics of the early 60's, when Lyndon Johnson signed the Civil Rights Act in 1964 and turned to an aid and said, "we've [Democrats] just lost the south for at least a generation." I wouldn't say all Republicans in the south are racist, but I suspect the majority of racist's in the south are Republicans to this day. Jeb Bush and Katherine Harris had gone a long way towards solidifying their base.

Throughout Florida, counties using the ES&S and Sequoia E-Touch voting machines showed an increase of actual votes over expected votes for Bush of about 29%. The increase of actual votes over expected votes for Kerry was about 24%. However in the counties using the Optical Scan machines manufactured by ES&S, Sequoia and Diebold the increase in actual votes over expected votes for Bush was 128%. The increase in actual votes over expected votes for Kerry were a staggering -21%. That's right, negative 21%. These are the state wide averages. In Liberty County there are 88.3% registered Democrats and 7.9% registered Republicans. The expected votes for Republicans were 237. The actual votes came in at 1,927, a 712% increase over the expected. The expected votes for Democrats were 2,667. The actual vote came in at 1,070, a negative 60% difference. [11]

There are literally dozens of examples, like the ones above, in county after county. Votes being lost in cyberspace or more votes being tallied than there are registered voters in a given precinct, faulty machines garnering dozens of complaints but kept in service all day, long lines due to there being fewer machines than there were in 2000 in a particular precinct, mainly in known Democratic areas, while adjacent precincts in the same county managed by the same county board of directors, in Republican areas, had more machines than in 2000. If done intentionally to create long lines then that would be a federal crime, violating the Voting Rights Act of 1965. And on and on it goes.

Another bizarre anomaly is the discrepancy in the exit polls. Exit polls early on showed John Kerry leading in almost all of the Battle ground states. In fact Karl Rove said on NBC's Meet the Press that early exit poll's on Election Day made him ill. Exit polls over the last fifty years have been extremely accurate. Instead of polling how people will likely vote, as is done in the weeks and months before an election, exit polling shows how people actually voted as they are leaving the polls. Americans have viewed the exit polls as a kind of confirmation of election results, a sort of standard to judge the legitimacy of their vote. This was apparent as late as the 2000 Presidential race when the major networks began calling Florida for Al Gore around 10:00pm the night of the election based on exit polls. They were confident in the historical accuracy of the exit polls. It later became evident there was a serious flaw, which caused them to retract their positions. This took them completely by surprise. I submit the Florida exit polls of 2000 were correct, based on the above examples and the 2004 exit polls were also correct and John Kerry won not only Pennsylvania, but Florida and Ohio as well.

For example, in states where paper balloting was used, the exit polls were very close to the actual vote count, within the margin of error. However, in states that heavily used the touch screens or the optical scanning machines, the exit polls were uncharacteristically skewed. New Mexico exit polls showed Kerry with approximately a 50% to 47% lead. The machine count was almost exactly opposite with Bush winning roughly 50% to 48%. New Hampshire's exit polls showed Kerry with a huge lead. Even though Kerry did carry New Hampshire, the machine count was within only a couple of points.

With the race being as close as it was, all the "experts" were saying it would come down to Florida, Ohio, and Pennsylvania. The assumption was Bush probably wouldn't win any of the states he didn't win in 2000 and Kerry wouldn't win any of the states Gore didn't win in 2000, therefore the winner would need two out of three of Ohio, Pennsylvania and Florida. On the morning of November 2nd, Tim Russert said whoever wins two of those three states will be the next

President of the United States. Exit polls in Pennsylvania showed Kerry with a huge lead, approximately 55% to 40%. The machine count had Kerry winning by just a couple of points. Ohio exit polls had Kerry roughly 52% to 47%. The machine count was almost exactly opposite with Bush winning roughly 52% to 47%. Florida was the same story as Ohio.

All of these things should be investigated however the Republican controlled Congress refuses to investigate. The voting machines and the use of them should also be investigated. When did we as a people agree to turn over our election process to private corporations? Corporations whose CEO's and top executives are open supporters of the incumbent party. Walden O'Dell, CEO of Diebold said in a 2003 fund raising letter for the Ohio Republican Party "I'm committed to helping Ohio deliver its electoral votes to the President next year." Corporations that claim their software codes are proprietary knowledge and therefore company secrets and only they can program their machines and retrieve the machine's information. They're doing the counting. And corporations that claim it would be cost prohibitive to have a machine produce a paper trail. We wouldn't walk away from our ATM machine after making a deposit without a receipt. Many of these ATM's are manufactured by Diebold. The machines that scan our groceries in the super market use the same technology used in the optical scan voting machines throughout the country, heavily in Ohio and Florida, yet we don't leave the grocery store without a receipt. We want to make sure we didn't pay .23 cents more than we were supposed to for that can of soup, but we'll walk out of the most important election of our lives knowing there's no way for a recount if the need should arise because there's no paper trail, which is in violation of Florida law. These corporations stand to make billions of dollars through government contracts-if the right people are elected.

On August 8th 2004, on CNBC's Topic A with Tina Brown, Bev Harris, author of Blackbox Voting, showed Gov. Howard Dean how to alter the votes that go into Diebold's Central Tabulators live on the air with a laptop computer. All the Diebold voting machines in a given county, for example, send their results to a central tabulator PC. A Microsoft Windows based computer, just like the one you're using right now. This is where any hacking would take place. Not at thousands of individual machines in a particular county.

Harris pointed out how Diebold uses a program called GEMS which she found on the internet while researching the 2002 Georgia election in which Max Cleland lost. "This is the official program that the county Supervisor sees" she said. She then instructed Dean step by step on how to open the GEMS folder and alter the numbers in a program similar to an EXCEL spreadsheet for a simulated election. When they closed the program and logged back in as an election supervisor would the program displayed the "new" numbers. "We just edited an election," Harris told Dean "and it took us less than 90 seconds." She also pointed out it would be nearly impossible for a county official to know the database had been tampered with. [12]

All of a sudden those damn exit polls, the one's that have historically been very accurate, are now looking problematic to say the least. Bush supporters call anyone who has questioned the outcome of the 2004 election "sore losers" and advise them to "get over it." The media in this country simply "corrected" their poll data and implied those questioning the results of the election were conspiracy theorists. Ironically, at the same time they were "reporting" on the fraudulent election in the Ukraine citing the exit polls. The Bush administration helped pay for the polling in the Ukraine (and in Georgia and Belarus) because of "the reliability of exit polling." During testimony before the House Committee on International Relations on December 7th 2004, Deputy Assistant Secretary of State for European and Eurasian Affairs, Ambassador John Tefft said the administration funded election observing efforts "to raise the bar for fraud by focusing our assistance in ways that would help to expose large-scale fraud such as parallel vote counts and independent exit polls." He then cited the discrepancy between the exit polls and the official vote count to argue the November 22nd Ukraine election was stolen. He also cited evidence of "illegal access to the Central Election Commission's computer system and illegally altered vote tabulation data."

The media has been very efficient in reporting the vote fraud in the Ukraine while all but ignoring an even greater amount of evidence the same thing is going on in this country.

What happened to us dropping our ballot in the non-descript grey metal box, without a corporate logo on the side of it, in front of a Civil Servant and volunteers from both parties overseeing the election process who count the votes and deliver them to election officials to be certified? I understand we are in the 21st century and I am confident we can use computers and technology in the voting process, but the process needs to be transparent and not for corporate profit, and not run by partisan hacks like Ohio's Secretary of State Kenneth Blackwell, or Katherine Harris in Florida in 2000. Any electronic machine chosen should, at the very minimum, provide a voter verified paper trail. And while it may prove very difficult to have a nation wide standard of voting because of the differences in laws from state to state, we should at least demand every state be uniform in its voting procedures.

Initially, only three members of Congress called for an investigation. On Nov. 5th John Conyers, Jr. (D-MI) Ranking Member of the House Judiciary Committee, Jerrold Nadler (D-NY) Ranking Member of the Subcommittee on the Constitution and Robert Wexler (D-FL) Member of Congress made an urgent request to the U.S. Government Accountability Office (GAO) to investigate "the efficacy of voting machines and new technologies used in the 2004 election." They also cited many of the troubling incidents written about here. On Nov. 8th they wrote a follow up letter to the GAO saying more than 30,000 complaints have been noted. They also had three more members of Congress sign on. Robert Scott (D-VA) Ranking Member of the Subcommittee on Crime, Terrorism and Homeland Security, Melvin Watt (D-NC) Ranking Member of the Subcommittee on Commercial and Administrative Law and Rush Holt (D-NJ) Member of Congress. As of yet no Republican members have come forward to support an investigation.

Unable to get an investigation in the Republican controlled house, John Conyers launched his own investigation. The goal was to prepare a status report before the joint meeting of Congress scheduled for January 6th 2005 to receive and consider the votes of the Electoral College. The report, along with its recommendations, was published in book form titled *What Went Wrong in Ohio*. It can be purchased at any of the major book sellers by anyone interested in the cold hard facts regarding the 2004 Presidential election. My copy cost a whopping $8.95. The evidence uncovered by the report is staggering and leaves little doubt that Bush's cronies did everything possible (illegally) to deliver Ohio to the President. It reads like a how-to manual for stealing a federal election. Using the instructions judges give to juries to only return a guilty verdict if the charges are proven "beyond a shadow of a doubt," one would have no choice but to return a guilty verdict after reading the Conyers report.

With this preponderance of evidence, there is still no investigation scheduled by Congress. One would think Republicans would want an investigation more than anyone else. Let's face it, a large number of people still think this President was not legitimately elected in 2000. We now have an election that is going to be viewed by at least half of the electorate as exponentially worse than the one in 2000. If I were accused of murder and I knew I was innocent, I would drag every shred of evidence I could think of to light to clear my name and my reputation. One would think the Republicans would want to legitimize the second term of this President who won by the narrowest margin of any incumbent in history and is talking about a mandate. Further attempts to block an investigation, by the

Republicans in Congress, should be viewed as a dereliction of duty and a cover-up.

Without a thorough investigation, all we are left with is a perception of impropriety and cover-up that is as dangerous as any real improprieties. Real improprieties can be dealt with to restore trust in the process. Only a thorough investigation can put the perception of impropriety to rest. Through investigations there will either be indictments and arrests, or impeachment, or exoneration. Trust in our election process is the only reason we abide by the laws of our elected officials. It's the only reason we trust our representatives to speak for us. Trust that we can remove them if they are not acting in our best interest. If the perception of impropriety, the perception that our election process has been corrupted, is allowed to stand, we will lose that trust. Then what? In 1801 Thomas Jefferson said, "That love of order and obedience to the laws, which so remarkably characterize the citizens of the United States, are sure pledges of internal tranquility." The only thing that keeps us from taking to the streets (internal tranquility) is the knowledge that we can remove politicians from office at our will.

Our founders foresaw potential threat to our democracy at some point in their future. They warned us to expect and prepare for "usurpation of power by people who care not a fig about your comfort." They understood the concept of absolute power corrupts absolutely long before the phrase became a cliché. Jefferson wrote about this numerous times.

1782. "We should look forward to a time, and that not a distance one, when corruption in this as in the country from which we derive our origin will have seized the heads of government and be spread by them through the body of the people; when they will purchase the voices of the people and make them pay the price. Human nature is the same on every side of the Atlantic and will be alike influenced by the same causes."

1787. "If once [the people] become inattentive to the public affairs, you and I, and Congress and Assemblies, Judges and Governors, shall all become wolves. It seems to be the law of our general nature, in spite of individual exceptions."

1812. "Unless the mass retains sufficient control over those entrusted with the powers of their government, these will be perverted to their own oppressions, and to the perpetuation of wealth and power in the individuals and their families selected for the trust."

1816. "No other depositories of power [but the people themselves] have ever yet been found, which did not end in converting to their own profit the earnings of those committed to their charge."

The founders also charged us, the people, to defend our own rights by staying informed and being participants in the process.

Jefferson said, "If a nation expects to be ignorant, and free, in a state of civilization, it expects what never was and never will be." Also, "There is only one force in the nation that can be depended upon to keep the government pure and the government honest, and that is the people themselves. They alone, *if well informed,* [italics added] are capable of preventing the corruption of power, and of restoring the nation to its rightful course if it should go astray."

The crimes against the American people began on Election Day 2000 with the theft of the Presidency and are continuing on a pace that will remove the Nixon administration from the top of the "most corrupt" list. The members of Congress who won't do their jobs by blocking further investigations (not only on vote fraud but many other issues) have to go before vote fraud becomes so widespread it will be impossible to get rid of them. The election reform legislation recommended in the Conyers report needs to be enacted immediately.

One last thought. If what we are seeing is the normal "bugs" and "glitches" of a fairly new electronic way of casting our vote, why then does virtually every one of these irregularities favor Bush. I'm not a statistician, but I would bet heavily the odds of that are astronomical.

3

The Real Reason for War with Iraq

"What a country calls its vital...interests are not things that help its people live, but things that help it make war. Petroleum is a more likely cause of international conflict than wheat."
Simone Weil

"In war, truth is the first casualty."
Aeschylus

There is a document, that's approximately ninety pages long, titled *Rebuilding America's Defenses*. (RAD) *Strategy, Forces and Resources for a New Century*, a Report by The Project for the New American Century, (PNAC), published in September of 2000 that everyone should be aware of. The RAD document is the topic of the next chapter, but first there needs to be an examination of the Project for the New American Century (PNAC) members. Many of them are currently serving in the George W. Bush administration. Many of them served in the Nixon, Ford, Reagan, and George H. W. Bush's White House. After leaving government during the Clinton years, some of them worked for a foreign government. All of these men are now back in the current George W. Bush administration. The one's that aren't specifically in the Bush administration are very much involved in an advisory position.

- Paul Wolfowitz—Head of the State Department's Policy Planning Staff from 1981-82 during the Reagan administration. Under Secretary of Defense for Policy under then Secretary of Defense Dick

Cheney from 1989-93 during the first Bush administration. Currently Deputy Secretary of Defense under Donald Rumsfeld.

- Richard Perle—Assistant Secretary of Defense during the Reagan administration. Currently Chairman of the Defense Policy Board, a Pentagon advisory panel.

- Donald Rumsfeld—Member of Richard Nixon's Cabinet from 1969-72 Chief of Staff and member of Gerald Ford's Cabinet from 1974-75. 13th Secretary of Defense from 1975-77. Currently Secretary of Defense.

- Dick Cheney—Special Assistance in the Nixon White House. Assistant to Donald Rumsfeld from 1974-75. White House Chief of Staff for Gerald Ford from 1975-77. Secretary of Defense during the first Bush administration from 1989-93. Currently Vice President of the United States.

- I. Lewis "Scooter" Libby—Department of State, Policy Planning Staff, Office of the Secretary 1981. Department of State, Director of Special Projects, Bureau of East Asian and Pacific Affairs 1982-85 during the Reagan administration. DOD, Principal Deputy Under Secretary for Strategy and Resources during the first Bush administration. DOD, Deputy Under Secretary for Policy During the first Bush administration. Currently Chief of Staff for Vice President Dick Cheney.

- Elliot Abrams—Assistant Secretary of State for International Organization Affairs during the Reagan administration. Indicted in 1991 by the Iran-Contra special prosecutor for giving false testimony to Congress in 1987 about his role in illicitly raising money for the Nicaraguan Contras. Pled guilty to two lesser offenses to avoid a trial and possible jail time. Pardoned by George H. W. Bush on December 25, 1992. (Merry Christmas). Served as President of the *Ethics* [emphasis added] and Public Policy Center in Washington D.C. since 1996. Special Assistant to the President and Senior Director for Democracy, Human Rights and International Operations 2001. Currently Director for Near East and North African Affairs at NSC. Includes Arab/Israel relations. Instrumental in running Mid-East policy.

- Richard Armitage—Deputy Assistant Secretary of Defense for East Asia and Pacific Affairs 1981-83. Assistant Secretary of Defense for International Security Affairs 1983-89 during the Reagan administration. In 1989 under the first Bush administration he was denied appointment as Assistant Secretary of Defense because of ties to the Iran/Contra scandal. Currently Deputy Secretary of State.

- William Kristol—Chief of Staff to former Vice President Dan Quayle. Editor of the Neo-Conservative magazine "The Weekly Standard." Chairman of the "Project for a New American Century." (PNAC). You may also recognize him from the Sunday morning news programs.

- Jeb Bush—Governor of Florida from 1998 to present. Brother of George W. Bush.

All of the persons above were signers of either PNAC's Statement of Principal's or other PNAC statements and letter's. The following "players" are important to understand how and why we are in a war in Iraq.

- Douglas Feith—Middle East Specialist at the NSC 1981-82. Transferred to DOD as Assistant Defense Secretary under Richard Perle during the Reagan administration. Currently the number three civilian at DOD as Undersecretary for Policy and head of Reconstruction Matters in Iraq under Donald Rumsfeld and Paul Wolfowitz.

- David Wurmser—State Department, Special Advisor to Under Secretary of State for Arms Control and International Security 2001-03. Office of the Vice President, Middle East Advisor 2003-present.

- Abram Shulsky—Served in the Pentagon under Assistant Secretary of Defense Richard Perle during the Reagan administration. Later joined RAND Corporation. Contributed to the PNAC document Rebuilding America's Defenses. Director of the Office of Special Plans prior to the invasion of Iraq.

PNAC was established in 1997 by a group of Neo-Conservatives who were ex-government officials during the Reagan/Bush years. Some held high government positions as far back as the Nixon/Ford years. By the early to mid 90's, after the fall of the Soviet Union, they saw the U.S as the preeminent Superpower and have been lobbying for U. S. domination of the world ever since.

Their plan urges the redrawing of the map in the Middle East and was actually written in 1996, during the Clinton years, while the men above were out of government. Richard Perle and Douglas Feith participated in a report titled *A Clean Break: A New Strategy for Securing the Realm* (ACB) that was going to advise newly elected Israeli Prime Minister Benjamin Netanyahu. Richard Perle was the study group leader. The Perle study group was set up by The Institute for

Advanced Strategic and Political Studies, an Israeli based Think Tank where David Wurmser was working.

ACB starts out urging Netanyahu to "Work closely with Turkey and Jordan to destabilize and roll back" Israel's neighboring Arab enemies, to "Change the nature of its relationship with the Palestinians, including upholding the *right of hot pursuit* [emphasis in original document] into all Palestinian areas" and to "Forge a new basis for relations with the United States-stressing self-reliance." Israel, it says, "can manage its own affairs. Such self-reliance will grant Israel greater freedom of action and remove a significant lever of pressure used against it in the past." Perle, Feith and Wurmser were advising Netanyahu to get the United States to pull out of the Arab-Israeli conflict so the Israelis could deal with the Palestinian "problem" as they saw fit.

The plan goes on to call for "reestablishment of preemption" and unprovoked strikes against Syria and Iran. "An effective approach would be if Israel seized the strategic initiative along its northern borders by engaging Hizballah, Syria and Iran, as the principal agents of aggression in Lebanon, including by: Establishing the precedent that Syrian territory is not immune to attacks emanating from Lebanon by Israeli proxy forces. Striking Syrian military targets in Lebanon, and should that prove insufficient, *striking at select targets in Syria proper.*" [Emphasis in original document] The ultimate goal would be toppling Iraq and installing a puppet government that would be friendly to Israel. "This effort [rolling back Syria] can focus on removing Saddam Hussein from power in Iraq [Syria's ally]-an important Israeli strategic objective in its own right-as a means of foiling Syria's regional ambitions...It would be understandable that Israel has an interest in supporting the Hashemites in their effort to redefine Iraq"

The document discusses how to gain support from the world, the American Government, and more importantly, the American people for the waging of regional war in the Middle East they were advocating. "To anticipate U.S. reactions and plan ways to manage and constrain those reactions, Prime Minister Netanyahu can formulate the policies and stress themes he favors in language familiar to the Americans by tapping into themes of American administrations during the Cold War which apply well to Israel. If Israel wants to test certain propositions that require a benign American reaction, then the best time to do so is before [The Presidential election] November, 1996." They point out:

- "Israel can take this opportunity to remind the world that Syria repeatedly *breaks* [emphasis in original document] its word.

- Syria has killed "tens of thousands of its own citizens

- Syria's *regime* supports the terrorists

- The *Syrian controlled Bekaa Valley in Lebanon has become for terror what the Silicon Valley has become for computers."* [Emphasis in original document]

- It is both natural and moral that Israel abandons the slogan 'comprehensive peace' and moves to contain Syria, *drawing attention to its weapons of mass destruction program."*

The first part of the ACB document which discusses withdrawal of the U.S. from the Arab-Israeli conflict was implemented in the first two weeks of the Bush administration. This was *the* first policy decision of the Bush administration. On January 30, 2001, ten days after Bush's inauguration, he gathered his new cabinet and stated "We're going to correct the imbalances of the previous administration on the Middle East conflict. We're going to tilt it back toward Israel." He also said, "If the two sides don't want peace, there's no way we can force them." After a short dialog with the meeting members, he said, "I don't see much we can do over there at this point. I think it's time to pull out of that situation." Colin Powel stressed that a pullback by the U.S. would unleash Sharon and the Israeli Army and "The consequences could be dire." Bush's response was, "sometimes a show of strength by one side can really clarify things." The conversation then turned to Iraq. Powel seemed stunned. And that was it. The U.S. would disengage from the Arab-Israeli conflict, a problem every President since Eisenhower considered paramount, to bring stability to the Middle East, through out their respective presidencies. Secretary of the Treasury Paul O'Neill who attended the meeting said, "ten days in and it was about Iraq." [1] He also thought "the dialog today had been mostly about the *hows*" and "when exactly, the *whys*-why Saddam, why now, and why this was central to U.S. interests-were to be discussed." [2] And "From the start, we were building the case against Hussein and looking at how we could take him out...It was all about finding *a way to do it.* [Emphasis in original] That was the tone of it. The President saying, 'Go find me a way to do this.'" [3] Five years after it was written for a foreign government, the ACB plan was now in motion.

The portions of ACB that advised Netanyahu of how to gain support from America for war is almost verbatim of the rhetoric the American people heard just before the March 2003 invasion of Iraq by the Bush administration. If you replace the word Syria with Iraq, it's chilling.

- [Iraq] repeatedly breaks its promises. Bush spoke of Iraq continually breaking its promise of U.N Security Council Resolutions of letting weapons inspectors in. Not true. After the Bush administrations demand that Iraq allow inspections to resume, in September of 2002 Saddam agreed to let inspectors back in, without conditions, and they did go in. Before their work could be completed, Bush gave them two weeks to evacuate in early 2003. They weren't going to find any WMD. A report by Tel Aviv University's Jaffee Center for Strategic Studies said, "Why did he [Saddam Hussein] not do everything possible to convince Western governments that he was 'clean,' retaining no weapons of mass destruction? The answer is that from Saddam's perspective, he did do everything to respond to every whim of UNMOVIC [the U.N. inspectors], but to no avail, since the real aim of the United States was regime change and not Iraq's disarmament of weapons of mass destruction."

- [Iraq] has killed tens of thousands of its own people. True. In the 80's during the Reagan-Bush administration, at a time when Iraq was our ally, and supported by the U.S. in its war against Iran they did use chemical weapons on thousands of Iranians and their own people. Weapons we provided to them and allowed them to posses. The helicopters used to deliver those chemicals were provided by the U.S.

- [Iraqi regime] supports terrorism. False. The 9/11 commission has found no evidence Saddam Hussein supported al Qaeda. In fact it is widely known that Usama bin Laden * was a threat to Saddam's power. Usama [a Wahhabi Muslim] issued a decree calling for Sadam's death. He considered Saddam an infidel and a thug and an oppressor of Muslim's. Saddam [a Sunni Muslim] reciprocated by issuing a decree of his own calling for Usama's death. Usama, he believed, was a religious zealot who wanted to return the Muslim world to a 14th century style theocracy.

- [Iraq] has weapons of mass destruction. Not true. We all now know that wasn't true. Those statements were designed to gain support for an invasion as per ACB. When no WMD were found, the reason for the war morphed into Saddam had the *capability* to manufacture WMD. Again not true. Seven months before 9/11, on February 24 2001, in Chiro Secretary of State Colin Powel said, "He [Saddam Hussein] has not developed any significant capability with respect to weapons of mass destruction. He is unable to project conventional power against his neighbors." He went on to say it was the U.S. policy of containment that had effectively disarmed the Iraqi dictator. On May 15 2001 Powel said Saddam had not been able to "build his military back up to or to develop WMD for the last ten years." America, he said, had been successful in keeping him "in a box." Two months later, Condoleezza Rice said, "Saddam does not control the northern part of the country," "we are able to keep his arms from him. His military forces have not been rebuilt." They were both proven right. We all watched on CNN as the invasion started and the U.S. Army was outside of Baghdad in about a week.

When it became clear Saddam didn't even have the capability to manufacture WMD, the reason for invading Iraq morphed once again. He was a brutal dictator who killed his own people and threatened the region. The U.S. was going to bring democracy. "Freedom is on the march." That sounds a lot like a Nation Building policy. On October 11, 2000 during the Presidential debate with Al Gore, then Governor Bush said, "I don't think our troops should be used for what's called 'nation building.'" A little later in the same debate he said, "I am worried about over committing our military around the world. I want to be judicious in its use. [To Jim Lehrer] You mentioned Haiti. I wouldn't have sent troops to Haiti. It was a nation building mission. And it was not very successful. It cost us billions." And "I'm going to be judicious as to how to use the military. It needs to be in our vital interest. The mission needs to be clear, and the *exit strategy obvious.*"

If we're going to use the "brutal dictator" criteria, then we'll have to take out the governments of Saudi Arabia and China, which are arguably, two of the worst violators of human rights in the world. Then there are Iran and Syria. Iran will probably be next. We can't forget North Korea, one of "the Axis of Evil." There has to be a few countries in South and Central America that probably fit the criteria, and while we're in this hemisphere, we might as well take out Cuba. And then there's Pakistan. General Pervez Musharraf was in the U.S. on December 4, 2004. At the White House President Bush said that Pakistan is an ally on the war on "terra". He said, "People don't think a Muslim country can be anything but a tyranny and the People of Pakistan have proven the cynics wrong." Mr. Bush needs a lesson in recent history. Musharraf seized control of Pakistan in a military Coup in 1999 when he ousted *elected* Prime Minister Nawaz Sharif. He has refused to relinquish command of the armed forces. Hence the reason his title remains "General" Musharraf. He is a military dictator that oppresses his people.

He pushed through a Constitutional amendment without parliamentary approval known as the Legal Framework Order (LFO) that gave him the power to sack the Prime Minister, dissolve parliament and recognize himself as both head of the Army and head of state. He was not elected, and there are no elections scheduled any time soon. While Bush was singing Musharraf's praises, the military dictator recently went on the record and criticized the U.S. for not providing enough troops on the Afghan/Pakistan border to capture or even locate Usama bin Laden. The Pakistanis have all but given up the search.

In the Presidential debates of 2004 with John Kerry, Bush, while speaking of his record on terrorism, said the A. Q. Khan terrorist network in Pakistan had been broken up and brought to justice. A. Q. Kahn is Dr. Abdul Qadeer Kahn, considered to be the father of Pakistan's nuclear program. (Yes, Pakistan has nuclear weapons and the capability to deliver them) His network is believed to have given nuclear technology to Iran, Libya, and North Korea, violating all kinds of *stuff*. He enjoys a larger popularity rating than Musharraf. After a recent attempt on Musharraf's life, it was believed that, had the attempt been successful, Dr. Khan could have become President of Pakistan. Not only was A. Q. Khan's network not broken up, nor has anyone in the network ever been *brought to justice*, as Bush said, but Musharref has pardoned Dr. Khan of any crimes. Also Musharraf has refused any attempt by U.S. officials or the International Atomic Energy Agency (IAEA) to interview Dr. Khan, insisting questions be passed through Pakistani officials. This filtering of questions is believed to be designed to avoid any duplicity by the Musharraf government in the turning over of nuclear technology to Iran, Libya, and North Korea.

There are only three conclusions to come to regarding Bush's statements about Pakistan, recently, and A. Q. Khan, during the debates.

1. He doesn't know the facts or doesn't understand them, which makes him stupid.

2. He doesn't think people will bother to look the facts up, which means he thinks we're stupid. Or

3. He's a liar and doesn't care what we think, and will say these things knowing his base will blindly follow.

In October, just before the 2004 Presidential election, the Iraqi Survey Group released its report saying Iraq eliminated its weapons programs in the 90's. The reason for war began to morph again. It has yet to hit the mainstream media, but it is bouncing around in the right wing echo chamber on the right wing cable shows like Fox's *The O'Reilly Factor* with Bill O'Reilly and on Sean Hannity, and right wing talk radio shows like Rush Limbaugh. It's the Oil for Food program angle, and it's coming to a mainstream network near you soon.

The Oil for Food program began in 1996. The U.N. allowed Iraq to sell oil to certain companies through vouchers that sanctions would otherwise prohibit. There were 4,734 of them worldwide, according to a U.N. appointed investigation headed by former U.S. Federal Reserve Chairman Paul A. Volcker. The proceeds were to be used to provide food and medicine for the Iraqi people who were suffering under post Gulf War sanctions since 1990. Not surprisingly, a lot of the money ended up in Saddam's coffers through skimming and kickbacks. Some estimates put the figure as high as 21 billion dollars. According to the list, four U.S. companies were allowed to participate in the Oil for Food program, Exxon Mobile which purchased $152 million, Texaco purchased $28.3 million, Chevron bought $140.2 million, and Phoenix which bought $162.25 million of Iraqi crude. So far there is no indication that any of the 4000 plus companies, on the list, did anything illegal in trading with Iraq through the program. Accusations on the right wing talk shows have been flying that Iraq bribed U.N. member countries (which have companies participating in the Oil for Food program) to oppose U.N. sanctions, specifically, France and Germany. As yet, there is no evidence of this. The insinuation is the U.S. had no choice but to stop the hemorrhaging of dollars to Saddam caused by U.N. corruption. What they aren't saying is there is evidence that the majority of the money Saddam stole, which some estimates put as high as 15 billion of the 21 billion, came from oil smuggled out of Iraq by truck and pipeline to Turkey and Jordan, both of whom are U.S. allies, prior to 1996, before the oil for food program began, which the U.S. and Great Britain were well aware of. The U.S. and Great Britain were the prime enforcers of the U.N. sanctions throughout the 90's. U.N. Secretary General Kofi Annan said, "We had no mandate to stop oil smuggling. There was a maritime task force that was supposed to do that. They were driving trucks through northern Iraq to Turkey. The U.S. and the British had planes [in the northern no fly zone] in the air. We [the U.N.] were not there." The right wing pundits are getting right in line with the RAD program, which we will see, seeks to undermine U.N. authority.

This is still a breaking story, and the scandal will be investigated, as well it should. It would best be left to another discussion at a later date.

The reasons given to the American people for the invasion of Iraq have changed so many times it's hard to keep up with. It started with Iraq being able to spread toxic chemicals over U.S. cities, among other terrible things, to Saddam was corrupt. We've been sold a Ferrari, but we received a Hyundai.

The Clean Break plan was authored by former very high level American government officials. Benjamin Netanyahu wisely rejected the plan at the time. However three things have happened to allow this plan to be dusted off and implemented.

First, a receptive George W. Bush was elected President in 2000. Most of the men above, and the authors of the ACB and RAD documents, after an eight year hiatus during the Clinton administration, would soon be taking their place in the highest levels of government once again. Is it co-incidence that all of these men are now back in this place at this point in time?

Second, in 2000 a receptive Arial Sharon, a Likud Party hardliner when it comes to the Arab situation in general and the Palestinian situation specifically, is now the Prime Minister of Israel.

And third, the attacks of September 11, 2001. They were determined to get their war with Iraq, with or without 9/11. The 9/11 attack allowed them to go directly, do not pass go, to Iraq, circumventing Syria and Iran. However, transforming the military into a military they envision for world domination would have been difficult without 9/11. In the 90 page document, *Rebuilding America's Defenses* (RAD), they write "the process of transformation [of the military] is likely to be a long one, absent some catastrophic and catalyzing event-like a new Pearl Harbor."

Although they did have to alter the plan slightly and go to Afghanistan first, because that's where Usama and al-Qaeda were, and that's what the American people were expecting. The American people and the world were united behind the Bush administration in the Afghan operation. However, Afghanistan was nothing more than a speed bump for them. Afghanistan was a token response by the Neo-Cons and the job there remains unfinished to this day.

On the morning of September 12 2001, Richard Clarke, the administration's Counterterrorism Czar, walked into a meeting in the West Wing of the White House. Kept on from the Clinton administration, he had written a plan (In January 2001) for the incoming Bush administration for strikes against al-Qaeda which sat collecting dust for almost eight months. He thought "Now we have the full attention of the bureaucracies and the full support of the President." He said, "I expected to go back to a round of meetings examining what the next attacks could be, what our vulnerabilities were, what we could do about them in the short term. Instead, I walked into a series of discussions about Iraq. At first I was incredulous that we were talking about something other than getting al-Qaeda.

Then I realized with almost a sharp physical pain that Rumsfeld and Wolfowitz were going to try to take advantage of this national tragedy to promote their agenda about Iraq. Since the beginning of the administration, indeed well before, [The ACB document and the RAD document were little known by most at the time, but Clarke would have known about them] they had been pressing for a war with Iraq. My friends in the Pentagon had been telling me that the word was we would be invading Iraq sometime in 2002." Later, on the evening of the 12th he said, "I left the video conferencing Center and there, wandering alone around the Situation Room, was the President. He grabbed a few of us and closed the door to the conference room. 'Look,' he told us, 'I know you have a lot to do and all…but I want you, as soon as you can, to go back over everything, everything. See if Saddam did this. See if he's linked in any way…' I was once again taken aback, incredulous, and it showed. But, Mr. President, al-Qaeda did this." "I know, I know, just look, I want to know any shred…" the President said. Clarke agreed to look again. "You know, we have looked several times for state sponsorship of al-Qaeda and not found any linkages to Iraq. Iran plays a little, as does Pakistan, and Saudi Arabia" "'Look into Iraq, Saddam'" the President said testily and left us." [4]

Discussing the Clinton administration officials briefing of the incoming Bush administration officials, the 9-11 Commission's March 24, 2004 Staff Report says, "Clarke asked on several occasions for early Principals Committee meetings on these issues [outlined in his January 25, 2001 memo] and was frustrated that no early meeting was scheduled. He wanted principals to accept that al Qaeda was a 'first order threat' and not a routine problem being exaggerated by 'chicken little alarmists.' No Principals Committee meetings on al Qaeda were held until September 4, 2001. The Principals Committee did meet frequently before 9-11 on other subjects, Rice told us, including Russia," Iraq and missile defense. (9-11 Commission, Staff Statement Number 8, "National Policy Coordination," pp 9-10).

On April 30, 2001, CNN reported, "unlike last year [during the Clinton administration], there's no extensive mention of alleged terrorist mastermind Osama bin Laden. A senior [Bush administration] official tells CNN the U.S. government [under Clinton] made a mistake in focusing so much energy on bin Laden and 'personalizing terrorism.'" [5] It was the Clinton administration's #1 priority. Besides overthrowing Saddam and missile defense, the new administration moved tax cuts for the rich, gutting the EPA, and privatizing Medicare and social security to the top of the agenda. Terrorism from non state sponsored groups like al-Qaeda fell to about six or seven on the priority list.

On the morning of September 11, 2001 National Security Advisor Condoleezza Rice was scheduled to give a major speech outlining President Bush's national security priorities. The speech was designed to promote missile defense as the cornerstone of a new national security strategy, and contained no mention of al Qaeda, Usama bin Laden or Islamic extremist groups. The speech was never given, for obvious reasons. [6]

The RAD report advocates the U.S. pull out of the Anti Ballistic Missile (ABM) Treaty of 1972, allowing the U.S. to resurrect the Reagan era Strategic Defense Initiative (SDI), or Starwars program. It also advocates nuclear expansion. "Of all the elements of U.S. military force posture, perhaps none is more in need of reevaluation than America's nuclear weapons. Nuclear weapons remain a critical component of American military power but it is unclear whether the current U.S. nuclear arsenal is well suited for the emerging post—Cold War world...there may be a need to develop a new *family* [emphasis added] of nuclear weapons designed to address new sets of requirements, such as would be required in targeting the very deep underground, hardened bunkers that are being built by many of our potential adversaries." The RAD report is not talking about nuclear weapons as we knew them in the 60's and 70's. Weapons that were deterrent, in the sense that both the U.S. and the Soviet Union knew the other side could cause "mutual destruction" and therefore neither side was willing to use them. The RAD report is discussing tactical nuclear weapons (AKA battlefield nuke's) that could potentially be used, as it says, against "deep underground bunkers." Make no mistake; these are not deterrent strategic nuclear weapons they are talking about.

In 1964, while a student doing his dissertation in the Political Science department at the University of Chicago, Paul Wolfowitz met a professor by the name of Albert Wohlstetter. Wolfowitz admired Wohlstetter's intellect and began working under his supervision to carry his ideas further. Before teaching at the University of Chicago, Wohlstetter had been an analyst at project RAND since 1949. RAND was started as a division in the Douglas Aircraft Corporation as a platform to connect research and development with military planning. It is a think tank which provides tools to government decision makers by analyzing every possible scenario and outcome of possible conflicts. Their job is to think the unthinkable. At least one of Wohlstetter's colleague's at RAND, Herman Kahn, believed a nuclear war with the Soviet Union was winnable. Do Wohlstetter and Wolfowitz share this view?

As we've seen, the Bush administration, before 9-11, was repeatedly warned about non-state sponsored organizations such as al Qaeda. Their focus was on

Empire building (and still is) as per the RAD philosophy. The real threat posed by terrorist organizations is not hi-tech long range weapons systems. A missile defense system would not have protected us from the attacks of 9-11. Before 9-11, and before the RAD document was published, al Qaeda, whom the Bush administration was warned about, used very low-tech fertilizer bombs to simultaneously attack the U.S. Embassies in Nairobi and Tanzania in 1998. They used readily available explosives to attack the USS Cole in Yemen in 2000. And they used box cutters to take control of commercial airliners on September 11. They knew this. But they still pursue strategies, policies and weapon systems to fight large scale battles around the globe as per RAD which will further enrich corporate defense contractors.

After the first Gulf war, Usama bin Laden left Saudi Arabia, angered by the Saudi Royals' decision to allow the U.S to remove Saddam from Kuwait and establish a military presence in the Holy Land. Bin Laden had urged the House of Saud to let him, a Saudi, and his army of Mujahedeen fighters, who had just recently defeated the Soviet military in Afghanistan do the job. They refused, in favor of the U.S. They weren't too keen on his brand of Islamic extremism, nor of the power he was gaining. He was becoming somewhat of a hero in the Muslim world after the defeat of the Soviets in Afghanistan. The same reason Saddam didn't want Al Qaeda in Iraq, one of the more secular countries in the Middle East. In a recent interview with UPI, the formerly anonymous author of the best selling book *Imperial Hubris: Why the West is Losing the War on Terror*, Michael Scheuer, said, "bin Laden is now possibly the Arab world's most popular leader," and the "problem the U.S. faced in fighting the war on terrorism *is its allies in the Arab world.* Since many of those leaders are unpopular among their own people...bin Laden is the only leader in the Islamic world, a heroic figure." [7]

Bin Laden and his Islamic extremist army went to Sudan and Pakistan mostly, where they began recruiting for a Holy War. They also have become active in places like Somalia, Chechnya, Philippines, the Balkans and other heavily Muslim areas. Soon, it became apparent to the Sudanese they could not bear the pressure bin Laden was bringing on them, and bin Laden moved to Afghanistan, where he was on September 11 2001. Experts like Richard Clarke, Paul O'Neill, and various high ranking military commanders have argued these areas are where the war on terrorism needs to be fought with both the full force of the U.S. military and with diplomacy and humanitarian aid. No one in the world would oppose us if we are going after Al-Qaeda wherever they are, with all the resources of the U.S. military, as was evident in Afghanistan when we had the full support of the world.

In June of 2002, Paul O'Neill discussed the second part of the equation-humanitarian aid-with the President, after a ten day trip to Africa. He had visited some of the poorest countries on the planet and believed one way to start to stem the flood of recruits to Al Qaeda and other Islamic terrorist organizations was to help these countries governments provide a better life for it's people by making measurable differences in HIV/AIDS education and treatment, hunger, and the area he thought the U.S. "should be able to make the greatest difference in the shortest time", constructing wells and bringing clean water. He also said, "The United Nations' goal of cutting illiteracy in half by 2015 and doubling per capita incomes in the poorest countries are not ambitious enough." He composed a memo to the President recommending an "action agenda" on these and other ideas and placed them in the broader context of foreign policy. "We are not going to dissuade countries from building destructive weapons and maybe aligning against us with just threats of force. We also need a nonmilitary side to our foreign policy, where the U.S. can start treating much of the beleaguered developing world—the source of so many of the threats to our security—in a way that show we value and respect them." [8] O'Neill would leave the White House in January 2003. The memo would get no further discussion, no policy or even an action agenda would be forthcoming. The Presidents small circle of advisors, entirely made up of the PNAC men listed previously have another agenda.

4

Making the Case for War as per RAD

"The people of England have been led in Mesopotamia [Iraq] *into a trap from which it will be hard to escape with dignity and honour. They have been tricked into it by a steady withholding of information. Things have been far worse than we have been told, our administration more bloody and inefficient than the public knows. We are today not far from disaster."*
Lieutenant Colonel T.E. Lawrence (Lawrence of Arabia) 1920.

If the *A Clean Break* (ACB) document is a blueprint for the Bush administration's policies in the Middle East, then the *Rebuilding of America's Defenses* (RAD) document, published in 2000, is a blueprint for the world. It is an extension of (ACB). It calls for a "Pax Americana" by securing complete control of land, sea, air, space and *cyber-space*. This will be achieved by waging "multiple simultaneous large scale wars" preemptively, with no regard for international opinion, the *denigration of the U.N.* and the abrogation of international agreements. (Such as ABM mentioned earlier) "The Cold War world was a bipolar world; the 21st century world is—for the moment, at least—decidedly unipolar, with America as the world's sole superpower." It states the main military threat(s) during the Cold War as "Potential global war across many theaters" and in the 21st century as "Potential theater wars spread across the globe." Speaking to U.N. type missions the U.S. would now perform, it says "these constabulary missions are far more complex and likely to generate violence than traditional 'peacekeeping' missions. For one, they demand American political leadership rather than that of the U.N. American troops in particular, must be regarded as part of an overwhelmingly powerful force."

On January 29 2002, during his first State of the Union address, President Bush declared North Korea, Iran and Iraq the "axis of evil." This theme was laid out for him the year before he became President. North Korea, Iran and Iraq are a common theme mentioned throughout the RAD document as the largest threat to America and her allies. Since the 2004 Presidential elections, the saber rattling has begun in earnest over both Iran and North Korea. On November 17, ABC, CBS and NBC all lead their newscast that night with the story that Iran is producing a gas used to enrich plutonium for a nuclear program. North Korea's nuclear program was also mentioned. You can't turn on the evening news lately without hearing about Iran and North Korea. Recently there have been stories on the evening news that al Zarqawi has reportedly been traveling freely across the Iran/Iraq border before the assault on Falluja. Iran Pursuing a WMD program? Iran harboring terrorists? Starting to sound familiar? Déjà vu all over again? Over the next few months, listen for the case against Iran to start sounding very much like the case against Iraq prior to the invasion in 2003. "American military pre-eminence will continue to rest in significant part on the ability to maintain sufficient land forces to achieve political goals such as removing a dangerous and hostile regime when necessary."

On unilateral military operations, the document says "If an American peace is to be maintained, *and expanded* it must have a secure foundation on *unquestioned* U.S. military preeminence." And "Indeed, it is the Air Force, along with the Army, that remains the core of America's ability to apply decisive military power when it pleases." Is this document starting to sound like Mein Kampf?

As RAD moves into the future of global conflict, it speaks of controlling space. "Control of the sea could be largely determined not by fleets of surface combatants and aircraft carriers, but from land and space based systems, forcing navies to maneuver and fight under water. Space itself will become a theater of war" The warrior of the future, in their world, will utilize "skin patch pharmaceuticals to help regulate fears, focus concentration and enhance endurance and strength." (It is important to note Donald Rumsfeld, Condoleezza Rice and others in Bush's circle have been Board Members of pharmaceutical companies).

By far the most frightening single sentence in the entire ninety page document is on page 60. "Advanced forms of biological warfare that can target specific genotypes may transform biological warfare from the realm of terror to a politically useful tool."

Another theme throughout the RAD document is the need for huge amounts of military spending due to the vast amount of technology needed for war of the future. However, according to RAD, while there will still be a need for a large number of ground troops, because of the technology that will be deployed, some troop units can be much smaller in size. "The U.S. would be unwise to accept the larger proposition that the strategic value of land power has been eroded to the point where the nation no longer needs to maintain large ground forces." However, in the situation in which we find ourselves in Iraq, where we are not fighting large armies on huge open battlefields, the report states, "The army must become more tactically agile, more operationally mobile, and more strategically deployable…Under the 'Land Warrior' program, some Army experts envision a 'squad' of seven soldiers able to dominate an area the size of the Gettysburg battlefield—where, in 1863, some 165,000 men fought." The "Land Warrior" program exists, as the authors point out "Even radical concepts such as those considered under the 'Land Warrior' project do not involve outlandish technologies or flights of science fiction. Many already exist today."

The RAD document, as the ACB document before it, has also been put into action. On September 20 2002, the Bush administration released a 31 page report titled *The National Security Strategy of the United States of America* [1] Like RAD it calls for preemptive attack against *perceived* enemies, and American internationalism. It's a plan for a permanent U.S. military and economic domination of every region on the planet. The plan refers to terrorism and the 9/11 attacks, however it mirrors the language of RAD, which was published two years prior, before the attacks of 9/11. The conclusion is the National Security Strategy document was not inspired by 9/11, but has everything to do with the PNAC agenda. *September 11 was the catalyst for moving their agenda forward.* Journalist Jay Bookman referred to PNAC as "a group of conservative interventionists outraged by the thought that the United States might be forfeiting its chance at a global empire." [2]

We are seeing the "test" of the "Land Warrior" portion of RAD in Iraq today. Defense Secretary Rumsfeld and the President both have been accused of bungling the planning of the war, and criticized for their handling of the occupation since the "end of hostilities" in May 2003, and of not having an adequate exit strategy. After reading RAD, it has become painfully clear that these men did not bungle anything. Their actions have been very deliberate. There is no exit strategy because they don't plan to exit the region. Read that sentence again. *There is no exit strategy because they don't plan to exit the region.* Their vision advocates expansion, not exiting. As long as the neo-cons of this administration are in power there will be conflict and a U.S. military presence in the Middle East. Their goal is to have an outpost (the first of many) sitting on top of the second largest oil reserve in the world. They have told us this themselves in the RAD and ACB documents written years before George W. Bush became President of the United States. An alarming number of Bush's inner circle and cabinet have signed one or both of these documents. They are:

- Dick Cheney
- Paul Wolfowitz
- I. Lewis (Scooter) Libby
- Abram Shulsky
- Richard Perle
- Elliott Abrams
- Richard Armitage
- Stephen Cambone
- John Bolton
- Robert Zoellick

This strategy will mean perpetual conflict in the Middle East region for many years to come, and under this policy, there will never be a shortage of extremists willing to carry out terrorist attacks on the United States. The debate over the last year has been centered on the "when" we're going to leave Iraq and "time lines" and if we even should leave. The real debate should involve "why" Cheney, Rumsfeld, and Wolfowitz and the other neo-cons don't have an exit strategy.

The RAD vision of the future army is being road tested right now. A smaller force than necessary is currently deployed in Iraq.

Before the invasion of Iraq, in February 2003, Army General Eric Shinseki (Army Chief of Staff 1999-2003) advised the Pentagon the Army would need *several* hundred thousand troops to secure a post war Iraq. At the time, Deputy Secretary of Defense Paul Wolfowitz publicly criticized the estimate as "wildly off the mark" and "outlandish" He also said, "the Iraqi's will greet us as liberators." Shinseki was subsequently replaced by Rumsfeld. Shinseki obviously didn't get the RAD memo. In April 2004, Shinseki stood by his pre war estimate of necessary troop levels in Iraq. "My concerns were that this was going to be more difficult than any of us would have liked, and was going to take more effort than others might have thought, the purpose of the military is to create a secure environment for real peace activities. If you do not create this safe environment, there are undesirable others who are only too happy to fill the void." This is exactly what we are seeing in Iraq today with the insurgency. On winning the war on terrorism, he said, "We need visionary leadership. Winning this war on terrorism will succeed not because we hunt down every extremist warrior, but because we're able to change the global environment for the better in some measurable way.

And to have any hope of creating that kind of change, it would take strong, *credible* leadership." It sounds like Shinseki did get the Paul O'Neill memo. Oh, that's right, O'Neill's gone too.

Marine General Anthony Zinni is also very critical of the Iraq "adventure." Commenting to the *San Diego Union-Tribune* on Defense Secretary Donald Rumsfeld's comments in April of 2004, in which Rumsfeld said he "could not have estimated how many troops would be killed in the past week", Zinni said, "I'm surprised that he's [Rumsfeld] surprised because there were a lot of us who were telling him that it was going to be thus," Zinni, was a Marine for 39 years and the former commander of the U.S. Central Command (CENTCOM). Out of uniform he served as the Bush administration's Special Envoy to the Middle East before his reservations over the war in Iraq and its aftermath caused him to resign and oppose it. "I spent two years in Vietnam; I've seen this movie before." General Zinni testified before the Senate Foreign Relations Committee one month before the war. "Senator Lugar asked me: 'General Zinni, do you feel the threat from Saddam Hussein is *imminent?*' I said no, not at all. It was not an imminent threat. Not even close. Not grave, gathering, imminent, serious, severe, or mildly upsetting," On CBS's 60 Minutes he said, "I think there was dereliction in insufficient forces being put on the ground, I think there was dereliction in lack of planning, the President is owed the finest strategic thinking. He is owed the finest operational planning. He is owed the finest tactical execution on the ground...He got the latter. He didn't get the first two." [3] It wasn't that the President and his inner circle weren't getting the finest strategic thinking and operational planning, they weren't listening. They weren't listening to men like Clarke, Shinseki, Zinni and others who had spent more than thirty years of their lives in the military, or the Pentagon, in intelligence and counterterrorism. General Zinni suffered consequences for providing the finest strategic thinking and operational planning as an expert in these matters. "I've been called a traitor and a turncoat" he said. This administration has no room for honest brokering, opposing views, or open debate. General Zinni and General Shinseki are not the only high ranking military leaders to speak out. Former General and National Security Advisor Brent Scowcroft, former CENTCOM Commander Norman Schwarzkopf, Supreme Commander of Allied Troops in the first Gulf War under Bush 1, and former NATO Commander Wesley Clark have all been vocal in their reservations about the leadership and war planning of this administration.

In answer to the question why we didn't go into Baghdad during the first Gulf war in 1990, George H.W. Bush wrote in his memoirs "Trying to eliminate Saddam would have incurred incalculable human and political costs. Apprehending him was probably impossible. We would have been forced to occupy Baghdad and, in effect, rule Iraq. There was no viable exit strategy we could see, violating another of our principals. Furthermore, we had been self-consciously trying to set a pattern for handling aggression in the post-Cold War world. Going in and occupying Iraq, thus unilaterally exceeding the United Nations mandate, would have destroyed the precedent of international response to aggression that we hoped to establish. Had we gone the invasion route, the United States could conceivably still be an occupying power in a bitterly hostile land."

Not only did the President not take any advice from his own father, (not just his father, but the only President, living or dead, in American history to have sent U.S. troops into a real shooting war in the Middle East, specifically Iraq.) he didn't even consult him. In the book *Plan of Attack* by Bob Woodward, Woodward asked the President if he consulted with his father before the invasion. Bush said, "No, I consulted a higher Father."

It's important to note here, that some of the PNAC men who are back in power, under George W., which served in the Nixon, Ford and Reagan White Houses, were not in the first Bush White House. George H.W. Bush was a much more moderate Republican than his son. There is evidence the first Bush, like Netanyahu, wisely rejected their militaristic ideology.

On January 26, 1998, the men profiled previously, Elliot Abrams, Richard Armitage, William Kristol, Richard Perle, Donald Rumsfeld, Paul Wolfowitz and other PNAC members, while out of government service, signed a letter to then President Clinton. In it, they discuss the "threat" of Saddam Hussein, and urge the President "to enunciate a new strategy that would secure the interests of the U.S. That strategy should aim, *above all*, [emphasis added] at the removal of Saddam Hussein's regime from power." They go on to say "The only acceptable strategy is one that eliminates the possibility that Iraq will be able to use or threaten to use weapons of mass destruction. In the near term, this means a willingness to undertake military action as diplomacy is clearly failing. [We now know this was not true. Sanctions and weapons inspections clearly worked, as there have been no WMD found to this day]. In the long term, it means removing Saddam Hussein and his regime from power. That now needs to become the aim of American foreign policy." Clinton, as did Netanyahu and the first George Bush before him, also rejected this radical strategy. It is no surprise that it has become the *aim* of American foreign policy for this administration, given the players. It is clear these men have been obsessed with Iraq since the early 90's.

We have been lied into a war. Bush, Cheney, Rumsfeld, Rice, Wolfowitz and others in this administration started right after September 11, 2001 telling us

Saddam had weapons of mass destruction. It was a fact, not conjecture, they said. That was a lie. For something to be a fact and not conjecture, then it would have to turn out to be true, otherwise it could never have been a fact. There were chemical belts around Baghdad. Saddam was pursuing a nuclear weapons program, Saddam had links to Al Qaeda, Saddam was developing anthrax, botulinum toxin, aflatoxin, ricin, gas gangrene, plague, typhus, tetanus, cholera, camelpox, hemorrhagic fever, small pox and hotdog thumb. O.K., I made up hotdog thumb, but they made up all the other things. They also told us Saddam could deliver these terrible chemical and biological weapons to the east coast of the United States via Unmanned Aerial Vehicles (UAV's) launched from freighters in the Atlantic. [4] They told us Saddam was an "imminent threat." They used that exact term dozens of times leading up to the invasion of Iraq. On Sunday morning March 14, 2004, roughly a year after the Invasion, and no nuclear, biological or chemical weapons were found, Bob Schieffer asked Donald Rumsfeld, on *Face the Nation*, why so many in the administration had used the term "imminent" or "immediate" threat when referring to Saddam Hussien. Rumsfeld said no one in the administration had used that term. Schieffer then read a few transcripts of him using those terms exactly. Rumsfeld was lying about lying. [5] Condoleezza Rice said we can't wait for the "smoking gun to be a mushroom cloud" over an American city. Nothing like stirring up Cold-War fears to get the population behind you.

A couple of quotes here would be appropriate.

Secretary of Defense Donald Rumsfeld: "Some have argued that the nuclear threat from Iraq is not *imminent,* that Saddam is at least five to seven years away from having nuclear weapons. I would not be so certain."

Vice President Dick Cheney to the VFW 103rd Convention in August 2002: "Simply stated, there is *no doubt* that Saddam Hussein now has weapons of mass destruction. There is *no doubt* he is amassing them to use against our friends, against our allies, and against us. And there is *no doubt* that his aggressive regional ambitions will lead him into future confrontations with his neighbors." O.K., for those reading this that want to argue semantics, I will concede, he didn't use the exact term "imminent threat." However, later in the speech he did say Saddam was a "mortal threat." I printed the transcript of Cheney's speech. It's six pages long and it's interesting to note here that after the opening comments on page one, page two is devoted to the attacks of September 11. At the bottom of page two he says "our armed services must have every tool to answer any threat that forms against us. It means that any enemy conspiring to harm America or our friends must face a swift, a certain and a devastating response." He could have been talking about Al Qaeda in Afghanistan. He could have been talking about Al Qaeda terrorists in Sudan, or Pakistan, or Somalia, or the Balkans, or Chechnya, or the Philippines, or any number of other places. But he wasn't. The last four pages of the six page speech were devoted exclusively to Saddam Hussein and Iraq.

President Bush speaking to the nation days before the invasion began: "Intelligence gathered by this and other governments leaves *no doubt* that the Iraq regime continues to possess and conceal some of the most lethal weapons ever devised."

Bush, Cheney, Rumsfeld and Rice were telling us Iraq was nothing but a supply dump of nuclear, biological and chemical weapons. We've been in Iraq for almost three years now and have nothing to show for it. Not a single weapon prohibited by any U.N. resolution. Just before the invasion, the U.N. weapon's inspectors found a few archaic conventional scud type missile's that had a range of 15 miles more than U.N. resolutions allowed, and destroyed them. That's hardly an imminent threat to the United States.

Every single reason this administration gave for going after Iraq, instead of terrorist groups in the places discussed above, have been false. Every time Bush, Cheney and Co. would mention 9-11, they would mention Saddam Hussein in the same sentence. They did this over and over, both before and after the invasion. These linkages have been proven false. The widely accepted argument is they were given bad intelligence. The evidence is that, not only did they know the intelligence was faulty, but that they themselves "cooked" the evidence against Iraq.

It's important here to take another look at Douglas Feith. He is not only one of the author's of ACB, that we discussed earlier, along with Richard Perle and David Wurmser, he has been an out spoken advocate of war in the Middle East and the overthrow of Saddam Hussein for more than a decade. Like all of the PNAC members listed above, Feith moves fluidly between government service and the corporate world, lobbying for sweetheart deals for companies they have ties to. Energy contractors, defense contractors, or pharmaceutical companies they have been board members of, or CEO's of and may possibly lobby for in the future. Dick Cheney's Halliburton, with their no-bid contracts worth billions in Iraq, gets the most press lately, but they all do it. In 1986 Douglas Feith founded the Feith & Zell law firm based in Israel. One of their major clients was Northrop Grumman. In 1989 Feith started another company called International Advisors Inc. In 1999 his firm Feith & Zell formed an alliance with Israeli based Zell, Goldberg & Co., [ZGC] which resulted in the creation of Fandz

International Law Group. Fandz assists regional construction firms to collaborate with contractors from the U.S. and other coalition countries in implementing reconstruction projects in Iraq. [6] Given Feith's current position in the Pentagon, it would be impossible to overestimate how perfect ZGC would be in assisting American companies in their relations with the U.S. government in connection with Iraq reconstruction projects. [7]

Hours after the attack on 9-11, an effort began to create a believable case showing Saddam's ties to al Qaeda. Rumsfeld, Wolfowitz, Feith and Perle called on David Wurmser to head a secret intelligence unit that would answer only to Feith. The unit was called the Policy Counterterrorism Evaluation Group. The unit was little more than a pro-war propaganda cell designed to produce evidence to support an attack on Iraq. The primary purpose was to counter CIA analysis that had consistently found no credible link between Al Qaeda and Saddam. [8]

Gregory Thielmann, who was in charge of military assessments in the State Department's Bureau of Intelligence and Research until 2002 said the makeup of the unit was suspect, indicating they had no interest in true analysis. Like Feith, Wurmser spent most of his career as a pro Israeli activist and had no background at all in intelligence. "Are they missile experts?" Thielmann asked. "Nuclear engineers? There's no logical explanation for the office's creation except that they [the Bush administration] wanted people to find evidence to support their answer about war." [9]

Retired Air Force Lt. Col. Karen Kwiatkowski [10] who worked in the Near East South Asia division at the Pentagon, was in the military for twenty two years, published two books, earned a master's degree from Harvard and is a lifelong conservative agreed. She said, "They'd take a little bit of intelligence, cherry pick it, make it sound much more exciting, usually by taking it out of context, often juxtaposition of two pieces of information that don't belong together." She also said most of the long time career Pentagon civilians in the office, and some of the military, were quickly being transferred out to make room for new appointments, mostly from neoconservative and pro Israeli think tanks. "What seemed out of place was the strong and open pro Israeli and anti Arab orientation in an ostensibly apolitical policy generated staff within the Pentagon. There was a sense that politics like these might play better at the State Department or the National Security Council, not the Pentagon, where we considered ourselves objective and hard boiled." [11]

Another source of intelligence for Perle, Feith, and Wolfowitz came from the Iraqi National Congress (INC) led by Ahmed Chalabi. Chalabi who was born in Iraq, but had been in exile in London for years, received a PhD from the University of Chicago, Paul Wolfowitz's alma mater. He also had a career in banking in Jordan. He was charged and has been convicted in absentia, in Jordan, for embezzlement and received a twenty two year sentence. Chalabi was introduced to Perle and Wolfowitz in 1985 by a University of Chicago professor. For years, Perle, Wolfowitz, and Feith hoped to install Chalabi as President of Iraq after the removal of Saddam. Unfortunately for them, virtually all the intelligence he gave the U.S. government about Saddam's WMD programs, supposedly from his contacts inside Iraq, turned out to be completely bogus. No one argues this, not even the White House. Seasoned intelligence officers understood the problem with using informants like Chalabi and his people, is that the more exaggerated their claims, the better their chances of asylum, or even large payments by CIA and other intelligence agencies were. It was a constant problem for the CIA during the Cold War. The U.S. paid millions of dollars to Chalabi for this intelligence, millions of tax payer dollars. As late as January of 2003, during his second State of the Union Address, and just two months before the start of the war, President Bush stood in front of us and used the bogus evidence of Iraqi WMD provided by Chalabi, and Feith's Pentagon unit, to sell us this war. That night Chalabi was sitting next to Laura Bush in the audience. It is also alleged, Chalabi was giving U.S. secrets to Iranian intelligence during this period. Chalabi has been cut off, but the job of Interim Prime Minister that Perle, Wolfowitz and Feith hoped to give to Chalabi, has gone to another high ranking INC member, Iyad Allawi instead. Indictments against Chalabi may be coming; however, the Bush administration is probably not to anxious to see him indicted in the U.S. There's no telling what he might say about them. He served his purpose.

Wurmser was the conduit for the "cherry picked" intelligence between the Policy Counterterrorism Evaluation Group at the Pentagon and the White House. Remember, Wurmser went from State to the Office of the Vice President as Middle East Advisor.

During the summer of 2002, Feith and Wolfowitz created another organization, with the Orwellian name Office of Special Plans (OSP). Abram Shulsky was picked to head it. Its most important responsibility was "media strategy." The office was Top Secret. Col. Kwiatkowski said, "We were instructed at a staff meeting that this office was not to be discussed or explained, and if people in the Joint Staff, among others, asked, we were to offer no comment." OSP had close ties to a parallel, ad hoc intelligence unit in Ariel Sharon's office in Israel. It was designed to go around Israel's own intelligence organization, Mossad. The purpose of the unit was to provide key people in the Bush administration "with more alarmist reports on Saddam's Iraq than Mossad was willing to authorize." OSP was not only getting cooked intelligence from its own intelligence unit, but also from a similar Israeli cell. Kwiatkowski said, "They pushed an agenda on Iraq, and developed pretty sophisticated propaganda lines which were fed throughout government, to Congress, and internally to the Pentagon, to try and make this case of immediacy, this case of severe threat to the United States." She said, "This was creatively produced propaganda spread across a network of policy makers. OSP needed to convince the remaining holdovers. Take Colin Powell for example. There was a lot of frustration with Powell; they said a lot of bad things about him in the office." She added "OSP had a very close relationship with Vice President Cheney's office."

Another thing which troubled Kwiatkowski was the sort of "enemies list" kept by OSP. In addition to Powell, another person targeted was Marine General Anthony Zinni. "He spoke out publicly about some of the things he saw. Before he was removed by Bush, I heard him called a traitor in a staff meeting. They were very anti anybody who might provide information that affected their paradigm. They were the spin enforcers." She also said the public heard what they were supposed to hear, what the OSP wanted them to hear. "The very phrases they used were blatantly false and not based on any intelligence. The OSP and the Vice President's office were critical in this propaganda effort. The Congress was misled, it was lied to. At a very minimum, that is subversion of the Constitution." [12]

This is how the propaganda machine worked. The "cooked" intelligence from OSP would be leaked to the media through the White House Iraq Group (WHIG), another secret group set up at the White House by Chief of Staff Andrew Card. Its function was to selectively leak information to the press. They would print stories quoting Iraqi informants and U.S. officials who commented on conditions of anonymity. When the stories broke, Senior White House officials, who had already set up appearances on the Sunday morning talk shows days earlier, would point to the news articles as proof of their wild claims and parrot the unnamed quotes they previously supplied. On Sunday September 8, 2002, the *New York Times* published a story titled *U.S. Says Hussein Intensifies Quest for A-bomb Parts* by Judith Miller and Michael Gordon. The article talked about aluminum tubes to enrich uranium, nuclear weapons, defectors describing Iraq's attempt to expand its biological and chemical arsenals, and mushroom clouds. (Pulitzer Prize winning journalist Judith Miller, it turns out, was nothing more than a good taker of dictation, often spewing the White House line on WMD. The Times has since issued a mea-culpa regarding stories of WMD during the run-up to the war). One line said, "all of Iraq is one large storage facility." That same Sunday morning, Dick Cheney, on *Meet the Press* said, "It's now *public*; Saddam has been seeking to acquire the kind of tubes needed for the production of highly enriched uranium." Condoleezza Rice was on CNN's *Late Edition* with Wolf Blitzer, saying "we don't want the smoking gun to be a mushroom cloud…" again. Colin Powell was on Fox News saying "specialized aluminum tubes we saw reported *just this morning*…" and Rumsfeld doing *Face the Nation* tied it all to September 11 saying "Imagine a September 11 with weapons of mass destruction."

Unlike a legitimate investigation, they weren't following the evidence, they already had their answers, they were forcing the evidence to fit. Senior State Department intelligence official Gregory Thielman said, "Instead of our leadership forming conclusions based on a careful reading of the intelligence we provided them, they already had their conclusions to start out with, and they were cherry-picking the information that we provided to use whatever pieces of it that fit their overall interpretation. There seemed to be an unseemly eagerness to believe any information which would portray the Iraqi threat as being extremely grave and imminent."

The war in Iraq is not going as planned. It's a disaster. Rumsfeld's (and the other PNAC members') "road test" of the future of warfare is leaving a lot to be desired. The U.S. media is not covering the failure in Iraq. There are reasons for this. In the Toronto Star, Antonia Zerbisias, in an article titled "U.S. Media Still Hiding Bad News From Americans" reported on a Pentagon strategic report to Donald Rumsfeld which said, "U.S. actions have not only failed, they may also have achieved the opposite of what they intended." In August of 2004, the CIA drafted a formal National Intelligence Estimate (NIE) which predicted a bleak future for Iraq through the end of 2005. The NIE described three possibilities. The best case scenario was a continuation of what we are experiencing now, (in august) the worst case scenario was all out civil war. Since then the violence has been steadily increasing, and what is happening now is starting to look a lot like Lebanon in the 70's. Every day we're told Iraqi *insurgents* are attacking Iraqi's who are aiding American's. In reality, it's looking more and more like Sunni's (sympathetic to Saddam) killing Shiite's and the formation of a Shiite militia to attack Sunni's.

President Bush, at the time, dismissed the August NIE as just a "guess." Amazingly, this is the same intelligence service whose intelligence he used just sixteen months earlier to justify the invasion of Iraq in the first place.

On December 7 2004, a *New York Times* article titled *Two CIA Reports Offer Warnings on Iraq's Path* by Douglas Jehl reported that "a classified cable sent by the CIA's station chief in Baghdad has warned that the situation in Iraq is deteriorating and may not rebound any time soon." The Times reported the cable echoed a briefing presented by a senior CIA official who recently visited Iraq. "Unnamed government official described the reports as 'an unvarnished assessment of the difficulties ahead in Iraq.'" They said the reports warned "the security situation was likely to get worse, including more violence and sectarian clashes." The Times article says, the appraisals, which follow several other such warnings from officials in Washington and in the field, "were much more pessimistic than the public picture being offered by the Bush administration."

Time Magazine reporter Michael Ware was interviewed (from Baghdad) on MSNBC's *Hard Ball with Chris Matthews* on November 13, 2004. Ware is an Australian journalist who has embedded himself with Iraqi insurgents. Currently he is embedded with the Army's 2nd Battalion, 2nd Infantry in Fallujah. Matthews asked "Are we winning this war?" Ware said, "As a journalist, I was free, until March of this year to travel the breadth of this country. Then, after April, [after the U.S. Army's first push into Fallujah, in which we pulled back] I was much more restricted to the confines of the metropolis of Baghdad. Well, we've lost Baghdad. Sitting in my own compound in the city, I'm prone to mortar fire. They have kidnap teams circling our block. A journalist was kidnapped 300 meters outside our gate. Zarqawi controls central nodes of the city, where he is within range of mortars directly impacting into the Green Zone and the U.S. Embassy. That doesn't feel like winning to me." On the invasion of Fallujah, he said, "Have we beaten the insurgency? No. No, I suspect we're far from that. I was interviewing cells weeks before the operation who had long fled. Documents I have from Zarqawi's people, which are after action reports on the previous uprising in April, show just how they did it then, evacuating the leadership. All indications are that they did this again, leaving a rear guard action behind to fight a suicidal death march." On comparisons to Vietnam, Ware said, "I try to shy away from analogies to Vietnam. But, sometimes it can be chilling. We do not control this country. We may have territory, but we do not have the substance of the people, nor the land. We're certainly encountering very similar insurgency practices, methods, techniques, tactics, a mind set that we did see in Indochina. And indeed, something that resonates with me to this day is the interviews I've done with senior insurgent leaders, the upper echelons, and they talk to me about reading Vo Nguyen Giap, the Vietnamese General. The manner in which they can dissolve back into the population [As did the Viet Cong] is almost magical. So, yes, we will see the insurgency continue to evolve as it moves almost with complete freedom of movement throughout the country."

Ware's words have proven to be prophetic. On December 21, 2004 a suicide bomber infiltrated the American base in Mosul and detonated a bomb, in a dining hall, which killed twenty two people including fourteen American soldiers and four American contract workers. The worst single day loss of life for the military since the war began.

Rumsfeld and Wolfowitz have been wrong regarding every aspect of the war in Iraq. Not just the pre war rhetoric about WMD and Iraq ties to bin Laden, or the imminent threat statements, but after the fall of Baghdad, the failure to have enough troops to secure historic archeological sites and to stop looting of Iraqi national treasures. They have failed to provide enough troops, to this day, to secure the general peace for average Iraqis. As General Shinseki said, "the purpose of the military is to create a secure environment." They ignored, or dismissed, reports by career military commanders concerning post occupation forces needed in Iraq. As Wolfowitz wrongly predicted, "We'll be greeted as liberators." In the speech Cheney gave to the VFW National Convention in August 2002, mentioned earlier, Cheney said, "As for the reaction of the Arab "street", Middle east expert Fouad Ajami predicts that after liberation, the streets in Basra and Baghdad are 'sure to erupt in joy.' Extremists in the region would have to rethink their strategy of Jihad." They failed to secure the borders of Iraq, resulting in the country being flooded with extremists who were not there before. They failed to see the potential for the insurgency we're seeing today. This was not unforeseeable; they had been warned of the potential by senior military strategists before the war even began. For almost two years now, they've been criticized for not providing enough equipment, or sub standard equipment, specifically, body armor and vehicle armor. These allegations were simply dismissed by Secretary of Defense Rumsfeld. Until the second week of December that is, while Rumsfeld was in Kuwait talking to more than 2000 Guardsmen on their way north to Iraq. A young Guardsman from Tennessee, Spec. Thomas Wilson asked "Why do we have to dig through local land fills for pieces of scrap metal and compromised ballistic glass to up armor our vehicles?" Cheers broke out from the more than 2000 troops present. Rumsfeld appeared momentarily shaken, and his answer was shocking. "You go to war with the Army you have, not the Army you might want or wish to have." He also said it's a matter of physics and not money however the next day no less than three companies came forward to say they were just waiting for the word from the Pentagon (for two years) to start production of the required armor. On December 13th, Former General Norman Schwarzkopf said he was angered by the Secretary's answer. It was as if he was saying that after four years, the Secretary of Defense had no control over the Army he was taking into battle, in effect blaming the military.

The right wing talk shows went into high gear the day after the story broke about Spec. Wilson's question. They said the Secretary was set up by a reporter who *fed* the question to Spec. Wilson, effectively ignoring the validity of the question itself. The fact is, the reporter who was imbedded in Iraq, and who had himself been traveling in unarmored Humvee's was not allowed to ask questions. The press is routinely shut out of such events. The embedded reporter scenario has come back to bite Rumsfeld in the ass. Early on, critics said that embedded reporters would report favorably on the war and not be as objective because they would not want to compromise troops in the field. What they failed to realize is that men in combat form a unique bond. And while the embedded reporters are not soldiers, they are in the same situation the troops find themselves in. The troops begin to like the reporters, and the reporters begin to like the troops. This is especially true when the reporter is on the side of the grunt. They share a common and profound experience together. The reporter, if allowed to, will echo the concerns of the troops. Another soldier, emboldened by Spec. Wilson, asked why her family had not received her paychecks since last June, another asked why she and her husband, who were members of a *volunteer* Army were being held over under the Stop Loss program, and when they could expect to go home. Rumsfeld's answer was the Stop Loss Program has routinely been used "for years, and years, and years, and people who sign up for military service are well aware of it." The truth is this program has never been used, and few veterans even know of its existence. It is in effect, as John Kerry said during the Presidential race, a back door draft.

Bush, Cheney, Rumsfeld and company are the people who say if you don't blindly follow this administration's policy in Iraq and their war on "terra," then you are not patriotic, you are un-American, and you don't support the troops. Clearly, they are not supporting the troops. Rumsfeld runs the war in Iraq as if he were still the CEO of Searle Pharmaceutical; it's all about the bottom line. He's running the war on the cheap. If the U.S. Army were a publicly traded company, the share holders would be ecstatic, but these are living, breathing and dying U.S. troops.

Senator John McCain (R-AR) has said he has no confidence in Secretary of Defense Donald Rumsfeld. He stopped short of calling for Rumsfeld's resignation. Senator's Joseph Biden (D-VT) and Chuck Hagel (R-NE) have also been very critical of Rumsfeld's handling of the Iraq war.

After the elections, half of the President's cabinet has resigned. While this may not be unprecedented, the strange thing is Rumsfeld (and his deputy, Wolfowitz) has been asked by the President to stay on. Strange to those looking at Rumsfeld's record of failures, but not so strange when you consider who he is, a PNAC member. None of them are going anywhere.

Rumsfeld has been under increasing pressure to resign by an increasing number of Republicans. The dissent seems to coincide with the question from reservist Thomas Wilson in Kuwait. Also the Abu Ghraib prisoner abuse scandal won't seem to go away. However, on Sunday December 19, 2004, on *This Week with George Stephanopoulos*, Andrew Card, the White House Chief of Staff, said Donald Rumsfeld is doing a *"spectacular"* job. Huh? During a rare press conference with Bush at the White House on Monday, December 20, 2004, Bush said that after he asked Rumsfeld to stay on he was pleased Rumsfeld accepted. Bush also said he knew Rumsfeld's heart. We'll have to wait and see if Rumsfeld does in fact stay after the inauguration. I'll make my prediction now. He's staying.

Since the election, the President's inner circle has gotten smaller. There doesn't seem to be any room for honest brokers in this administration. Paul O'Neill said, "What became clear to me is that the presence of me Colin [Powell] and Christie [Todd Whitman] helped convince people that this would, actually, be an administration that would look hard for the best solutions, without regard for which party had claimed an idea first or some passing political calculation. That's what the three of us were kind of known for, for being non-ideological, for walking across political borders and looking for common ground. Thinking back about how all of us started to be banged up so early on, from the inside, it now seems like we inadvertently may have been there, in large part, as cover." [13]

President Bush, by his own admission, doesn't read newspapers or even lengthy reports. He does not put any weight in opinions of those out side of his ever tightening inner circle. He has said, "What's in the newspapers worth worrying about? I glance at the headlines just to kind of get a flavor of what's moving. I rarely read the stories." He continued "I get briefed by people who have probably read the news themselves, I also understand that a lot of times there's opinions mixed in with news." He went on to say "the best way to get the news is from objective sources. And the most objective sources I have are people on my staff who tell me what's happening in the world." [14] Paul O'Neill had attended many meetings with the President, both large and one on one. During one cabinet meeting on March 19, O'Neill watched Bush closely. He threw out a few general phrases, a few nods, but there was virtually no engagement. The cabinet secretaries had worked for weeks on detailed reports. It was troubling to O'Neill that Bush asked no questions, there were so many worth asking. O'Neill had been made to understand by various colleagues in the White House that the President should not be expected to read reports. In his personal experience, the President didn't even appear to have read the short memos he sent over. [15]

There is a lack of curiosity of complex issues. The reason for this has been explained, again, by the President himself. Throughout his first term he made many references to his "instincts." He said he makes decisions based on his "gut." Senator Joe Biden said when he was at the White House a few months after the fall of Baghdad to express concern of, among other things, troop strength to secure the country, the disbanding of the Iraqi Army, and the threat of an insurgency movement, the President was unflappably sure everything was going to be just great. Biden said, "But Mr. President, how can you be so sure when you know you don't know the facts?" Bush stood up and put his hand on the Senator's shoulder and said, "My instincts, my instincts." These statements are references to his religious faith. His first term has been defined as the faith based Presidency. Bush's religious faith in and of itself *should* be no cause for concern. The vast majority of U.S. Presidents, if not all of them, have been men of faith, Christians. The problem is the President is making decisions which affect the entire planet based on faith alone. If faith is used to simply certify one's righteousness, then there is no longer room for discussion. On June 17, 2004, at the White House, in response to a reporters question regarding the 9-11 commission's finding there was no link between Iraq and al Qaeda, Bush said, "The reason I keep insisting that there was a relationship between Iraq and Saddam and al Qaeda is because there was a relationship between Iraq and al Qaeda." Period. End of discussion. We see Bush has surrounded himself with the tightest, most secretive inner circle in recent history. We know what their agenda is. He doesn't' read much and is not interested in outside influence, and doesn't ask questions. This preternatural certainty of things not based on any fact, but rather some sort of gut instinct is both scary and dangerous.

Richard Nixon would have briefs prepared for him by the different departments. He would spend hours reading them and other sources of fact on the issue at hand. When he gathered his advisors, he would ask dozens of pointed questions. If they didn't have answers, he would dress them down and send them out to get answers.

George H. W. Bush had scores of people, especially his military commanders, working tirelessly for months to put together a real coalition, made up of virtually every Muslim country in the Middle East to oust Saddam Hussein from Kuwait. The war was over quickly and by most accounts was a huge success.

Bill Clinton was known to be a tireless reader who would read one or two hundred page reports in a night. When he gathered his advisors, he would demand facts on all sides of the issue. After meeting with his advisors, he was known to get on the phone and call people who were experts on the issue at hand outside of his administration, sometimes other foreign leaders. When he was comfortable he had all the facts, he would make a decision.

These men, as well as most other Presidents, understood a mistake at the level they were operating at could produce catastrophic results. They considered it their obligation to have all the facts, all the time.

One hundred years from now, history will undoubtedly recognize September 11, 2001 as arguably the worst tragedy that has ever happened to the U.S. But that generation will probably not be discussing what happened, but rather what this generation did about it. Did we try to understand why young men would strap explosives to their chest and blow themselves and countless innocent people up? Or did our leadership give us simplistic slogans like "they hate our freedom" and "they hate our way of life" to be repeated by their followers over and over?

The terrorists themselves have said it is U.S. policy they are fighting, not our way of life. A policy decades old of supporting repressive regimes like that of the Shah of Iran, Saddam Hussein, the Saudi Royal Family, the Kuwaiti Royal Family, Pakistan, Jordan, and the list goes on and on. Usama bin Laden said, after 9-11, the U.S. would invade and occupy an oil rich Muslim country. We have turned him into a prophet in the eyes of the Muslim world by invading Iraq, which had nothing to do with 9-11, as we've been discussing. There is no negotiating with the extremists. They don't seem to want anything now except to kill infidels, particularly Americans and Jew's. Michael Scheuer, the former CIA analyst, said we don't have any choice now but to kill thousands upon thousands of people. Unfortunately, he is probably right. Iraq has become the recruiting poster for Islamic extremists throughout the world. But while we're eradicating terrorists is our leadership trying to prevent future terrorism by doing the things O'Neill and Shinseki talked about, bringing a better way of life to people, who currently have no hope, and stemming the flow of recruits into terrorist organizations.

Some may ask why it is the responsibility of the United States to solve the problems of the world. The answer is, because we are 5% of the world's population, yet we consume 25% of the world's resources. First and foremost, it's a moral obligation of the richest country on the planet. The second reason is purely selfish, simply put; it is in the best interest of our national security, for the reasons stated above. Undoubtedly, this is going to be a huge challenge. The historians one hundred years from now are going to be asking if we met these challenges.

Or were we waging war with no regard for the longer term solutions. It seems we are doing the latter, which makes this administration clearly incompetent. Did we allow a few militaristic ideologues to lead us down the path of empire building, furthering their agenda which is not in the best interests of the people of the United States? If we were going after terrorists in places where they are, like North Africa, Pakistan and Afghanistan we would have the world behind us, we wouldn't be going it alone. However the PNAC members would probably not be able to build the military they envision for world domination, and increase defense spending which would greatly increase the bottom line of the defense and energy contractors they worked for and will lobby for in the future. Did we try to solve problems we were faced with, or did we use 9-11 to try and force our brand of democracy down the throats of people, who have a couple of thousand years of culture on us, at the barrel of a gun.

During the 2004 Presidential debates, John Kerry said, "No President through all of American history, has ever ceded, *nor would I*, the right to preempt in any way necessary to protect the United States of America. But if and *when* you do it, you have to do it in a way that passes the test, that passes the global test where your countrymen, your people, understand fully why you're doing what you're doing, and you can prove it to the world that you did it for legitimate reasons." The Bush campaign twisted and distorted what Kerry meant by "global test" to say Kerry would require a "permission slip" from other countries to protect the U.S. Read the statement again. Kerry was clearly talking about *after* America used military action, and that any war waged by our government, in our name, which will potentially kill American troops had better be justifiable to the American people first and then to the world. The reason the American people and the world were behind the U.S. operation in Afghanistan is because that operation met the "global test" Kerry was talking about. The invasion of Iraq doesn't.

Chapter seven of the U.N. Charter, Article 51 says "Nothing in the present Charter shall impair the inherent right of individual or collective self-defense if an armed attack occurs against a member of the United Nations." Under U.N. Charter, chapter seven, we could, and should be going after Al Qaeda in any country we find them, preferably with the co-operation of that country's government, or without it, if that turns out to be the case.

In 1837, then Secretary of State, Daniel Webster, in response to a British attack on an American ship, set U.S. precedent when he spelled out the conditions for justified "anticipatory self-defense." He wrote "It could only be justified when the threat is "instant, overwhelming, and leaving no choice of means, and no moment for deliberation." It is a winnable argument to say Al Qaeda is still an imminent threat to the U.S. Al Qaeda was, and still is in Afghanistan, and the Talliban government was a puppet of Al Qaeda. Currently, International law does provide for preemptive war when it is in defense of an imminent attack.

Author Peter Singer, Professor of bioethics at Princeton University, wrote "In his preamble to the National Security Strategy, Bush takes a very different position from that taken by Daniel Webster and by the U.N. Charter. He says that 'as a matter of common sense and self-defense, America will act against such emerging threats *before they are fully formed.*' [Emphasis added] One problem with this view lies in the risk of a government manufacturing a case for a preemptive war when it actually has other motives for going to war." [16] This is exactly what is happening. This *new* interpretation of preemptive war is as per RAD.

It is clear that the intelligence that has put us in Iraq has been massaged, manipulated, and cooked by a group of militaristic neo-conservatives bent on seeing their vision through to fruition without regard for the interests of the United States. Moreover, the real threat of Al Qaeda and Al Qaeda type organizations are unaddressed while the neo-cons make their plans for Iran and Syria.

The conclusion is the war in Iraq does not meet the "test to our own countrymen", it does not meet U.N. Charter chapter seven article 51, it does not stand up to the precedent laid out by Webster in 1837 and it is in violation of international law.

Newsweek reports in early December 2004, a previously secret memo written just two weeks after 9-11 by Justice Department lawyer John Yoo to White House counsel Alberto Gonzales, was posted on an obscure portion of the website of the Justice Department's Office of Legal Counsel. There was no notice to the public or the news media, and there was nothing on the site calling attention to the memo. The memo, titled *The Presidents Constitutional Authority to Conduct Military Operations Against Terrorists and Nations Supporting Them* states there are effectively "no limits" on the President's authority to wage war. Yoo argues "The President may deploy military force preemptively against terrorist organizations or the States that harbor or support them, whether or not they can be linked to the specific terrorist incidents of 9-11." And "the President's decisions are for him alone and are unreviewable." What is striking is it goes beyond the joint Congressional resolution passed on September 14, 2001, which gives the President the authority to attack only those connected with 9-11. Yoo argued that what Congress authorized didn't matter saying, "It should be noted here that the Joint Resolution is somewhat narrower than the President's constitutional authority," [17] but that will probably be argued. The constitution is pretty clear on who can authorize war. And it's not the President.

While this memo argues, the President has broader powers than anything we've seen before, it essentially says we have a right to preemptively strike Al Qaeda in any country they may be, as per international law, as was discussed earlier, especially since 9-11. Iraq was not one of those countries. The memo was written two weeks after 9-11 in response to questions from the White House to Justice. Yoo does not mention Iraq specifically, but he provides the framework for striking terrorists. This memo is the motive for the "cooked" evidence against Iraq. The PNAC members who had been advocating war with Iraq for ten years would have to make Iraq fit into the legal parameters laid out by the Yoo memo. Iraq had to have been harboring terrorists and/or have weapons of terror. Both arguments, as we have seen, have been presented, and both arguments have been proven to be completely false.

We need visionary leadership, not slogans like "there's an old poster in Texas that says wanted dead or alive" Bush talking about capturing Usama bin Laden on September 17, 2001. It's been over 1,180 days since he said that. On March 13, 2002 during a White House press conference, in response to a question about Bush rarely talking about bin Laden, Bush said, "I don't know where he [bin Laden] is. You know, I just don't spend that much time on him, to be honest with you." In response to a follow up question, he said, "And again, I don't know where he is. I-I'll repeat what I said. I truly am not that concerned about him." And slogans like "Freedom's on the march" and my personal favorite, from the deck of the USS Abraham Lincoln, standing under a sign which said, "Mission Accomplished", on May 1, 2003 "Major combat operations in Iraq have ended." That was over two years ago.

There is not a more frightening statement of the PNAC doctrine than Richard Perle's concept of "total war." He says, "No stages, this is total war. We are fighting a variety of enemies. There are lots of them out there. All this talk about first we are going to do Afghanistan, then we will do Iraq…this is entirely the wrong way to go about it. If we just let our vision of the world go forth, and we embrace it entirely and we don't try to piece together clever diplomacy, but *just wage total war*…our children will sing great songs about us years from now." [18] Sieg Hiel!

Update to chapter's three and four [added since original writing in December 2004]

Some very interesting developments have broken since the writing of *The Real Reason for war with Iraq*. The first deals with Richard Clarke's testimony before the 9-11 commission and Clarke's previous secret testimony before the Joint Inquiry. During the public 9-11 investigation, Clarke testified extensively about the January 25, 2001 memo to then National Security Advisor Condoleezza Rice in which he laid out plans for urgent action by the new administration to roll up the al-Qaeda network within the next three to five years making them a "rump group" like others formerly feared but now largely defunct terrorist organizations in the 1980's. "That goal can be achieved if adequate resources and policy attention are devoted to it" he writes. Attached to the January 25, memo was a December 2000 paper titled *Strategy for Eliminating the Threat from the Jihadist Networks of al-Qida: Status and Prospects* and a 1998 paper titled *Pol-Mil Plan for al-Qida* known as the Delenda Plan. These two attachments which accompanied the January 25, memo to Dr. Rice were written during the Clinton administration and were provided as a review of what Clark and his team at Counterterrorism had been doing up to that point. Clarke asked numerous times for early principal's meetings on the subject.

During the 9-11 hearings, Commission Member Timothy Roemer asked Clarke, "Do you get a response to this urgent request for a principals meeting on these [the Jan. 25, memo]."

Clarke responded, "I did get a response, and the response was that in the Bush administration I should, and my committee, counterterrorism security group, should report to the deputies committee, which is a sub-Cabinet level committee, and not to the principals and that, therefore, it was inappropriate for me to be asking for a principals' meeting. Instead there would be a deputies meeting." Clarke's group had been demoted.

Roemer: "A memo comes out that we have seen on September 4. You are blunt in blasting DOD for not willingly using the force and power. You blast the CIA for blocking Predator. You urge policy makers to imagine a day after hundreds of Americans lay dead at home and abroad after a terrorist attack and ask themselves what else they could have done. You write this on September 4th, seven days before September 11th.

Clarke: "That's right"

As is policy with the Bush White House, they began a campaign to destroy Clarke's credibility. Clarke was ready for them because he saw what happened to

Joe Wilson and his wife, Valerie Plame when Wilson disputed Bush's claims in the 2003 State of the Union Address that Iraq was attempting to acquire yellow cake uranium from Niger for a WMD program, Plame's role as a CIA operator was leaked to the press. There were also attacks on Generals Eric Shinseki and Anthony Zinni and former treasury secretary Paul O'Neill for speaking out against Bush administration policies.

During Clarke's public testimony before the 9-11 commission, Jim Thompson, former Republican Governor of Illinois, charged Clarke with changing his story. He referred to a 2002 off-the-record background briefing Clarke had given to Washington Journalists. Clarke's name was "leaked" to his attackers which is unethical at best. While Clarke may have put a positive spin on the briefing (He was still at the White House at the time) there is nothing inconsistent with his statements.

On March 25, 2004, speaking from the Senate floor, Mitch McConnell (R-KY) again referring to the 2002 background briefing said Clarke is now "singing an entirely different tune. This is a man who lacks credibility...clearly he has a grudge of some sort against the Bush administration." These attacks didn't go anywhere because clearly Clarke's testimony was not contradictory with his earlier statements.

So, Bush shill and Republican Majority leader, Senator Bill Frist tried a different tact. He attacked Clarke's closed door testimony to the Joint Inquiry into 9-11 by implying Clarke's closed door testimony differed from his public testimony and that Clarke may have "lied under oath", a very serious charge. But Frist has no idea what Clarke said in the closed door hearing. Frist, along with Speaker of the House Denny Hastert, has called for Clarke's testimony to be declassified. To their surprise, Clarke, knowing what he said during the closed door hearing, has agreed. He has also called their bluff by calling for Rice's testimony to be declassified along with the January 25th memos to her. Dr. Rice testified "The fact is that what we were presented on January 25th was a set of ideas and a paper, most of which was about what the Clinton administration had done." Rice also testified there was no "actionable intelligence" before 9-11. Clarke has also made it clear that his testimony, and Dr. Rice's testimony, should not be "selectively" released, as the Bush administration is prone to do, but be completely declassified. When this happens we'll see who perjured themselves.

After Clarke's "bring it on" attitude, the Republicans have quietly backed away from their "demand" his testimony be declassified. But Clarke hasn't. The January 25th memo and the two attachments have been declassified and they say exactly what Clarke said they'd say. They contain much more than "a set of ideas" and a paper as Dr. Rice has said.

The memo, titled *Presidential Policy Initiative/Review—The Al-Qida Network* says, in the very first two sentences, "…we propose major Presidential policy reviews or initiatives. We *urgently* need such a Principals level review on the al Qida network." The memo's call for covert funding for the Afghanistan Northern Alliance, "significant program growth in the FY02 budget for anti al Qida operations by CIA and counterterrorism," and a response to the attack on the U.S.S. Cole and says "a decision is needed now." The memos urged the use of unmanned Predator aircraft equipped with Hellfire missiles giving them a "see-it, shoot-it" capability. (This was rejected by the CIA).

Bush and Rice claim, and the administration's supporters believe the Clinton administration had done nothing about al-Qaeda, however, the attachments to the January 25th memo provided to Rice, which were written at the end of the Clinton administration, show Clarke's group had identified the al-Qaeda organization and their areas of operations in Somalia, Sudan, Egypt, Uzbekistan, Philippines, Libya, Yemen, Chechnya, Morocco, Tunisia, Saudi Arabia, and Central Asia. Outside of these mostly Muslim countries they identified cells in Canada, Ireland, England, Israel, Italy, Turkey, Germany, Spain, Belgium, Thailand and the United States.

The memos provide an overview of what worked during the Clinton administration and discusses al-Qaeda plots which were thwarted such as the plot to destroy the N.Y.-N.J. tunnels, multiple attacks around the world targeting American citizens, three of which were scheduled for January of 2000 in Jordan and an attempted attack on a U.S. Navy ship in Yemen prior to the successful attack on the Cole. In addition to disrupting plots, the "U.S. found and brought to the U.S. for trial al-Qida operatives in Jordan, Egypt, Pakistan, Malaysia, South Africa, Kenya, Tanzania, Germany and the United Kingdom. Other al-Qida operatives not indicted in the U.S. were brought to [redacted] where they were wanted by authorities."

Overt military action is also discussed such as the 1998 attack on al-Qaeda facilities in Afghanistan, which specifically targeted bin-Ladin, and Sudan. These were the cruise missile attacks which Clinton critics claimed accomplished nothing more than blowing up a tent and killing a camel, and accused him of attempting to divert attention from the Monica Lewinski scandal. They were more concerned with impeaching Clinton for lying about an affair with a White House intern than they were about al-Qaeda.

One of the more chilling observations Clarke made in the memo was a plot by a Manila cell, which was thwarted in 1993, that *"was preparing bombs for six U.S. flag 747's* [and] was funded and trained by al-Qida."* These memos were loaded with "actionable" intelligence and specific recommendations contrary to Dr. Rice's testimony. All of Clarke's recommendations from going after al-Qaeda funding to overtly attacking al-Qaeda and Taliban training camps and covertly funding the Northern Alliance to arming Predator aircraft and pressuring other governments, were implemented by the Bush administration—after September 11th.

Clarke had been asking for a serious discussion on al-Qaeda for the first seven months of the Bush administration. During the 9-11 hearings, when asked if having deputies meetings instead of Cabinet level meetings slowed the process down Clarke replied, "It slowed it down enormously, by months." He explained the al-Qaeda issue took more of a back seat to other issues. After a few deputies meetings, which ended around July, Clarke testified "we were ready for a Principals meeting in July. But the principal's calendar was full and then they went on vacation, many of them in August, so we couldn't meet in August, and therefore met in September." Seven days before 9-11 Clarke finally got his meeting.

During Bush's vacation in August of 2001, in Crawford, Texas a reporter asked Bush what he would say to critics who accused him of taking to much vacation time. Bush responded, "They don't understand how work gets done. It's amazing what you can accomplish with phones and fax machines."

Also during the same month, there was another memo to the administration. This one was from the CIA now known simply as the Aug. 6th PDB (Presidential Daily Briefing). During her testimony before the 9-11 commission, Condoleezza Rice also said this brief had no "actionable intelligence" either and that it was just an historical document. It's true it didn't have a map of New York with a big red "X" over Manhattan with the date September 11th penciled in, but when asked to read the title of it for the 9-11 commission she said, "I think it's title was 'bin-Laden determined to strike in the United States.'" This memo cites a source as saying, "Bin Ladin wanted to hijack a U.S. aircraft to gain the release of 'Blind Shaykh' Umar Abd al-Rahman." It goes on to say the FBI had information that "indicates patterns of suspicious activity in this country consistent with preparations for hijackings or other types of attacks, *including recent surveillance of federal buildings in New York."* And the very first paragraph says in part, "Bin Ladin implied in U.S. television interviews in 1997 and 1998 that his followers would follow the example of [1993] World Trade Center bomber Ramzi Yousef and 'bring the fighting to America.'" [1] Its not clear to this day whether Bush read this memo or not.

What is clear is this administration has made it a policy to reverse everything "Clinton." The Clinton administration had made terrorism a number one priority throughout the 90's with Clarke playing a major role. Knowing what we know now, that the Bush administration was briefed in January of 2001, during the transition, that al-Qaeda would be their number one problem by Clarke and Sandy Berger the out going National Security Advisor and that they had in their possession the January 25th memo and the two attachments written earlier which were not merely a set of ideas but detailed analysis and solid recommendations and that the CIA warned in August of 2001 about bin-Ladin wanting to attack in the U.S. with airplanes, one can only conclude the Bush administration's priorities were elsewhere, specifically on tax cuts for the wealthy, dismantling Social Security, gutting the EPA, usurping Congressional authority and cooking up ways to invade Iraq. The Bush/Cheney administration is incompetent at best and criminally negligent at worst.

Of all the countries mentioned in Clarke's memos and the August 6th PDB, there is absolutely no mention of al-Qaeda in Iraq. They're there now however and they are still in all the other places identified by Clarke, undoubtedly growing stronger, thanks to the recruiting boon the U.S. invasion has provided them.

Another intriguing piece of recent news since the writing of *The Real Reason for War with Iraq* can be found in Bush's FY2006 budget request. In it is funding for the new *family* of nuclear weapons discussed in the RAD document in that chapter. With the Project for the New American Century (PNAC) members taking their place in the Bush administration in January 2001, Donald Rumsfeld's pet project grew legs. Known as the Robust Nuclear Earth Penetrator (RNEP) project, Congress has continually cut the funding and late in 2004 cut the funding completely from the '05 budget which was projected to grow to almost $500 million through 2009.

But Rumsfeld refuses to give up. The *Washington Post* recently obtained a memo from January 10, 2005 from Rumsfeld to then Secretary of Energy Spencer Abraham which says, "I think we should request funds in FY06 and FY07 to complete the study," Rumsfeld wrote. "Our staffs have spoken about funding the RNEP study to support its completion by April 2007." He added, "You can count on my support for your efforts to revitalize the nuclear weapons infrastructure and to complete the RNEP study." [2]

The FY06 budget request, released in February 2005, provides for $8.5 million, $4 million for the department of energy and $4.5 million for Rumsfeld's

Department of Defense for research and development of the RNEP project. The administration plans to spend an additional $26 million through FY07. Unlike earlier requests, the FY06 budget does not include a cost projection past 2007. Some in Congress have accused the administration of trying to slip the RNEP funding past Congress without fully disclosing the cost. [3]

The *Washington Post* also reported that "sealing off underground facilities could be done as well with smart, precision guided conventional weapons, a position supported in 2003 by Adm. James O. Ellis Jr., then head of the U.S. Strategic Command. They also have said that no casing could dig deep enough to prevent the nuclear warhead's explosion from sending tons of radioactive debris into the atmosphere." [4]

How does the Bush administration expect to further a non-proliferation agenda internationally while at the same time declaring to the world, the U.S. is seeking to invent a new family of nuclear weapons? Hopefully Congress will reject the funding for this one more time.

Another major development since the writing of *The Real Reason for War with Iraq* is the release of the Downing Street memos. [5] The first memo (there are nine to date) was published in London's *The Sunday Times* on May 1, 2005. It was the minutes of a July 23, 2002 meeting with Prime Minister Tony Blair attended by, among others, the British Ambassador to the United States, David Manning, the head of British intelligence, Sir Richard Dearlove, (known as "C" in the memo), Foreign Secretary Jack Straw (the equivalent of our Secretary of State), Defense Secretary Geoff Hoon and the Attorney General Lord Goldsmith. The minutes begin "This record is extremely sensitive. No further copies should be made. It should be shown only to those with a genuine need to know its contents."

The most damning portion of the meeting takes place right at the beginning. "C reported on his recent talks in Washington. There was a perceptible shift in attitude. Military action was now seen as inevitable. Bush wanted to remove Saddam, through military action, justified by the conjunction of terrorism and WMD. But the intelligence and facts were being fixed around the policy."

This is a full eight months before the U.S. lead invasion of Iraq, however Bush said he did not decide to go to war until after Colin Powell's speech to the United Nations on February 5, 2003, only six weeks before the invasion began.

Until recently, the memos received very little attention in the United States, to the amazement of Europe and the rest of the world. Some American news outlets took the position this was old news and did not need re-hashing. As we've seen in the chapter *The Real Reason for the War with Iraq* this is, in a way, old news, however the media didn't report what people like Col. Kwiatkawski and Gregory Thielmann have been saying for years. Paul O'Neill and Richard Clarke did get some attention in the mainstream media but follow up stories were almost non-existent and the White House was effective in painting these people as "disgruntled" former White House employee's, moreover the Bush administration was also able to, with help from a complacent media, create an impression the intelligence was simply wrong, misleading the American public. What makes these memos news worthy is they are an inside look at what the Bush administration was planning long before they were willing to admit it, and the observations were from officials from another government. They also corroborate what Kwiatkawski, Thielmann, O'Neill, Clarke and others have been trying to tell us.

At the White House in June of 2005, Blair was asked about the leaked memo, specifically was the intelligence being "fixed around the policy?" He replied, "Absolutely not." He offered as proof the fact that the coalition went to the U.N., after the date on the memo, to force Saddam to let weapons inspectors back in to Iraq. The inference was they had not made up their minds to use force. The minutes from the meeting Blair attended offer a different reason for going to the U.N.

Straw said, "It seemed clear that Bush had made up his mind to take military action…But the case was thin. Saddam was not threatening his neighbors, and his WMD capability was less than that of Libya, North Korea or Iran. We should work up a plan for an ultimatum to Saddam to allow back in the U.N. weapons inspectors. This would also help with the legal justification for the use of force."

Lord Goldsmith said, "…the desire for regime change was not a legal base for military action." And they probably would not be able to rely on earlier U.N. resolutions.

Blair agreed "The Prime Minister said that it would make a big difference politically and legally if Saddam refused to allow in the U.N. inspectors." And there is the reason for going back to the U.N. from the people involved themselves.

The Brits were worried about the legalities of the war. If Saddam rejected the new U.N. resolution they could use that as justification for war. The problem was, Saddam didn't reject the U.N. and inspectors did go back in. Just prior to the invasion, Bush ordered them to leave. Nothing was going to stop them from their war.

On this side of the pond the Bush administration was also concerned with creating conditions which would make the war legal. According to the Downing Street memo, Defense Secretary Hoon, "cautioned that many in the U.S. did not think it would be worth going down the ultimatum route." (Bush would later concede to Blair's insistence on going to the U.N. because of Blair's concern that even if the British didn't go in with the Americans, the U.S. would still be using U.K. bases which would have legal implications for England). The Bush administration was taking a different approach. They were attempting to gain support by manipulating intelligence to make Saddam fit within the parameters of the Yoo memo as discussed in *The Real Reason for the War with Iraq.*

These memos from Great Britain should not come as any great shock to anyone. The fact that they do is testimony to the disservice of the media and the success of the Bush administration's deception perpetuated on the American people. Even without the Downing Street memo's, the preponderance of evidence the Bush administration was planning for war well before September 11th as far back as the first few days of the Bush administration is overwhelming. In fact, the members of PNAC, many of whom are at the highest levels of our government, have told us with their words and through their writings of their desire to invade Iraq as far back as at least 1997.

Defense Secretary Hoon also told Blair, "...the U.S had already begun 'spikes of activity' to put pressure on the regime." And "...the most likely timing in U.S. minds for military action to begin was January [2003], with the timeline beginning 30 days before the U.S. Congressional elections."

The war started in March 2003, very close to the date Hoon spoke about. Was Blair's Secretary of Defense suggesting the timing of the invasion was partly politically motivated? Historically Presidents have been given great latitude during times of war and public opinion tends to support a President during crises, especially when the public doesn't know all the facts. We tend to want to believe in our government. If Bush was politicizing the war to help Republicans get elected this would be the most abhorrent thing any President had ever done. But it's the first part of Hoon's statement which should raise the most questions. "The U.S. had already begun spikes of activity." What did he mean by that?

In an article in *The Nation* dated June 1st 2005 by Jeremy Scahill titled *The Other Bomb Drops* there are some clues as to what Hoon was talking about. Scahill reports, "*The Sunday Times* of London recently reported on new evidence showing that 'The RAF and U.S. aircraft doubled the rate at which they were dropping bombs on Iraq in 2002 in an attempt to provoke Saddam Hussein into giving the allies an excuse for war.'" Much of this was happening while Hans Blix's U.N. inspectors were on the ground in Iraq. They were targeting "...western air-defense facilities, clearing the path for Special Forces helicopters that lay in wait in Jordan. Earlier attacks had been carried out against Iraqi command and control centers, radar detection systems, Revolutionary Guard units, communication centers and mobile air-defense systems." These operations were more than enforcing the no-fly zone; they were softening targets in the spring of 2002 in preparation for an invasion. The war had begun!

Scahill quotes Rear Admiral David Gove, former deputy director of global operations for the Joint Chiefs of Staff as saying, "U.S. and British pilots were essentially flying combat missions." Also in October of 2002 the *New York Times* reported U.S. pilots were using southern Iraq for "practice runs, mock strikes and real attacks against a variety of targets." [6] These combat operations were occurring in the spring and summer of 2002, approximately nine months before Bush said he made up his mind to use military action and at least four months before the October 2002 Congressional authorization to use military force.

Under the three branch system of government as laid out by the Constitution of the United States, the Legislative and the Judicial branches are charged with providing checks and balance over the Executive branch. Therefore they would be derelict in their duties if they did not confront the President with evidence of potential wrong doing. There is nothing more patriotic than the legitimate questioning of the people we charge with running our government. With the evidence Congress has, they are obligated to hold hearings to determine whether the Bush administration lied to Congress, and the American people, which resulted in the war with Iraq. And did they begin the war long before telling the American people that war was a "last resort," before the October 2002 Congressional authorization. If the hearings find this is in fact the case then under the Constitution they are also obligated to start impeachment proceedings. If they do not begin hearings then they themselves should be subject to impeachment or other actions as prescribed by the Constitution. This is exactly what Clinton was impeached for. For *lying to Congress* about a sexual affair with a White House intern.

5

U.S.A., Inc.

"The liberty of a democracy is not safe if the people tolerate the growth of private power to a point where it becomes stronger than their democratic state itself. That, in its essence, is fascism-ownership of government by an individual, by a group."
Franklin D. Roosevelt

In 1886, there was a Supreme Court decision which would change the course of American history from that day forward. It still affects us to this day. It was the case of Santa Clara County v. Southern Pacific Railroad. [118 U.S. 394 (1886)] The court ruled that a corporation has the same status and rights, under the Constitution, as that of a living, breathing human being. Well, sort of.

Southern Pacific Railroad had for years disputed the way Santa Clara County had been taxing the land and right of ways the railroad used. For six years they refused to pay *any* of the taxes levied by Santa Clara County. The dispute finally ended up in front of the Supreme Court. The Chief Legal Advisor for Southern Pacific was S. W. Sanderson. He had been an attorney for the nation's largest railroads for twenty years. He would present six different defenses. One of the defenses was that when the state assessed the value of the railroads property, it accidentally included the value of the fences along the right of way. The County, not the state, should have assessed the fences. But the main defense would be that because Southern Pacific was a "person" under the 14th Amendment of the Constitution, local governments couldn't "discriminate" against it by having different laws and taxes than any other person, by assessing its property at full value without making deductions as it does on a person's mortgage.

O.K, I know what you're thinking. How the hell is a railroad a "person." This is where a simple tax case that would have ended up on the back burner of history, or buried in some boring law book gets a little complicated.

The 14th amendment, section 1 says:

All persons born or naturalized in the United States, and subject to the jurisdiction thereof, are citizens of the United States and of the state wherein they reside. No state shall make or enforce any law which shall abridge the privileges or immunities of citizens of the United States; nor shall any state deprive any person of life, liberty, or property, without due process of law; *nor deny to any person within its jurisdiction the equal protection of the laws.* [Emphasis added]

The 14th amendment's purpose, written in 1868, was the freedom of the slaves; however, there is evidence the use of the word "person" in the 14th amendment instead of the more correct legal phrase "natural person" was intentional.

The terms "natural person" and "artificial person" were over 100 years old. It was recognized there were similarities between corporations and humans. They could both enter into agreements, they could both sue, both could be taxed and both were subject to the law and the penalty of the law. Even though there were similarities, there also needed to be a separation of the two, therefore, corporations were commonly referred to as "artificial persons" and humans were referred to as "natural persons."

One of the Senate committee members, who wrote the 14th amendment, was Senator Roscoe Conkling of New York. Conkling, who later became a railroad lawyer, testified in 1882, as a paid witness for the railroads, he'd slipped the "person" language into the amendment to ensure corporations would one day receive the same civil rights Congress was giving to freed slaves.

This brings us to the 1886 Santa Clara Supreme Court case. Though this was not the first time corporations had argued for "personhood" in various courts, it is the first time any court ruled on the argument. Well, again, sort of.

During the proceedings Chief Justice Morrison R. Waite said to the attorneys "The court does not wish to hear argument on the question whether the provision in the 14th Amendment to the Constitution, which forbids a state to deny to any person within its jurisdiction the equal protection of the laws, applies to these corporations. We are of the opinion that it does."

In the written record of the case, court recorder J.C. Bancroft Davis noted "The defendant corporations are persons within the intent of the clause in section 1 of the 14th Amendment to the Constitution of the United States, which forbids a State to deny any person within its jurisdiction the equal protection of the laws."

In the 1960's, author and legal historian Howard Jay Graham found the personal papers of Chief Justice Waite on file with the Library of Congress. Among them was a letter from Davis to Justice Waite which asked "In opening the Court stated that it did not wish to hear argument on the question whether the 14th

Amendment applies to such corporations as are parties in these suits. All the Judges were of opinion that it does. Please let me know whether I correctly caught your words and oblige."

Waite replied "I think your mem. in the California Railroad Tax case expresses with sufficient accuracy what was said before argument began. I leave it to you to determine whether anything need be said about it in the report inasmuch as *we avoided meeting the constitutional question in the decision.*"

Waite was saying they never ruled on the Constitutional question of corporate personhood. When Waite said they didn't rule on the Constitutional question it was because they didn't need to. Waite told the attorneys we don't wish to hear the Constitutional question, so move on from there. Southern Pacific had presented six different defenses, one of which the court made its decision on. The fence issue and who should assess it. The official ruling said in part "As the judgment can be sustained upon this ground, *it is not necessary to consider any other questions raised by the pleadings.*"

Author Thom Hartmann notes in his book *Unequal Protection: The Rise of Corporate Dominance and the Theft of Human Rights* that Waite recognized corporations were persons (of the artificial kind) and did not wish to hear that argument. The notes written by court reporter Davis in the summary of the case in which he acknowledges Waite's statement are not part of the official decision. However they were interpreted to be part of the decision by other courts and therefore have become precedent.

After the 1886 Supreme Court "decision", corporate attorneys lined up to argue for corporate personhood. They would cite the 1886 "decision" and win, setting the precedent for future cases, and even if the decision had been wrongly cited, and ruled on, it's now part of our law.

There was no majority opinion by the Supreme Court, no dissenting opinion written on the subject of corporate personhood. No state or federal legislature passed it, or even debated it. There was no Constitutional Amendment. The misinterpretation that the case summary was the decision of the court, a decision that a Constitutional Amendment about ex slaves had converted *artificial* entities into the legal equivalent of *natural* persons, would begin an abuse of the Constitution, by corporations, that is still plaguing us to this day.

Over the next twenty four years, from 1886 to 1910, there would be 307 14th Amendment cases brought before the Supreme Court. Nineteen dealt with African American issues, 288 were suits brought by corporations seeking the rights of natural persons. [1]

The implications of this are huge. Corporations could now argue the States, which chartered the corporations, should be constrained by the 14th Amendment from exercising power over them. Since corporations have been considered persons, without that pesky adjective *artificial* attached, they would soon argue, successfully, for protection under the 4th Amendment which says:

> The right of the people to be secure in their persons, houses, papers, and effects, against unreasonable searches and seizures, shall not be violated, and no Warrants shall issue, but upon probable cause, supported by oath or affirmation, and particularly describing the place to be searched, and the persons or things to be seized.

The key Supreme Court case here was Hale v. Henkel [201 U.S. 43 (1906)]. The court ruled a subpoena issued by a federal grand jury to the secretary of a corporation, MacAndrews & Forbes Company, amounted to an unreasonable search and seizure. The grand jury was attempting to investigate whether the corporation was in violation of anti trust laws, which naturally required the papers of the corporation, to determine if there existed grounds for an indictment.

In 1970, the Occupational Safety and Health Act (OSHA) was enacted to help employees get a safe working environment. The act allowed for surprise inspections of work places. In the Supreme Court case Marshall v. Barlow's, Inc. [436 U.S. 307 (1978)], the court struck down the surprise inspections citing the 4th Amendment. They ruled OSHA inspections required either the corporation's permission or a warrant. The "Constitutional rights" of the corporation superceded the rights of natural persons.

The implications were not lost on everyone. Beginning in the early 1870's, corporations began arguing for personhood to remove government restraint. In 1872, fourteen years before the Santa Clara case, a case came before the Supreme Court known as the Slaughterhouse Cases [83 U.S. 36 (1872)]. It was the first 14th Amendment case to be heard by the Supreme Court. Justice Samuel F. Miller writing for the majority, said:

"They [Negroes] were in some states forbidden to appear in the towns in any other character than menial servants. They were required to reside on and cultivate the soil without the right to purchase or own it. They were excluded from many occupations of gain…These circumstances forced upon the statesman who had conducted the Federal government in safety through the crises of the rebellion [the Civil War], and supposed that, by the 13th Amendment, they had secured the result of their labors, the conviction that something more was necessary in the way of Constitutional protection to the unfortunate race who had suffered so much. They accordingly passed the 14th Amendment.

'We repeat, then, in the light of this recapitulation of events, almost too recent to be called history, but which are familiar to us all, and on the most casual examination of the language of these amendments, no one can fail to be impressed with the one pervading purpose found in them all, lying at the foundation of each, and without which none of them would have been even suggested; we mean the freedom of the slave race, the security and establishment of that freedom, and the protection of the newly made freeman and citizen."

Justice Miller was clearly saying the 14th Amendment was designed exclusively for the recently freed slaves.

After the Santa Clara case, corporations had finally attained the same status of natural persons, but there was opposition to this ridiculous idea. In 1938, the Supreme Court sided with the corporation claiming rights of a person under the 14th Amendment in the case Connecticut General Life v. Johnson [303 U.S. 77 (1938)]. In writing the dissenting opinion, Justice B. Hugo Black said:

"I do not believe the word 'person' in the 14th Amendment includes corporations…A constitutional interpretation that is wrong should not stand. I believe this Court should now overrule previous decisions which interpreted the 14th Amendment to include corporations.

'Certainly, when the 14th Amendment was submitted for approval, the people were not told that the states of the South were to be denied their normal relationship with the Federal Government unless they ratified an amendment granting new and revolutionary rights to corporations. This Court, when the Slaughterhouse Cases were decided in 1873, had apparently discovered no such purpose. The records of the time can be searched in vain for evidence that this amendment was adopted for the benefit of corporations. It is true [303 U.S. 77, 87] that in 1882, twelve years after its adoption, and ten years after the Slaughterhouse Cases, supra, an argument was made in this Court that a journal of the joint Congressional Committee which framed the amendment, secret and undisclosed up to that date, indicated the committee's desire to protect corporations by the use of the word 'person.' Four years later, in 1886, this Court in the case of Santa Clara County v. Southern Pacific Railroad decided for the first time that the word 'person' in the amendment did in some instances include corporations. A secret purpose on the part of the members of the committee would not be sufficient to justify any such construction. The history of the amendment proves that the people were told that its purpose was to protect weak and helpless human beings and were not told that it was intended to remove corporations in any fashion from the control of state governments.

'No word in all this amendment gave any hint that its adoption would deprive the states of their long recognized power to regulate corporations."

Justice Black seems to have been worried about corporate power and the dismantling of government authority over corporations. So worried, in fact, he urged the other Justice's to overrule the ruling of the 1886 Supreme Court. It's also interesting that he wrote about how the word person got into the 14th Amendment without the term "natural" in the first place. From this we know at least some on the Court were well aware of the deception.

The colonial rebels in 1776 weren't to keen on unrestrained corporations either. You may remember learning about The Dutch West India Company in eighth grade history. This was one of the most powerful corporations in history. It was the Microsoft times ten of its day. Chartered in 1621 by the Dutch Republic, it soon swallowed the United New Netherland Company, which had been trading around the mouth of the Hudson River. The company built Fort Orange on the site of Albany, N.Y. in 1624, Fort Nassau on the Delaware River, Fort Good Hope on the site of Hartford on the Connecticut River, and Fort Amsterdam on the southern tip of Manhattan Island, in 1626, which was called New Amsterdam, what we now know as New York City. Its charter prevented anyone from trading from the African coast between the Tropic of Cancer and the Cape of Good Hope or on the American coast between Newfoundland and the Straights of Magellan without the company's permission. They were a monopoly of mega proportions. Even the empire of England could not afford to antagonize the Dutch because of its wars with France and Spain, so the Dutch corporation was permitted on the lands England claimed. Their sole purpose was wealth and power. They would attain both. They were so powerful they effectively became the government, and *appointed* governors in their area of operation, including what would become the United States. By the end of their existence, in 1791, their primary commerce was the African slave trade.

The recent memory of the Dutch West India Company was not lost on the founding Fathers. The conspicuous absence of any mention of corporations in the constitution is testimony to the fact they were not interested in protecting corporations. In the early 1800's Thomas Jefferson wrote:

"I hope we shall crush in its birth the aristocracy of our moneyed corporations which dare to challenge our government in a trial of strength, and bid defiance to the laws of our country."

Jefferson was not arguing against the existence of corporations, rather unregulated corporations open to corruption and bribery which was challenging the power of the new democracy he helped form. The greatest democracy ever created in the history of civilization and a democracy that, at the time, was still on shaky legs and trying to survive.

By the late 1800's, with very little regulation, and with their newfound rights and protections afforded to natural persons under the Constitution which allowed them to participate in the political process, and huge amounts of money, big business bought their first President. In 1896, William McKinley became the 25th President of the United States. His financier and campaign manager was Marcus Alonzo Hanna. Hanna ruled Ohio politics, a state as important then as it is now. He believed in unrestricted corporate power and cared little for the average worker. Corruption and bribes were the way things worked in his world. He once said, "Some men must rule; the great mass of men must be ruled. Some men must own; the great mass of men must work for those that own." He helped McKinley get elected Governor of Ohio in 1891 and again in 1893. That year he rescued McKinley from bankruptcy. By the 1896 Presidential race, he had built a huge powerful base of corporate contributors that was unprecedented at the time, and was successful in seeing McKinley's rise to the White House to become a rubber stamp President for their agenda's. They also believed "Free immigration provides a labor surplus. Immigrants can be worked twelve hours a day; by mixing nationalities they can be hindered from organizing; when they are maimed or worn out, others take their places. They need not be supported during hard times; when injured they can be sent to public hospitals for repair. Handled intelligently, ignorant men are cheaper than machines. And out of labor surplus come strike-breakers." [2] With the exception of Woodrow Wilson's term, Republican administrations and corporate cronyism would rule until the inauguration of Franklin D. Roosevelt on March 4, 1933. This was the era of the Robber Barons.

Corporations were now *the* major influence on the political landscape. Without their support, a politician could expect little success. With their [financial] influence of politicians they were able to get District Attorneys and judges appointed. Judges who would strike down minimum wage laws, worker compensation laws, energy and utility regulation, child labor laws, and other laws, that protected citizens from corporate abuse throughout the early part of the 20th century, allowing corporations to amass even more wealth and power. Corporate "personhood" had changed the relationship between corporations and government in a way the Founding Fathers had not intended, and allowed the wealthiest people to corrupt elected officials and control the government, and the people. Union members became the victims of violence perpetuated by "corporate armies" that considered them criminal's. Many at the time believe this imbalance of wealth and power, and the corruption of the government, contributed to the coming crisis.

The following are quotes from a speech given by Theodore Roosevelt before the Convention of the National Progressive Party in Chicago in August, 1912. This speech could be given today.

"As a people we cannot afford to let any group of citizens or any individual citizen live or labor under conditions which are injurious to the common welfare. Industry, therefore, must submit to such public regulation as will make it a means of life and health, not of death or inefficiency...

'The present conditions of business cannot be accepted as satisfactory. There are too many who do not prosper enough, and of the few who prosper greatly there are certainly some whose prosperity does not mean well for the country.

'We heartily approve the *prosperity, no matter how great, of any man, if it comes as an incident to rendering service to the community;* [Emphasis added] but we wish to shape conditions so that a greater number of the small men who are decent, industrious and energetic shall be able to succeed, and so that the big man who is dishonest shall not be able to succeed at all.

'Our aim is to control business, *not strangle it,* [Emphasis added] and above all, not to continue a policy of *make-believe strangle* [Emphasis added] toward big concerns that do evil, and constant menace toward both big and little concerns that do well. Our aim is to promote prosperity, and then see to its proper division.

'It is obvious that unless the business is prosperous the wage-workers employed therein will be badly paid and the consumers badly served. Therefore not merely as a matter of justice to the business man, but from the standpoint of the self interest of the wage worker and the consumer *we desire that business shall prosper;* but it should be so supervised as to make prosperity also take the shape of good wages to the wage worker and reasonable prices to the consumer. While investors and business rivals are insured just treatment.

'Through control by commission [regulatory bodies empowered by the people] we may secure freedom for fair competition, elimination of unfair practices, conservation of our natural resources, fair wages, good social conditions, and reasonable prices.

'The only effective way in which to regulate the trusts [corporations] is through the exercise of the collective power of our people as a whole through the governmental agencies established by the Constitution for this very purpose.

Grave injustice is done by the Congress when it fails to give the National Government complete power in this matter; and still graver injustice by the federal courts when they endeavor in any way to pare down the right of the people collectively to act in this matter as they deem wise; such conduct does itself tend to cause the creation of a twilight zone in which neither the Nation nor the States have power. Fortunately, the Federal Courts have more and more of recent years [as of this speech in 1912] tended to adopt the true doctrine, which is that all these matters are to be settled by the people themselves, and that the conscience of the people, and not the preference of any servants [elected officials] of the people, is to be the standard in deciding what action shall be taken by the people." [3]

Teddy Roosevelt was just a tad ahead of his time. The Robber Barons brand of unrestricted corporate power wouldn't come to an end until October 29th, 1929. America blamed (rightfully so) the Robber Barons for the disaster they were living.

The Great Depression of the 1930's would pave the way for Franklin Roosevelt and his New Deal agenda. With F.D.R's appointments of Supreme Court Justices and other Federal appointments, he was able to make many of his social programs "stick." Programs like minimum wage, health care, workers compensation, and social security, and child labor laws. Some of the same programs Teddy Roosevelt had talked about two decades earlier. Programs that would help build a strong middle class and would curb some of the powers of unrestrained corporations, returning rights to the working class. New Deal Democrats would occupy the White House for 28 of the next 36 years. Corporations would not lie down and quietly accept regulation.

Corporate Polluters and Modern Day Robber Barons

All the way back to the time of the Roman's, nearly all civilized nations recognized the importance of environmental rights. Ancient Rome's Code of Justinian guaranteed the use of the "public trust" or commons to all citizens. Such shared resources which cannot be privately "owned." Air, flowing water, public lands, wandering animals, fish in the ocean etc...

In 14th century England, clean air laws made it a capitol offense to burn coal in London. Violators were subject to execution.

After the 1870's the Robber Barons successfully stole the rights to the "commons" from the American people. Starting with the industrial revolution and into the post war industrial boom and into the second half of the 20th century, large factories were dumping toxic waste by-products into our lakes, rivers, and streams, belching clouds of toxic smoke into the air, and creating thousands of toxic dump sites and land fills.

By the 1960's this ongoing disaster was beginning to get some attention. There were reports of people coming down with mysterious diseases and cancers. In some areas, instances of birth defects rose sharply. Some community's water supplies were becoming contaminated and Lake Erie was declared dead.

On the first Earth Day in 1970, some 20 million people protested the destruction of the environment. That same year President Richard Nixon created the Environmental Protection Agency (EPA) whose mission was "to control and abate pollution in the areas of air, water, solid waste, noise, radiation and toxic substances." Over the next couple of years, Congress passed twenty eight environmental statutes, including the Clean Air Act, the Clean Water Act and the Endangered Species Act. The EPA was charged with enforcing these laws and holding violators accountable.

With the inauguration of President Ronald Reagan in 1981 came the first attacks on the EPA. One of Colorado's worst polluters, Joseph Coors, brewing and energy magnate, who founded the Mountain States Legal Foundation (MSLF) that was made up mainly of private energy companies and whose purpose was to fight environmental regulation, was a strong Reagan supporter. Coors, along with James Watt, who would become Reagan's Secretary of the Interior, and was President of MSLF, recommended Anne Gorsuch to the Reagan Transition Team for the EPA administrator position. Gorsuch's husband, a cattle baron who had vowed to destroy the Bureau of Land Management, was selected to head; you guessed it, the Bureau of Land Management.

Gorsuch worked as a corporate attorney while serving two terms in the Colorado House of Representatives. As a legislator she was a member of a clique known as the "crazies," whose agenda mainly consisted of opposition to federal energy and environmental policies. The "crazies" fought the EPA Denver regional bureau on the use of strict sanctions to bring the Denver area into compliance with federal clean air statutes. The "crazies" were often allied with MSLF. As head of the EPA, one of her first priorities was to appoint former corporate lobbyists from the paper, asbestos, chemical and oil industries to head agency departments. Departments whose jobs it would be to oversee paper, asbestos, chemical and oil industry. How many of these appointee's went back to their respective industries as heroes after their stint with the EPA with lucrative contracts and government contacts in hand? Her next priority was to cut the EPA budget by 50%, and EPA personnel by 23%. These Personnel were instrumental in enforcing regulatory laws. Under her tenure, the number of cases brought to court by the EPA declined by 50%. It would be an understatement to say corporate polluters were ecstatic.

By 1982 the House Energy and Commerce Committee, chaired by John Dingell (D-MI) was investigating Gorsuch's agency's use of Superfund monies. Money that was supposed to be used for the cleanup of toxic waste dumps. On December 16th 1982, because of her failure to turn over documents to Congress, the House, by a wide margin, voted her in contempt of Congress. Her policies would create a firestorm of controversy and investigations of sweetheart deals with polluters, including Coors. She would be driven out of the EPA along with twenty three of her cronies. Her assistant administrator for Solid Waste and Emergency Response, and former corporate public relations specialist, Rita Lavelle, would go to jail for perjury.

Reagan's choice for the Department of the Interior, James Watt, didn't fare much better. A proponent of dominion theology and an advocate of unregulated corporatism, Watt once said, "Clear cutting of old growth forests is a good thing because trees cause pollution." Coming from anybody other than the head of the Department of Interior this could be called ignorant. Coming from the head of the Department of the Interior, it would be fair to ask how this blithering idiot got this job. During a Senate hearing, while Watt was doling out Federal lands to industry, he was asked "if he agreed that natural resources should be preserved for future generations?" He replied: "I do not know how many future generations we can count on before the Lord returns."

If he is saying that he believes that allowing big industry to destroy our environment for profit because it won't affect my children or grandchildren because they won't be here anyway, then that is unacceptable and offensive. It's fine if he chooses to believe that, but most of us probably don't want him setting U.S. domestic policy based on that belief alone. The Christians I know don't pretend to know when the Lord will decide to return. According to them it could be this generation or a thousand generations from now. And isn't there anything in the Bible about protecting the Earth. I'm not talking about a quote, "Thou shall not pollute" but what about the concept of respect. What about "waste not, want not." Maybe he feels protecting our environment is a waste because we should exploit it now since it won't matter in the near future. That's a debate for theologians and philosophers.

In 1983, more than a million people, including all 125 American Indian tribes signed a petition demanding Watt's removal. Watt was later indicted on twenty five felony counts of influence pedaling.

How did these people get appointed to these positions? If it wasn't for huge amounts of corporate dollars to candidates like Reagan and the Republican National Committee, from the energy, cattle, oil and logging industries, and people like Coors and their foundations like Mountain States Legal Foundation, the Competitive Enterprise Institute, the Heritage Foundation and others, they couldn't.

Under the current George W. Bush administration, corporate cronyism is the worst it's been in a hundred years. The corporate shills, in and around this administration, makes Reagan's appointee's look like advocates for Greenpeace. It started just days after Bush was inaugurated the first time. In January 2001, President Bush tasked Vice President Dick Cheney with setting up an energy task force. The National Energy Policy Development Group, or NEPD, began meeting secretly with representatives and lobbyists of the energy industry. The energy industry, by the way, that gave over $26.7 million in political contributions, *78% (almost $21 million)* of which went to the RNC and the Bush/Cheney campaign during the 2000 election cycle. [4] This would prove to be a very wise "investment." Corporations like Southern Co., Cinergy and FirstEnergy, all facing EPA lawsuits would help re-write the countries energy policies that would gut the Clean Air Act (More on that in a moment). In March 2001 an E-Mail from a Southern Company lobbyist to DOE urged *reform* of the Clean Air Act and related enforcement actions. The suggestion was included in the administrations new energy policy. [5] The Bush administration pressured the Justice Department to drop dozens of investigations against the worst polluters.

This tampering with Justice Department investigations by the executive branch is almost unheard of. The three branches of government, the executive, judicial and legislative branches, were designed to be independent of each other and provide a check and balance system on each other (Separation of powers). I say almost unheard of. Attorney General of the United States John Mitchell (judicial branch) would have gone to prison, had he not died first, in 1974 for conspiring to obstruct justice with the Nixon administration (executive branch) in the cover up of the Watergate break in. The difference being Nixon was trying to cover his own ass while Bush is protecting his corporate pals.

The NEPD Task Force was a who's who of the energy industry. They are now at the highest levels of government. When Dick Cheney resigned as CEO of Halliburton to accept the nomination as Vice President he received a $36 million severance package in the form of stock options payable over several years, although he stated in 2003 he had "severed all my ties with the company, gotten rid of all my financial interest. I have no financial interest in Halliburton of any kind and haven't had, now, for over three years." In September 2003, a report issued by the Congressional Research Service stated the deferred options of the type Cheney is receiving "are among those benefits described by the Office of Government Ethics as 'retained ties' or 'linkages' to one's former employer." [6] That is because the value of the options is directly related to how well a company is doing financially. Halliburton received no-bid contracts in Iraq worth billions of dollars. Not to worry Dick, they're doing just peachy.

In his capacity as chairman of the NEPD Task Force, Cheney also met with Enron (which trades electricity and natural gas) CEO Kenneth Lay who's input for energy policy included, among other things, not allowing carbon dioxide to be regulated as a pollutant. Carbon dioxide is a by product of drilling for natural gas and of coal fired power plants and is considered to be one of the main causes of global warming by virtually the entire scientific community with the exception of Bush administration appointed scientists. The United States derives half of its electricity from coal fired plants. In contrast Mexico derives only eight per cent of its power from coal and Canada produces sixty percent of its electricity from hydropower. [7] Lay also was able to recommend two nominees for the Federal Energy Regulatory Commission which oversee the markets Enron operates in. The Presidents selection of Pat Wood to head the FERC was one of them. When the two Republican slots were filled by Bush, they had the backing of Enron. [8]

Another NEPD member, Gale Norton, Bush's Secretary of the Interior, met with petroleum companies that wanted to lease federal lands. Remember James Watt, Reagan's Secretary of the Interior and President of Coors's Mountain States Legal Foundation? Norton started her career as an attorney defending mining companies and oil companies at MSLF. An advocate of opening the Arctic National Wildlife Refuge to oil drilling, she followed Watt to the Department of Interior in the 80's.

Norton is also a strong advocate of federal deregulation and delegating regulatory duties, in environmental matters, to state and local governments. The problem is pollution transcends state lines and the federal government, in this case, is much more efficient in bringing law suits against offenders whose pollution has traveled downstream through three states. President Bush has promised smaller government. He's keeping that promise in the one place the federal government *should* be involved.

Norton holds an extreme libertarian view of the "takings clause" of the Fifth Amendment of the Constitution which says, "No *person*…shall be deprived of life, liberty, or property, without due process of the law; nor shall private property be taken for public use without just compensation." This is her argument against government regulation restricting the exploitation of federal lands by corporations. Sound familiar? She is using the argument that corporations have the same rights as natural persons and therefore are protected under the Constitution. "Federal courts should permit such regulation to go forward only if the public (taxpayers) pay compensation for the economic burden such regulations impose" on corporation. [9] She is advocating that taxpayers pay corporations billions not to pollute.

However, in 1887 a Kansas beer brewer argued that a prohibition law in that state was a taking under the Fifth Amendment. The Supreme Court ruled against him stating, "A government can prevent a property owner from using his property to injure others without having to compensate the owner for the value of the forbidden use." This "nuisance clause" is the basis upon which the government has been able to establish health and safety regulation, and environmental standards and is exactly what Norton argues against. In the Harvard Journal of Law and Public Policy, Norton argued for "a major shift in takings jurisprudence" away from this precedent. "We might even go so far as to recognize a homesteading right [for corporations] to pollute or to make noise in an area. This approach would eliminate some of the theoretical problems with defining a nuisance."

The logging, mining and oil industries have all brought law suits against the government claiming the protection of wetlands, wild life and establishment of wilderness areas are all regulatory takings, therefore under the takings clause, they should be compensated. With an ally in George W. Bush and Gale Norton, and Bush's appointments of like minded Federal Judges over the last four years, there is little standing in their way. The appointment of Gale Norton is a blatant payback by the Bush administration to the energy industry that donated millions of dollars to elect him President.

Norton's Deputy Secretary of the Interior also carries a lot of water for the coal and oil and gas industries. J. Steven Griles worked for James Watt during the Reagan administration where he met Gale Norton. As is typical of this administrations revolving door where one moves between politics, the corporate world and back to politics, Griles left government in 1989 to become a lobbyist with National Environmental Strategies, a firm that represented the mining industry. He later started his own lobbying firm; J. Steven Griles & Assoc. which represented oil and mining interests through the 90's including the Coal Bed Methane Ad Hoc committee and Dominion Resources. [10] During his stint at the Department of Interior under Watt in the 80's, Griles helped the coal industry in its efforts to conduct mountaintop removal strip mining in the Appalachians. A brutal practice that involves removing the trees and topsoil from a mountain peak and then blasting away layer after layer of rock until the mountaintop is gone exposing the coal. By the mid 90's thousands of tons of debris were dumped into valleys permanently burying almost 1,000 miles of mountain streams.

During the Clinton administration the practice of mountaintop removal was rolled back significantly. Clinton sought to strengthen government oversight of these practices. In 1998, W. Michael McCabe and other senior EPA officials called for a broad review of federal policies for mountaintop mining. In a settlement with environmental activists, the administration agreed to a closer scrutiny of mining permits and a thorough scientific review, called an environmental impact statement. McCabe said, "We would not go forward with the fill rule except as part of this comprehensive approach." [11]

However, shortly after Bush took office in 2001, administration officials publicly promised to remove the legal bureaucratic roadblocks, to the mining permits, of the Clinton administration. Griles, the former coal industry lobbyist, said in August 2001, to the West Virginia Coal Association: "We will fix the federal rules very soon." And now that Norton and Griles are back, the practice has not only become acceptable again, but the dumping of mining debris into valleys and streams is now protected. The Bush administration simply reclassified the debris from "objectionable waste into legally acceptable fill." The Bush administration calls this a "clarification." [12] More accurately it's a payback to the coal industry which makes their previously illegal activities legal.

Another member of Cheney's NEPD Task force and recipient of large amounts of corporate dollars was newly appointed Secretary of Energy Spencer Abraham. Abraham met with, among others, the National Mining Association and the National Petrochemical and Refiners Association which also made detailed policy recommendations. [13] In 2000, during a failed run at the Senate, Abraham received $700,000 from the big hitters in the auto industry. He also received $178,674 from The Coalition for Vehicle Choice, a coalition of 139 companies that opposed setting fuel economy regulations. [14] Abraham helped defeat the fuel efficiency standards for American automobiles that would have raised fuel economy standards. Another pet project of Abraham's is opening the Artic National Wildlife Refuge to drilling. The Artic Refuge will yield approximately 3.2 billion barrels. At peak production, in 2027, that would be about two per cent of the oil Americans are projected to use. Studies done show that by phasing in fuel efficiency standards, the one's Abraham opposed, to 40 miles per gallon by 2012, technology Detroit has, the nation could save fifteen times more oil than the ANWR could produce. [15] Spencer Abraham resigned at the end of Bush's first term. Bush's pick to replace him is Sam Bodman.

Bodman came to the Bush White House as Deputy Secretary of the Commerce Department in 2001. He later became Deputy Secretary of Treasury. Like Gale Norton and Spencer Abraham, Bodman favors giving oil companies access to the ANWR for drilling. An energy bill which was approved by the House in 2003, but died in the Senate, did not include the ANWR provision. However it did include billions of dollars in tax breaks for the oil and gas, nuclear power and coal industries and a repeal of the Public Holding Company Act, a consumer protection law that slows utility consolidation and some liability protections for companies that use MTBE, a gasoline additive known to pollute ground water. [16] Bodman said that passing comprehensive energy legislation is among the most important matters before Congress this year, and the Republican controlled Congress is expected to have enough votes to get it done with the ANWR provision this year. Before coming to the Bush administration, Bodman was Chairman and CEO of Cabot Corporation, the forth largest polluter in Texas in 1997. In that year, under pressure from environmentalist groups to do something about the pollution from oil refineries, then Governor George W. Bush commissioned oil company executives to propose a plan. They did. It was a *voluntary* program that allowed polluters to decide on their own how much to cut pollution. Bodman was part of the group that drafted the legislation that Gov. Bush signed into law that allowed Cabot and others to continue to emit the same level, and in some cases more, toxic emissions into the Texas skies. [17]

Cheney's NEPD Task Force is in violation of federal law. While there is nothing wrong with the President, Vice President and cabinet members meeting in secret, when advisory panels outside of government meet with the executive branch, it is to be transparent by law. In 1972 the Federal Advisory Committee Act (FACA) was enacted by Congress. Its purpose was to ensure advice given to the executive branch by the various advisory committees, task forces, boards and commissions formed by Congress and the President, be both objective and *accessible to the public.*

The meetings with Cheney's task force, during the first three months of Bush's administration, with energy corporations, and the exclusion of any environmental concern, prompted Congressman Henry Waxman (D.-Ca.), the ranking member of the committee on Government Reform, and John Dingle (D.-Mi.), the ranking member of the Energy and Commerce Committee to draft a letter to both Cheney and the comptroller general, David Walker, the head of the General Accountability Office (GAO) asking for the list of members of Cheney's energy group and their input in developing the energy policy, as per FACA. Cheney refused to provide the information saying the GAO was intruding into the heart of executive deliberations among members of the Presidents cabinet, which are protected and not subject to FACA. The Vice President misstated this numerous times. The GAO reminded the Vice President they were asking for information on the development of policy and the players, not deliberations between cabinet members, and in fact the GAO did have statutory authority to intrude into the heart of executive matters as they are the oversight of the executive branch. Cheney still refused to comply, prompting the GAO to file suit against the executive branch for the first time in the history of the United States.

FACA says in section 2, paragraph B, sub-paragraph 5:

> The Congress *and the public* should be kept informed with respect to the number, purpose, *membership, activities,* and cost of advisory committee's; and [sub paragraph 6] the function of advisory committees should be *advisory only,* and that all matters under their consideration should be determined, in accordance with law, by the official, agency, or officer involved. [18]

The GAO is a non partisan group that undertakes such investigations whenever they are requested to do so by either the chairman of a particular committee or the ranking minority member of any of the committees or subcommittees created by Congress no matter what party they are.

The GAO requested this information because of Waxman's and Dingle's request. The information they are requesting will help them determine who benefited from the President's energy policy and if the energy policy was in fact written, not by the government, but *for* the government by the energy industries that stand to benefit from the policy with no regard for the people of the United States, who have to live with these abhorrent policies. And this has to be the only reason for the Vice Presidents refusal to turn over any documents regarding his task force to the GAO.

In June of 2004, the Supreme Court, including Cheney's duck hunting buddy Scalia, who refused to recuse himself from the case involving Cheney v. the GAO, [*Walker v. Cheney*] sided with Cheney. This controversy is not over. The Supreme Court simply kicked it back to the lower courts. If this stands, it will be another attack on the checks and balances provided by the Constitution. In the book *Worse than Watergate* by John W. Dean, Dean writes, this raises the "fundamental question about the very nature of our system of checks and balances. If the GAO could not get the information it requested, then there was a black hole in the federal firmament-a no-man's-land where a President and Vice President could go free from Congressional oversight." [19]

One of the worst pieces of environmental legislation to ever come down the pike is President Bush's "Clear Skies Initiative." This bill, written by the energy industry lobbyists on Cheney's advisory panel, [20] is designed to effectively gut the New Source Review (NSR) provision of the Clean Air Act. NSR, which has been an essential part of the nations clean air laws for over 35 years, in basic terms, says that when facilities such as power plants, refineries and industrial factories upgrade, or install equipment that would increase emissions, they must bring their pollution control equipment up to the standards of current technology. During the Clinton administration, and into the first few months of the Bush administration, lawsuits had been filed against 51 of the worst polluters in the energy industry, which were in violation of the NSR provision, in 13 states. While these plants produce only 11% of the nation's fossil fuel electricity, they are responsible for more than 25% of the nation's harmful emissions. Their emissions cause over 9,000 deaths and 170,000 respiratory attacks annually. [21] Bush's Clear Skies Initiative replaces NSR with a national "cap and trade" policy. This effectively guts NSR in three ways.

First, the Plantwide Applicability Limit change to NSR, or (PAL) would cap power plants emissions based on their most polluting 24 month period in the last five years. Other facilities such as refineries and chemical plants cap would be based on any 24 month period in the last ten years. Plants can now avoid emission control requirements that were required previously under NSR, even if they upgrade or install additional equipment, simply by showing they are generating less pollution than they were during the 2 year period, say, six years ago, or five years ago etc...In effect they will now be allowed to increase emissions, in many cases, back to where they were up to ten years ago.

Secondly, the Clear Skies "Clean Unit Exclusion" allows facilities that have upgraded pollution controls in the last ten years to be excluded from the NSR provision for ten years from the date of the upgrade. For example, if a factory made changes that required them to upgrade their pollution controls two years ago, they can now add equipment that significantly increases pollution for the next eight years and will be excluded from upgrading pollution controls during that period, in effect increasing emissions. The EPA recently announced their intention to increase the ten year look-back to fifteen years.

And thirdly, the "Routine Maintenance" change to NSR under Clear Skies would exempt modifications that it classifies as "routine maintenance repair and *replacement*" based on a cost threshold below which these modifications escape NSR review. This would allow older dirtier plants to make upgrades without requiring additional pollution controls previously mandated under NSR and would "grandfather" older facilities at their current pollution levels.

The trade portion of the cap and trade program of Clear Skies permits utilities to buy emission "credits" from cleaner facilities to meet an overall industry target, which will result in little if any net reduction of pollution, and will continue to allow the industry to continue polluting in greater quantities for longer periods of time.

One of the most dangerous pollutants expelled into the air and water by these industries is mercury. The National Resources Defense Council (NRDC) reports "mercury is a potent neurotoxin that threatens the brains and nervous systems of fetuses and young children. A number of neurological diseases are linked to mercury exposure, including learning and attention disorders and mental retardation. Mercury may also be linked to the recent increases in autism, Parkinson's disease and Alzheimer's disease, according to experts." [22] The EPA has revised previous estimates showing mercury exposure poses a danger to twice as many children in the U.S. as previously thought. 630,000 of the 4 million babies (one in six) born each year are at risk of contracting a mercury related developmental problem. The CDC estimates that one in twelve women of childbearing age has a mercury level in the blood that poses a concern. The Bush administration rescinded an EPA ruling which classified mercury as a dangerously toxic chemical and reclassified it as a less hazardous substance allowing it to be part of the cap and trade program under the Clear Skies Initiative. This provision of Clear Skies is called the "Clean Air Mercury Rule."

The National Wildlife Federation says the Bush administration's proposal would give power plants another decade before controlling mercury levels. Felice Stadler, a mercury policy expert at NWF says "That's more than five times as much power plant mercury pollution for more than a decade longer. That pace is not only too slow; it's a roll-back of existing Clean Air Act requirements at a time when much more work needs to be done." [23]

NWF also reports mercury "a heavy metal that descends from polluted air into water, works its way *up* the food chain. It is especially dangerous to people and wildlife that eat fresh water and marine fish. High mercury levels in waterways have spurred officials in *44 states* to issue warnings to people to restrict or avoid eating fish caught from lakes, streams and coastal waters."

A stop at NRDC's website produces dozens of articles, research and reports on the environmental record of this administration with titles like EPA balks at recommended mercury reduction technology, EPA resists further mercury studies, White House altered scientific findings on mercury threat, EPA uses utility company memos to craft controversial mercury policy, EPA's mercury pollution plan mirrors industry's recommendations, EPA moves to reclassify mercury as non-toxic, EPA delays report on mercury risk for children and on and on. They are all worth reading. [24]

NSR was intended to be a technology forcing provision that would promote the reduction of dangerous toxic emissions over a period of time at all plants. As factories upgraded equipment over the years they would be required to also keep up with the latest technology in pollution control. Someday, possibly, the emission coming from the old smokestacks may be completely harmless and totally scrubbed of all toxins. However, with the Clear Skies Initiative pollution control technology will see a decline in progress because there will no longer be demand for it.

Clear Skies has done nothing more than create loopholes in the NSR provision of the Clean Air Act to be exploited by the people who wrote the policy in the first place. The argument by the multi billion dollar industries, that NSR is cost prohibitive, is without merit because the upgrades to pollution control is done over a period of many years. Since the early 70's the Clean Air Act has worked and worked well, dramatically reducing pollution in our skies, lakes, rivers and streams. Bush's Clear Skies will set environmental standards back decades and further enrich an already obscenely rich group. You have to wonder who comes up with names like Clear Skies Initiative. It's actually pretty brilliant. Who could possibly be against something with a title like Clear Skies? If you are, you must be for pollution.

In an interview on the Al Franken show on Air America Radio, Christine Todd Whitman, Bush's first head of the EPA later replaced by Michael Leavitt, was asked if their [The administration's] "goal from the beginning was to gut NSR." Her one word answer was simple. "Yes"

If it were just the energy industry buying the government that would be bad enough, but unfortunately, energy is not the only industry buying a seat at the Bush administration table.

6

From Timber and Logging to the Automotive Industry

"Wilderness is not a luxury, but a necessity of the human spirit."
Edward Abbey

During the 2000, 2002 and 2004 election cycle's, the timber industry in the northwest alone, gave a whopping $1.55 million to the Republican National Committee and the Bush/Cheney campaign. [1] Shortly after the devastating fires during the 2002 fire season, where we watched over 3,700 homes destroyed, the Bush administration came up with a "solution" in The Healthy Forests Initiative (HFI). The White House website states HFI will "reduce the threat of destructive wildfires while upholding environmental standards and encouraging early public input during review and planning processes. The legislation is based on sound science, and will protect threatened and endangered species." [2] Once again, with a name like Healthy Forests, how could anyone be opposed to it?

HFI hypothesizes that forests are overgrown creating huge reservoirs of fuel awaiting ignition. Fire requires three elements: heat, oxygen and fuel. We can't control the heat or the oxygen, but we can control the fuel by cutting down trees in selected areas. This sounds logical, however, an in depth look at what Healthy Forests actually proposes shows yet another payoff by the Bush administration to big industry.

HFI will not protect the communities the Bush administration is supposedly so concerned about from devastating fires as the White House website suggests. HFI eliminates the "Roadless Rule" enacted in January 2001, which limits logging in areas where there are currently no roads. The Roadless Rule protected nearly 60 million acres of national forests. This amounts to only about one third of the nations total national forest system mostly in the back country miles and miles away from populated areas. Cutting large fire-resistant old growth trees in these areas would actually increases the potential for fires in several ways. According to the National Resources Defense Counsel, the scientific community consensus (excluding Bush administration appointed scientists) based on a fifteen year study shows large wildfires are more likely to occur in areas outside of roadless areas. (Populated areas are where responsible thinning should take place). Opening up these ancient pristine forests will make them more susceptible to fire by "First, cutting down trees and building roads opens up the forest and lets in sunlight and wind, both of which dry out the forest and increase flammability. Second, when removing trees, loggers often leave behind collections of highly flammable materials such as brush, limbs, twigs, needles and saplings, which are difficult to remove. Third, opening up forests promotes the rise of new flammable undergrowth in a short period of time. Fourth, logging operations compact soil so that water runs off instead of soaking in evenly to keep the soil moist and trees healthy and fifth, logging and roads introduce disease and pests, which damage trees left behind making them more flammable."

HFI will not protect environmental standards as the White House also suggests. "Roadless areas are havens for fish and wildlife, whose habitat in many other forest areas has been fragmented or entirely destroyed. They provide habitat for more than 1,600 threatened, endangered or sensitive plant and animal species, and include watersheds that supply clean drinking water, unpolluted by development, for *millions of Americans.*" [3]

The forest road network is already eight times as big as the interstate highway system. The timber supply that was off limits to the timber industry by the roadless rule was less than 1% of what is now being produced [4], but it's the dollar amount that drives this bus.

HFI also does not "encourage early public input during review and planning" as the White House website says. In May of 2003 the Healthy Forests and Restoration Act (H.R. 1904) which passed in the House of Representatives implemented HFI and removed the Appeals Reform Act of 1992. HR 1904 makes it almost impossible for the public to participate by giving citizens limited time to file objections and imposing heavy filing fees and bond requirements. Moreover, logging projects can proceed before any outcome is reached.

HR 1904 guts the National Environmental Policy Act (NEPA) that previously required environmental impact statements and alternatives to agency actions, a public appeals process and mandatory input from *non-federal* scientists. Simply put, under the guise of "hazardous fuel reduction," virtually all logging projects could escape NEPA.

HFI allows the Bureau of Land Management and the Forest Service to pay logging companies for their "management" of public lands since they are doing us the huge favor of removing hazardous fuel from our old growth forests. This is a government subsidy to a multi billion dollar industry, corporate welfare. Just like the energy policy written by the energy industry, the Healthy Forests Initiative is a boon for the timber and logging industry. They already have access to more than two thirds of public lands, but they want it all. They're willing to buy it and Bush is willing to sell it to them, even though the vast majority of public comment is against it.

Fact: In May 2000, then Governor Bush met with timber industry executives in Portland. Each attendee contributed $100,000 to the Republican Party for a forty five minute meeting. In March 2003, Mark Rey and Carl Rove met with timber executives again in Portland. Pledge forms were distributed urging companies to contribute up to a maximum $275,000 to the public relations campaign to promote HFI. The Oregonian reported: "It's yet another sign of how closely the Bush administration is working with an industry it regards as a key part of its support base." In May 2004, the Bush/Cheney campaign announced its Oregon Natural Resources Leadership Team. Seven of the eight members have a timber industry background. The campaign named Steve Swanson, President of the Swanson Group, a timber company based in Glendale, as the team's chairman. Swanson had donated over $75,000 to the GOP and George W. Bush. [5]

The timber industry doesn't try to hide its motive for the large campaign contributions. In August 2003, Max Merlich, Vice President of logging operations for Columbia Helicopters said, "Columbia put a lot of time and money into getting Bush elected and we are going to get this Bush Healthy Forests Initiative rammed through so we can get to work and get the job done." [6]

I wonder who Bush appointed to oversee the U.S. Forest Service. That would be Mark Rey, Under Secretary for Natural Resources and Environment, who is responsible for the management of 155 national forests, 19 national grasslands, and 15 land utilization projects on 192,000,000 acres of publicly owned lands in 44 states. Until his appointment as Under Secretary for Natural Resources in 2001, Rey spent most of his career as a timber industry lobbyist:

- 1976–1984: National Forest Products Association.

- 1984–1989: Vice President of Public Forestry Programs for the National Forest Products Association later became the American Forest and Paper Association.

- 1989–1992: Executive Director of the American Forest Resource Alliance, a coalition of 350 timber corporations formed by the National Forest Products Association to oppose a plan, known as option 9, to designate habitat in the Pacific Northwest for the endangered northern spotted owl. Rey publicly promoted the idea that the Endangered Species Act unfairly restricts business. (Sounds familiar; like he's arguing that corporations are being treated unfairly under the takings clause of the Fifth Amendment).

• 1992—1994: Vice President of Forest Resources for the American Forest and Paper Association (AF&PA).

From 1995 until his appointment, Rey was a staff member with the U.S. Senate Committee on Energy and Natural Resources. He was instrumental in drafting Senator Larry Craig's (R-ID) 1997 National Forest Management Act, which sought to eliminate citizen oversight and make timber harvest levels mandatory and enforceable, while making environmental standards un-enforceable. The act would have allowed the U.S. Forest Service to fine citizens up to $10,000 for filing appeals to halt timber sales for an "improper purpose." [7]

Bush often talks about lessening the United States' dependence on foreign oil, but the rhetoric does not stand up to the scrutiny of the administrations actions.

The Bush administration is in perpetual payoff mode to their largest contributors at the expense of all the rest of us. With cheerful, rosy names like "Clear Skies" and "Healthy forests," they have successfully convinced large groups of their followers they are working for their best interests. They convince their base that drilling in the Artic National Wildlife Refuge is the answer to lessening our dependence on foreign oil, even though the data shows this to be far from the truth. But, we don't want to confuse them with the facts. Such facts as oil is a finite resource, and we should be talking seriously about alternative energy and renewable energy, not short term solutions, and not "clean coal." What an oxymoron! During the late 70's with the gas shortages and oil embargo, President Carter had solar panels placed on top of the White House. Not because that would magically solve the energy crises or even provide enough energy to power the whole building, but because it made the statement that this country needed to move, and would move in that direction. When Ronald Reagan moved into the White House in January of 1981, the first thing he did was to remove those solar panels.

People who disagree with the Bush administrations policy of deregulated, free-for-all, corporate plundering of the environment that sustains us, and allowing a select group to write bills that remove oversight and enforcement of their previously illegal dumping of toxins into our air and water, and, in many cases, plundering their own companies and dumping their stocks for millions mere months before the company files chapter 11 while thousands of middle and low level employees see their 401k's become worthless, all the while telling everyone everything's fine, (take a breath) are called tree huggers, or worse, socialists, or even worse communists.

Every group has their share of extremist whack jobs (just look at our current government), and the environmentalist group is no exception. However, the vast, vast majority of people, who probably wouldn't necessarily classify themselves as "environmentalists," believe the protection of the environment is important. They love freedom and democracy and support the concept of capitalism, just not this extreme form of free-for-all capitalism. They believe in making these corporations play by rules. Rules that empower us to regulate how these corporations affect our lives. They believe in doing this through our elected officials who *we the people* charge with administrating the agencies that are created to oversee and enforce laws that protect us. They don't believe that a small minority, who has enough money to buy a seat at the Vice Presidents Energy Task Force table, should be able to write legislation that benefits only them, and be able to cut us, the people affected, out of the process. They don't believe the constitution says "by the corporations for the corporations," or "by the rich for the rich," or "by the king for the king." They believe, because they can read, that it says "by the people for the people."

They believe Mr. CEO of XYZ Corporation is free to pull down five, ten, twenty million dollars, or what ever, a year as long as he's playing by the rules. They're not arbitrarily against corporate welfare. It might be palatable if the government wants to give the energy industry subsidies of tax payer dollars and tax breaks as long as this welfare was not going to subsidize the top executives golden parachute clauses, but to R&D alternative energy for example. What incentive does a corporation in the energy industry have right now to even look at alternative energy? The answer is none. They've bought a President who is pandering to them because he's one of them. We are getting nothing in return for the subsidies and tax breaks they've gotten. There is no incentive forcing them to do the hard work of moving alternative energy technology forward. They have convinced millions of people this is science fiction and a vehicle that gets 50 or 60, or even 80 miles to the gallon is cost prohibitive and would cost the consumer $100,000 for a car the size of a 1978 Honda Civic.

Bullshit. You can buy a hybrid gas/battery car right now. A car designed by Japanese engineers for Japanese manufacturers. Should we allow the Japanese to flood the U.S. automobile market again as they did during the energy crisis of the 70's, or should the U.S. lead in this technology? Is this vehicle feasible for everyone right now? Probably not. Would anybody argue that giving a government subsidy to the Big Three in Detroit and a tax break to consumers who purchased one of these vehicles to further this technology and possibly keep the cost to the consumer down is a bad idea? Probably not.

This thinking is not revolutionary, the technology is there but it won't move forward without leadership from Washington.

There are three prototype automobiles sitting in the big three's museums right now that have gotten 70 to 80 miles per gallon. One was manufactured by Ford, one by GM and one by Daimler Chrysler. They were the result of a ten year project called the Supercar initiated by the Clinton Gore administration in 1993. The goal was to have the most fuel efficient vehicle ever built in production sometime between 2004 and 2007. Al Gore spoke of the program during the 2000 campaign as one of the answers to the United States' dependency on foreign oil. The EPA has reported that increasing fuel efficiency standards by a mere 10 miles per gallon would virtually end our need to import oil from the Persian Gulf region. On the surface the program seemed to be a huge success, however behind the scenes things weren't going so well. The auto manufacturers were complaining to their government contacts that they were concerned about the cost of such a vehicle and their ability to sell this to the U.S. consumer. They also realized the huge profits which could be made by selling what the consumer, at that time, really wanted; SUV's. In the late 90's, America was experiencing the good life. Government surpluses, a booming stock market, a strong economy, low gas prices and a world at peace, or so the average person thought. Any turmoil the world was experiencing was "over there."

With the election of George W. Bush in 2000, the Supercar project would die. During the first couple of months of the Bush administration, while Cheney's closed door energy task force was meeting, GM sent a position paper to senior energy policy advisors, dated April 2, 2001, criticizing fuel economy standards, and stating "a better approach takes a longer-term vision of moving to a hydrogen economy with fuel cells." A much longer term vision, hydrogen fuel cells present a whole new set of problems and is decades away, so for now, the big auto makers will not have to divert monies to fuel efficiency research, which they already spent approximately $1.5 billion on with the Supercar, preserving their profits by continuing to sell large, gas guzzling SUV's.

Apparently, the Cheney task force was listening because a week later Energy Secretary Spencer Abraham told reporters funding for Supercar would be cut. On January 9, 2002, Abraham stood at a Detroit auto show with the CEO's of the big three and announced a new project called Freedomcar which would be hydrogen powered. It's interesting to note that even though backers of hydrogen technology and, Abraham's own agency, the Energy Department, admitted it would be at least 20 to 35 years before these cars would see U.S. hi-ways, the Freedomcar has a smaller budget than Supercar did, and unlike the Supercar project there are no deadlines to actually produce anything and little oversight. [8]

Even if scrapping the 80 miles per gallon technology that already exists in Supercar and going with hydrogen technology is the right thing to do, and for sake of argument we'll assume this to be true, a very basic look at this administration's past actions versus their rhetoric presents some doubt as to their motive of moving us towards a hydrogen economy. Hydrogen is not readily available in nature and therefore has to be produced by us. It can be produced at any energy producing facility, such as a hydro-electric facility, or a nuclear plant, or a coal burning energy facility.

The energy industry that we've been talking about, the one that contributed heavily to Bush, and the one the Bush administration seems to work the hardest for, the oil and gas and coal industry, has been buying up the hydrogen technology patents and the companies that are leading in hydrogen technology and positioning themselves to be the leading producers of hydrogen if and when we as a country move in this direction.

Experts say the exhaust from a hydrogen powered car is pure water. A car that runs on hydrogen would produce water so pure one could literally drink from the tail pipe. The multi-billion dollar question, then, is why manufacture such an environmentally friendly vehicle and at the same time be producing the fuel for it at coal fired power plants? The answer is:

1. The Bush's are not going to see their corporate pal's in the energy industry cut out of the action or

2. The corporate pal's in the auto industry are going to claim cost concerns, as they've done in the past, and nothing will come of hydrogen technology.

With no push from the federal government, or from consumer groups, it is unlikely the big three will make any significant progress on the Freedomcar. They fought mandatory seatbelts decades ago; they fought against making air bags a standard feature for years, even though the research showed, during those years, the life saving benefits to the driving public. Ralph Nader made his career in the 60's and 70's pressuring the big three and Congress on such consumer issues. The big three's argument was the same then as it is now, cost, however when pushed, they managed to make it happen.

The cost prohibitive argument is very frustrating. What if John F. Kennedy's speech, in 1962, was "We choose to send a man to the moon in this decade and return him safely to…oh wait, that would be cost prohibitive. We can't do that." This country found the $300 billion to make it happen. I'll leave it to the economists to determine what that figure would be in today's dollars adjusted for inflation. That challenge also produced new industries and awoke millions of kids' imaginations and drove them into math and the sciences and created millions of new jobs.

This administration has found, as of this writing, over $300 billion to fight a war in Iraq, under the guise of fighting the war on "terra" as Bush puts it. A war, that according to Paul Wolfowitz wasn't supposed to cost more than $50 billion because "Iraq oil revenue's will fund the war." But, give him a break, its not the first time he's been wrong. He's under a lot of pressure, what with being selected by Bush to run the World Bank and all.

They've found another couple of billion to fund the tax cuts to the richest 1% of our population, tax cuts that were given in a time of war which has never been done in the history of any country. Tax cuts which have plummeted this country into the worst deficits in history, and the Bush administration refuses to consider rolling back even a portion of the tax cuts to fund the war, and is causing them to cut almost every program under the sun including health benefits to Iraq veterans.

Under another created crisis (Saddam being one) they are proposing the privatization of Social Security, which would cost about $1.6 trillion. (See chapter 12) And on and on it goes.

What we need is visionary leadership. If we as people demanded that corporations could no longer donate millions of dollars to buy political favor, and no longer recognized them as having the same rights as living breathing persons, but recognize they need to be protected from each other *and not from us, the people,* and demanded that our elected officials work for us, and if we could take back our government and restore it to what it was originally intended to be, a government by the people, for the people, in the span of one generation, we would ensure our democracy, and freedoms, and way of life for many generations to come.

Maybe the short term solution of drilling in the ANWR might be acceptable if we knew these energy corporations were also working on the longer term alternatives to fossil fuel. Possibly, through government funding, (which would mean rolling back some of the tax cuts to the wealthy, but again we'll get to that later) creating new industry, just as the space program of the 60's did, which would create millions of new jobs and create new challenges. When has America ever backed down from a good challenge? The President has the authority, right now, to say we're going to drill in ANWR *and* we're going to make fuel efficiency standards of 40 miles per gallon mandatory by [insert date here]. But he won't do it. He won't call for any corporate fat cat to sacrifice in any way. However, he will ask 1600 American soldiers from Middle America to sacrifice (Over 1600, as of this writing).

Will we ever see Death Valley dotted with thousands of windmills manufactured by a corporation that formerly operated dozens of coal fired power plants? Will we ever see fields of solar panels manufactured by General Electric? Who knows? Is it possible? The answer is absolutely yes. It is *possible* if we demand it, but not if we allow a small group of narrow minded militaristic, corrupt, corporate cronies to steal the future from us.

Is it beyond the scope of possibility to see "conservationists" and "environmentalists" allied with big energy corporations? Why not, because it's never happened before? If big energy corporations were not allowed to buy politicians and were pressured to put the hundreds of millions of dollars they currently spend on political campaigns, advertising and public relations towards the R&D of new alternative fuel technologies, it could happen. We the people would have to return our voice to the political arena and force politicians to change the way corporations are viewed freeing them from answering to corporate lobbyists. Unfortunately, most people can't walk into their Congressmen's office and get a meeting unless you're carrying a 300 lb. bag of cash. But you can call and E-Mail them. They will respond. They may not be able to read each and every E-Mail, but they have staffers that do. If hundreds of E-Mails came to them on a certain topic, the message would get to the "boss." It's also unfortunate most people don't know who their senators are and even less know who their representatives are. [9]

I'm reminded of Senator Bobby Kennedy's speech while he was running for President in 1968 on a platform of opposition to a wrong war of his time, which the anti-war movement of the 60's was ultimately proven right, and civil rights, which were being largely opposed and he said (quoting George Bernard Shaw), "Some men see things as they are, and ask why? I dream of things that never were and ask why not?"

He was absolutely right. Why not? Where is that vision today? Where is the protest and outrage today? Why are there not a million people in the streets demanding our rights back?

How does Bush, who speaks about "erring on the side of life" and makes statements like "we are a culture of life," reconcile the fact that, because of his policies, mercury is no longer considered a dangerous toxin? These are policies that mirror the energy industry's memos almost verbatim.

How does Bush sell the argument that carbon dioxide emissions from power plants and automobiles is not a contributing factor to global warming, a fact that is accepted by virtually the entire scientific community world wide? They simply cite the stock answer, any time they need to dispute facts, from right wing funded conservative think tank scientists like the ones at Cato that, simply put, says "there's not enough evidence to make a conclusion." Just like with the war in Iraq, they've shown that they can, and will, make the evidence say anything that supports the policy they're pursuing.

Bush himself has told those of us who are listening who he works for. At the Alfred E. Smith memorial dinner, while campaigning for President in October of 2000, with camera's rolling, he told the $800 a plate crowd, "This is an impressive crowd, the haves and the have-mores. (Laughter) Some call you the elites; I call you my base." (Laughter and applause).

On April 21, 2005 the energy bill written by the energy industry lobby, passed in the House. This bill, as did the one in 2003, provides billions in tax breaks (nearly $10 billion) and subsidies to the energy corporations, including $2 billion for oil and gas research in the Gulf of Mexico. Unlike the 2003 bill, this one opens the Artic National Wildlife Refuge in Alaska to oil and gas drilling. It also eases environmental regulation to build more refineries in economically depressed areas and gives the Federal Energy Regulatory Commission (FERC) override authority if local municipalities object to the project. It cuts the number of special blends of gasoline currently required to ease air pollution. It provides a mere $700 million for new ethanol production. The provision that provides protection from law suits for the makers of the gas additive MTBE also remained in the bill. MTBE is responsible for the contamination of the water supplies in over 1800 communities in 29 states with an estimated clean up cost of over $29 billion. They've known this for decades. Since no one will be able to hold the producers of MTBE accountable any longer, the cost of the clean up will fall on the shoulders of the tax payers of those states.

Imagine a family member being diagnosed with cancer. And it is learned that it is from MTBE contaminated water. Then imagine you discover that the companies that manufactured it and the companies that used it knew of the potential contamination problem for years. Then you discover there's nothing you can do about it. None of the manufacturers of this pollutant can be sued or held accountable in any way. Apparently, this is what the Bush administration considers a frivolous law suit. This scenario could be reality for hundreds of thousands of people.

The bill does call for a ban on MTBE, but not for another decade, and gives the makers of MTBE $1.7 billion in *transition aid* to convert to other products. Think about this. The tax payers are going to have to pay $1.7 billion to companies that manufacture and use a toxic ground water pollutant to stop, and we're going to give them another decade to do it.

A move to add a provision to Bush's energy bill which would require auto makers to increase fuel economy standards to 33 miles per gallon over the next decade was defeated on a Republican Party line vote. Automobiles account for roughly 70% of the countries oil usage. House Democratic leader Nancy Pelosi of California accused Bush of trying to exploit people's anxiety over high gas prices to gain support of the bill, but even Republican supporters of the bill admit it does little to lower prices at the pump. Pelosi also called it a giveaway to the energy industry and said, "It's anti-consumer, anti tax-payer, anti-environment and fails to address major concerns of people across the country."

The one or two good things in the bill, such as extending daylight savings time by two months which will help to cut some energy usage, and offering tax breaks to homeowners to install more energy efficient windows and insulation seems to be nothing more than a token gesture to swing some law makers who may have been on the fence.

Bush said this is a step towards lessening our dependence on foreign oil and he talks about the importance of alternative energy, however, once again his rhetoric does not stand up to the scrutiny of his administration's policies. He is proving once again that he is working hard for the wrong "persons," the corporate kind, not the breathing kind.

One final point on MTBE: one of the largest producers of MTBE is a company called SABIC which stands to gain the most from liability protection in the energy bill. SABIC is largely owned by the Saudi government, which is for all practical purposes, the Saudi Royal Family. A member of the Royal Family is SABIC's chairman who has an office in Houston, Texas and a research facility in Sugar Land, Texas. A foreign owned corporation is prohibited from donating to political campaigns directly, but they can hire lobbyists. That is exactly what SABIC has done. They retained the firm of Miller & Chevalier, a Washington

D.C. lobbying firm to lobby lawmakers on MTBE matters. From 1998 to 2004, SABIC has paid $1.5 million to Miller & Chevalier ranking them number two in terms of amount spent during that time frame. [10]

7

Big Pharmaceutical and the FDA

"Half of the modern drugs could well be thrown out of the window, except that the birds might eat them."
Dr. Martin Henry Fischer

Congressman W.J. "Billy" Tauzin (R-La.), the principal author of the White House backed Medicare Prescription Drug Bill that President Bush eagerly signed into law in 2003, gave the pharmaceutical and health care industry their pay off for helping to elect Bush President. During the 2000, 2002 and 2004 election cycles, the pharmaceutical and health services/HMO's gave $118.9 million to political campaigns; over 74% went to Republican candidates the RNC and Bush/Cheney. [1] Tauzin was also the recipient of hefty contributions from the big pharmaceutical and health care industries.

This spending does not include the millions the drug industry spent to hire lobbyists from over 100 lobbying firms, including 21 former members of Congress.

What did the pharmaceutical and health care industry get for their $118 million? The bill gives $100 billion, nearly a third of the $395 billion the bill will cost over 10 years, for incentives to insurers to provide coverage and drug benefits to the elderly in effect privatizing the system by enticing seniors out of Medicare and into for-profit managed care plans, (and who will benefit from that). Seniors opting to leave traditional Medicare to receive the drug benefit will lose the guarantee of care under Medicare and assume the risk of paying for their own care and there are few, if any, restrictions on the private plans. Experts predict that seniors in managed care plans will face higher premiums, increased deductibles and higher co-payments. Also, seniors will not be allowed to buy additional coverage such as the current "Medigap" plan to compensate for shortfalls in coverage. Furthermore, those receiving Medicaid benefits (the poorest of the poor and the disabled) who also qualify for Medicare will loose their "wrap around" coverage leaving them behind in an under funded Medicare program.

Proponents of the Medicare bill, and the administration cite support from the AARP (in 2003) as proof the bill is in the best interest of the country's senior citizens, however when it was learned that the AARP's conflict of interest in that $635 million in annual revenues would come from insurance company royalties, drug discount cards and fees charged to celebrities to advertise for the bill, and that they helped write the bill and stand to make ten's of millions of dollars after the bills passage, some 15,000 members resigned and thousands more took to the streets around the country to protest on the day the bill was signed into law.

The Bush administration not only lied to the seniors in this country, and to the rest of us tax payers, but to their own party members in Congress as well. In his 2003 State of the Union Address, Bush said the cost of the bill would not exceed $400 billion. That figure was arrived at because there were moderate Republicans in the house who had reservations about the bill in the first place, but were told the cost would not exceed $400 billion. Without these Republicans, the bill had no chance of passing. For months before the vote, the administration's own analyst, Richard S. Foster, the chief actuary for the Centers for Medicare and Medicaid Services had concluded the cost would actually be in excess of $551 billion. Cybele Bjorklund, the Democratic staff director for the House Ways and Means health sub-committee said Thomas A. Scully, a former health industry lobbyist, then director of the Medicare Office, told her he ordered Foster to withhold information [about the cost of the bill] and that Foster would be fired for insubordination if he disobeyed. After the vote, Knight Ridder Newspapers obtained a copy of an e-mail written by Richard S. Foster to colleagues that corroborates Bjorklund's claims, which says "This whole episode which has now gone on for three weeks has been pretty nightmarish. I'm perhaps no longer in grave danger of being fired, but there remains a strong likelihood that I will have to resign in protest of the withholding of important technical information from key policy makers for political reasons." [2]

Soon after Bush signed the bill into law, the White House revised its projected cost of the bill to $534 billion without offering an explanation or breakdown of the estimate.

Representative Sue Myrick (R N.C.), one of the Republicans lied to by the Bush administration said she was "very upset" when she learned about the actual cost of the bill, and "I think a lot of people probably would have reconsidered [voting for the bill] because we said that $400 billion was our top of the line."

Actually the cost could be almost double the $551 billion estimate Foster came up with. On February 9, 2005 the *Washington Post* reported "The White

House released budget figures yesterday indicating that the new Medicare prescription drug benefit will cost more than $1.2 trillion in the coming decade." [3]

Naturally, the White House disputes the *Washington Post's* claims. On the official White House website, on February 9, 2005, they put out a fact sheet saying, "Setting the record straight-Medicare drug benefit estimates unchanged. Myth: Today's *Washington Post* story headlined '*Medicare Drug Benefit May Cost $1.2 Trillion'* is simply wrong...The White House is seeking a correction from the *Washington Post.*" The next paragraph of the fact sheet explains the Center for Medicare Services (CMS) "estimated the cost of the first ten years of the program (2004-2013) at $534 billion." They explain that these figures include 2004 and 2005 costs and the bill President Bush signed in 2003 does not take effect until 2006. So they're saying that if you subtract 2004 and 2005, we're back to the $395 billion figure. But 2006 to 2013 is not ten years. However, if Bush explained it this way to the American people during his State of the Union Address, or to members of his own party, he would have lost support for it. The very next point in the fact sheet says "The FY 2006 budget includes a cost estimate for the Rx drug benefit for a different 10 year time frame, 2006-2015. The 2006-2015 CMS net estimate of federal spending on the Medicare prescription drug benefit is $723 billion." Still a whopping $328 billion above the $395 billion the administration promised the bill would cost over the next ten years. So, they sold this by saying it would cost $395 billion over a ten year period, however the ten year period they talk about requires one to subtract two of those years, 2004 and 2005. Is this making anybody else's brain bleed? After the bill was signed into law, they said the correct time frame is 2006 to 2015, and that is going to cost $723 billion. But again, that's not how it was sold. No matter which ten year period you choose to use, the cost far exceeds the $395 billion price tag Bush promised. These are convoluted smoke screens, double talk and bait and switch tactics that have kept everyone arguing over the numbers and successfully diverted attention from the real point of all of this. And that is, the only people who have benefited from this bill are Bush's corporate pals; the big drug manufactures and the health care industry.

The next point they make is "The $1.2 trillion does not take into account savings to the government from premium payments, state payments, and savings from the Medicaid system." These would be the people discussed earlier, the poorest of the poor and the disabled who would, under this bill, no longer qualify for Medicaid. [4]

$723 billion or $1.2 trillion, who knows, the cost could conceivably exceed $1.2 trillion. Remember the Iraq war was not supposed to cost more than $50 billion. If the *Washington Post* did decide to correct the numbers as the White House has asked, they could change the headline from "*Medicare Drug Benefit May Cost $1.2 Trillion*" to "*Medicare Drug Benefit May Cost $723 billion, nearly 85 % more Than the Bush Administration Promised.*" The body of the story could remain unchanged.

One of the provisions in the bill the drug makers lobbied hard for is the provision which prohibits the government (Medicare) from exercising its buying power and negotiating with drug companies for lower priced drugs. The ability to collectively bargain with drug manufacturers for lower prices for senior citizens would make sense if you had the best interest of the senior citizen in mind and not the welfare of the pharmaceutical company of which your father was a board member. (George H. W. Bush was a board member of Eli-Lilly). The reality is the Medicare Prescription Drug Bill passed the House and the Senate and was signed into law by Bush has this provision intact. The government cannot negotiate with the drug companies. The result is higher prices for prescription drugs for seniors across the board and record profits for the drug manufacturers. And the prices will continue to climb.

Prices for popular brand name prescription drugs rose 7.1% in 2004, more than twice the general inflation rate, the biggest rise in five years, with 2003 increases being 7%. Any savings senior citizens may have realized from the prescription drug bill have already been offset by the drug manufacturer's price hikes, and then some.

The Medicare bill also prohibits the re-importation of drugs from Canada or anywhere else, which greatly benefits the big drug manufacturers. The drugs in question are manufactured in the same facilities that manufacture drugs for the U.S. market. However, because of price control agreements, some places like the Canadian market pay lower prices. When exported back to the U.S. American citizens could save as much as 40% for their prescription drugs. Before the prescription drug bill was signed into law, Pfizer and GlaxoSmithKline informed Canadian pharmacists they would no longer sell drugs to wholesalers, but instead would sell directly to the pharmacies. Don Sancton, a spokesman for Pfizer, said, "The objective of us having more customers as direct clients is for us to better enforce our terms of sale, which are that our products are only to be sold in Canada for Canadian patients and that they are not for export." AstraZeneca and Wyeth told its customers it would investigate any unusually large orders from its Canadian clients to ensure shipments were not being sent out of the country. [5]

What could their motive be? Could it be BILLIONS OF DOLLARS! It doesn't take a mathematical genius or a corrupt CFO to figure this out. Deep throat, Bob Woodward's informant during his investigation of Watergate in the early 70's, said it best when he told Woodward to "follow the money."

Clearly, the pharmaceutical manufacturers are not interested in seeing lower drug prices in the U.S. market. Neither is the Bush administration. Can you hear the champagne corks popping the day Bush signed the Medicare bill?

While the pharmaceutical industry has successfully stopped any chance of prescription drugs from being re-imported from companies in Canada to pharmacies in the U.S. (and let's be clear here and reiterate, we're talking about drugs manufactured in the same facilities that supply the U.S. market, not something manufactured in a third world country) it is still legal for individuals to obtain drugs from Canadian pharmacies, however the Canadian Health Minister Ujjal Dosanjh has indicated Canada may restrict the practice of cross-border sales of prescription drugs to individuals. The reason: the pharmaceutical companies are pressuring the Canadian government by threatening to limit the sale of drugs for Canadian citizens if they don't stop cross-border sales to U.S. citizens. If they could, given time, they will make low income, elderly and disabled American citizen's criminals.

In a letter to President Bush, dated January 5, 2005, Jim Doyle (Gov. of Wisconsin) and Rod Blagojevich (Gov. of Illinois) said in part, "We are now seeing the potentially devastating effects of an industry that can threaten to deprive millions of Americans from accessing safe prescription drugs. Your administration has allowed this disturbing trend to continue, siding with the pharmaceutical companies over U.S. citizens.

"Minister Dosanjh stated in a recent interview that you discussed the prescription drug reimportation issue with Prime Minister Paul Martin during your visit to Canada on November 30, 2004. Less than two weeks later, Minister Dosanjh, who has noted your opposition to prescription drug reimportation, abruptly announced that Canada was considering ending cross-border sales. While it is unclear what message you delivered to the Prime Minister about reimportation, we urge you now to discourage him from cutting off two million Americans from this safe, affordable option.

"We urge you to make it clear that the position of the U.S. government is that we will not allow drug companies to restrict supply, and that cross-border sales that provide life saving medication to millions of Americans is no threat to Canada's drug supply."

The Governor's may be unclear what the message was, or they're too diplomatic to state the obvious, but it is blatantly clear Bush was the delivery boy for the pharmaceutical industry's message. Stop this cross-border bullshit or suffer supply shortages, period.

The Bush administration has said everything from "drugs from other countries are potentially dangerous" (even though they're manufactured in the U.S.) to they're protecting us from terrorist attacks on imported drugs. It's not just the White House making these ridiculous claims, according to a report released by U.S. Representative Bernard Sanders (I-VT.), more than half of the FDA commissioners who claim these things have strong financial ties to the pharmaceutical industry. We import meat from Argentina and Uruguay, fruit, sugar, coffee and tobacco, among other things, from the Caribbean (Check out the Caribbean Basin Initiative) and Mexico is the largest supplier (next to U.S. farmers) of fresh and frozen vegetables to the U.S. market. Surely, drugs manufactured in the U.S. should be safe to *re-import* from Canada.

And what about Billy Tauzin, the author of this wonderful piece of legislation that so favors the pharmaceutical and health care industry? He's announced he will be leaving Congress at the end of the current session. He has cited the stock answer all politicians use when they leave office voluntarily. Whether they've been at it so long they just need to quit or whether they're being investigated for corruption or child molestation, the answer is always to spend more time with the family.

"Leaving will not be easy" Tauzin wrote in his resignation letter, "but I believe this year is the right time for me and my family." How much time Tauzin will be spending with his family will depend on his work schedule as the new chief lobbyist for the D.C. lobbying group, the Pharmaceutical Research and Manufacturers of America (PhRMA) which will reportedly earn him $2,000,000 a year, representing the very corporations that stand to make billions from the legislation he just wrote and saw passed. What's astonishing is this huge conflict of interest, (at best it's a conflict, at worst its criminal) doesn't seem to register on the national conscience. Where is our forth estate formerly known as the press? Where is the outrage! Is this acceptable to the sheep in this country? These people who wrote this bill just screwed this country's grandmother's, and are going to pay off the triggerman with $2 million a year for fulfilling his part of the deal.

After stepping from the political side to the corporate side of the Washington revolving door, he can now teach a younger Congressman how to keep the corporate donors happy by writing legislation they (or now he) dictate while selling it to your constituents with flowery names like Prescription Drug Care *Benefit for the Elderly*. And you too, son, can retire from politics "to spend more time with your family."

While the Bush administration is preventing millions of people from procuring affordable, sometimes life saving drugs from Canada, vaccines manufactured, distributed and injected into millions of children in the United States (and around the world) are proving to be a serious health risk.

A mercury based preservative called Thimerosal invented by drug giant Eli-Lilly has been added to childhood vaccines for years to increase the life of the product, also increasing profits, and has recently been shown to be a factor in increased cases of Autism. According to the National Autism Association, the disorder has increased over 1000% since 1990 nearing epidemic status.

While Autism has been recognized by the medical community since the 50's, the disturbing thing about the more recent cases is symptoms did not occur at birth, but soon after an infant received vaccinations at age two. An FDA study determined that during the 90's children receiving vaccines under the Universal Childhood Immunization Schedule were receiving as much as 40 times the amount of mercury considered safe by EPA guidelines. These numbers were confirmed by the National Research Council's report published in July 2002.

Representative Dan Burton (R-IN.) along with others in Congress from both parties has pleaded with the department of Health and Human Services (HHS), which has jurisdiction over the FDA, to immediately ban vaccines containing Thimerosal. However, HHS has allowed big pharma to "phase out" Thimerosal.

In a letter to HHS by Rep. Burton, he writes "We all know and accept that mercury is a neurotoxin, and yet the FDA has failed to recall the 50 vaccines that contain Thimerosal. On their own website, the FDA states 'lead, cadmium, and mercury are examples of elements that are toxic when present at relatively low levels'...Our children are the future of this country. As a Government we have a responsibility to do everything within our power to protect them from harm, including ensuring that vaccines are safe and effective. Every day that mercury containing vaccines remain on the market is another day HHS is putting 8,000 children at risk. Given that Thimerosal free vaccines are available, and the known risk of mercury toxicity, to leave Thimerosal containing vaccines on the market is unconscionable." [6]

As we've seen with this administration, the corporate person's interests will win out over natural person's interests, including children and the elderly, every time.

However, the drug companies have found themselves in a bit of a conundrum. On the one hand downplaying the effects of Thimerosal keeps them hugely in the black profit wise. For example, UNICEF, the World Health Organization's parent body, buys 40 % of all vaccines which contain Thimerosal for third world countries from Merck. Eli-Lilly has licensing agreements with drug companies in 40 countries that produce the product. On the other hand, if it were found to be the case that these companies were found liable for damages because they knew about the health risks of Thimerosal, the resulting class action suits would rival the suits brought against tobacco and asbestos combined.

At a CDC committee meeting, developmental biologist Robert Brent stated, "The medical/legal findings in this study are horrendous. If an allegation was made that a child's neurobehavioral findings were caused by Thimerosal containing vaccines, you could readily find a junk scientist who would support the claim with a 'reasonable degree of certainty.' But you will not find a scientist with any integrity who would say the reverse with the data that is available…So we are in a bad position from the standpoint of defending any lawsuits if they were initiated, and I am concerned."

So, Brent is saying they would not be able to find a reputable scientist to dispute a "junk scientist", as he says, with the data available, data that comes from the EPA and the National Research Council. Sounds like reputable scientists are not afraid of disputing "junk scientists" but rather of disputing reputable sources like the EPA and the National Research Council.

By mid 2002 the Thimerosal law suits the corporations and Brent were concerned about were happening. Eli-Lilly and the others that make up the biggest of the big in the pharmaceutical industry had a way out of their legal conundrum. In June of 2002, President Bush appointed Eli-Lilly's CEO, Sidney Taurel, to a seat on the Homeland Security Advisory Council. Just prior to this strange appointment Bush had signed the Homeland Security Act. A massive bill that no Congressman had actually read, and was pushed through in the aftermath and fear created by 9-11. Buried in the bill was a provision which protected Lilly and other pharmaceuticals from parents, who believed their children were harmed by Thimerosal, from bringing lawsuits against drug companies.

No one knows how a provision which protects drug companies from lawsuits ended up in a homeland security bill. Well, somebody knows, but their not talking. The provision was ultimately removed from the bill.

Recently some suspects in the protect-the-drug-companies-by-slipping-in-a-provision-in-the-3000-page-Homeland-Security-Act-that-no-one's-going-to-read case have emerged. This year, senator's Bill Frist (R-TN), Judd Gregg (R-NH), Jeff Sessions (R-AL), Mike DeWine (R-OH), George Allen (R-VA), Rick Santorum (R-PA), Mitch McConnell (R-KY), and Jim DeMint (R-SC) introduced a bill calling for sweeping changes in pharmaceutical product liability. The Protecting America in the War on Terror Act of 2005 (S.3.IS) includes a provision very similar to the one that attempted to protect drug companies from accountability in 2002 called Vaccine Injury Compensation and Vaccine Litigation Reform. Once again, this provision designed to protect corporations from product liability has been intertwined with a homeland security bill. [7]

The Protecting America in the War on Terror Act includes raising the death benefit to the families of soldiers killed in Iraq and Afghanistan to $100,000 from $12,000. No Congressman or senator will vote against that, nor would any of their constituents expect them to. And therein lies the problem with shameless corporate shills who would use the families of American soldiers in this manner. I do not envy the senator, who understandably wants to raise the death benefits for the families of fallen soldiers, but at the same time is finding it hard to vote for the protection of corporate fat cats because of a provision, in an otherwise good bill, that shouldn't be there. And how is the politicizing of this bill by Frist and the others supporting the troops? Any senator who voted against a bill that gives the families of soldiers killed in action more money would be committing political suicide. You can hear the raspy voice of the guy that does the voice-overs for action movies, during the 2006 elections "Senator John Doe voted against the families of our brave soldiers. How can he possibly serve as your senator?" Screen fades to our opponent smiling with the American flag blowing in the wind superimposed behind him.

One final point on Thimerosal; it has been completely ban from veterinary use in the United States.

Expanding the Market (and Profits)

Since its inception in 1906, all of the FDA's funding has come from the U.S. Treasury. That changed in 1992 when a law was passed requiring drug companies to pay money directly to the FDA for the drug review and approval process. The Prescription Drug User Fee Act (PDUFA) of 1992 that was most recently re-authorized by the Public Health Security and Bioterrorism Preparedness and Response Act of 2002 were enacted to reduce tax payer funding of the review process. Critics argue this is industry funding to the FDA which gives pharmaceutical companies and their lobbying arm, PhRMA, too much influence.

In an interview on PBS's Frontline the Director of Public Citizen's Health Research Group, Sidney Wolfe, M.D. said, "Starting ten years ago, the influence was exerted by their directly funding, paying cash right up front, for FDA review. So in many ways, the FDA started looking upon the industry as their client, instead of the public and the public health, which should be the client." He believes this client relationship "has resulted in some drugs getting approved that shouldn't; drugs being put on a faster track than they should have." [8]

Director of the Center for Medical Consumers in New York City, Arthur A. Levin, in an April 2002 article titled Drug Company Influence Over the FDA wrote "My long running concerns about the erosion of the FDA's independence as a regulator over the last decade have only been heightened recently…I worry that the faster review process is the reason that a number of drugs approved over the last five years had to be withdrawn due to safety concerns."

Since Levin's article we've witnessed the disaster of Vioxx, Celebrex, Bextra and other widely prescribed drugs.

Discussing the re-authorization of the Prescription Drug User Fee Act, Levin writes, "The newly negotiated increases in user fees will now pay for more than half of FDA's expenses for pre-approval reviews. This growing dependency on industry cash to pay salaries of the review staff entrusted to carry out what is arguably one of the agency's most important public safety responsibilities is problematic. It suggests the FDA is being relegated to the role of consultant rather than regulator…I find it disturbing that this latest agreement was negotiated behind closed doors without inviting advocacy organizations to participate when the 'nuts and bolts' of the agreement were being decided…Unfortunately, Congress seems to be convinced that getting new drugs to people faster is by definition a good thing. No doubt the campaign contribution largesse of the drug industry helps to mute any Congressional criticism of the agreement. And having three former drug company executives in cabinet level positions doesn't hurt either." [9]

Under the guise of using less tax payer money and putting some of the financial burden on drug companies to get their products approved, the government has put the FDA in a position of depending on drug corporations for funding. This is in effect the partial privatization of the Food and Drug Administration and the result will be that drug companies will be able to fast track their products by exercising their new found leverage over the agency that formerly forced them to bring safe and efficient drugs to the market and discourage the FDA from rejecting drugs when the industry's research is marginal, thereby bringing more drugs to the market faster and expanding the market, and profits, with a reduced regard for safety.

We've seen this happen recently with Vioxx and Celebrex, to name just two, that had to be pulled from the market over safety concerns. The preliminary investigations seem to show Vioxx initially produced no more side effects than a placebo in the short term showing both groups had a stroke or heart attack occurrence of approximately 7.5 per 10,000, however, after 18 months of use the Vioxx groups stroke or heart attack rate increased to 15 per 10,000, almost a 100% increase over the placebo group. By then Vioxx was being prescribed to millions of people. Sometimes new drugs need three to five years before the long term affects can be determined. Had the research continued before the approval phase thousands of people may have avoided serious health problems.

Another problem with drug companies funding the review and approval process is that in 1991, almost all the trial research was done at academic institutions the drug manufacturer had little if any control over. Currently, the majority of testing is done at for-profit contract research facilities where the corporations can, to a much greater extent, control the results of data.

This experiment of having drug companies pick up some of the tab for review and approval should have ended in 2002. The Bush administration would never have signed the 2002 re-authorization bill had the drug companies opposed it. On the contrary, the drug companies are perfectly comfortable with it. Whatever costs they incur because of this bill will be offset by being able to reduce their research and development costs, since it will be easier to get drugs approved with less evidence of risk, and bringing more drugs that are increasingly more expensive to market faster.

The vast, vast majority of tax payers in this country do not oppose paying taxes when insured their tax dollars are not being pissed away but being used responsibly for agencies such as the EPA and the FDA, agencies that are administrated properly by the elected officials we hire to protect us. And almost all tax payers would oppose the cutting of funding to these agencies if they knew the shortages in tax dollars would result in big industry being able to manipulate the outcome of these agencies decisions at the harm to the average citizen. Again, the Bush administration is keeping their promise to reduce government in the one place the federal government is best suited to be effective.

Most tax payers would oppose appointing former corporate executives and lobbyists, who have ties to the industries they are tasked to oversee, to these agencies especially when their ideology is corporations should not be regulated in any way that interferes with the bottom line, consumers be damned.

A great way for the pharmaceutical industry to increase their profits is to simply reformulate or "tweak" an existing drugs inactive ingredients, and renaming it, just prior to the patent expiring, thereby extending the patent and preventing generic drugs that can be as much two thirds cheaper to the consumer from entering the market. While a company has the right to try and increase their sales and profits, and there is at least one advantage to doing this in that this "new" drug is, for all practice purposes, the same as the one it is replacing, therefore the approval process is much easier, and in many cases the drug has proved to be safe and effective. One, then, could ask what's wrong with this practice. The main problem is the consumer continues to pay high prices since they don't have the option of choosing a generic brand and on top of that these "new" drugs are always marketed as somehow better, justifying a hefty price increase sometimes as much as double the price, [10] in effect hitting the consumer with a "double-whammy." Since the approval process is much cheaper for the drug company, and the R&D costs were already covered from the sales during the first go-round, this is borderline unethical profiteering.

In August of 1994, more than one person was arrested for driving down to south Florida after Hurricane Andrew and selling $250 chain saws to people who had just suffered the worst natural disaster in history, at that time, for $500.

This brings us to the marketing of drugs in this country. In Canada, and every other industrialized country, strict regulation on how drug companies can advertise coupled with price controls help keep cost to consumers affordable. Advertising was also regulated in the U.S. until 1997 when the law was significantly relaxed. Since then the drug corporations expenditures for advertising has surpassed that of R&D. In 1991 the pharmaceutical industry spent $55 million on advertising. By 1998, one year after the regulation on drug advertising was relaxed in the U.S., the industry was spending $1.8 billion on advertising, by 2001 they were spending in excess of $2.5 billion on advertising, and that investment is paying off.

By 1998 consumers were spending $93.4 billion on prescription drugs compared to just over $50 billion five years earlier, an eighty four per cent increase.

A study conducted at the University of British Columbia looking at how drug advertising affects what patients ask for found people in Sacramento were twice as likely as people in Vancouver to ask for new, more costly, brand name drugs. The study also showed people who asked for specific drugs they'd seen advertised got them 75% of the time.

In Canada the law states an advertisement can only state the drugs proper name, common name, price and quantity for purposes of price comparison. They cannot make claims as to effectiveness. The law is modeled on the World Health Organization's criteria for the ethical marketing of pharmaceutical's and designed so that when a person in Canada sees an advertisement for a new drug that may be an option to what they are taking, it may prompt them to discuss this with their physician to make an informed decision. In the United States, since the pharmaceutical companies are no longer burdened with such restrictions in their advertising, the ads appear to be more of an "educational" nature and therefore people will demand what they saw on "the TV" as the University of British Columbia study has found. However there is absolutely no evidence that a thirty second spot run forty times a day on TV in the U.S. equals "education." On the contrary, the FDA in recent years has had to admonish some companies like Bristol-Myers Squibb, Wyeth, Eli-Lilly and others because their advertising down played risks and overstated benefits.

The pharmaceutical lobby has been pressuring Canada's equivalent of the FDA to remove restrictions on advertising in that country so they would more closely resemble the U.S.'s form of advertising. One group lobbying for the de-regulation of Canada's laws on advertising is Advocare, a patient advocacy group that claims they want patients to be better "educated" apparently by saturating them with thirty second advertising spots dozens of times a day. Advocare receives a large portion of their funding from the pharmaceutical industry.

If Canada succumbs to the efforts of the pharmaceutical lobby, consumers in this country will no longer need to bother with going to Canada to get their drugs, Canada's drug prices will soon be just as un-affordable as they are here. Hopefully Canada will place more importance on the breathing person than on the corporate person, and resist the free-for-all corporate attitude unlike the current government in this country.

More Expanding the Market: When the Government Requires the Medication of Children

In 1995 Texas Governor George W. Bush implemented a plan called the Texas Medication Algorithm Program (TMAP) to screen school children and school employees for mental health disorders. In July 2004 President Bush unveiled a sweeping mental health initiative that would take TMAP national and recommends the screening of 52 million students and 6 million adults who work in the public school system. It started in April 2002 as the New Freedom Commission on Mental Health. The commission concluded that schools were in a "key position" to screen for a new market for antipsychotic drugs.

Allen Jones, an employee of the Pennsylvania Office of the Inspector General wrote in a whistle blower report that, "the political/pharmaceutical alliances are poised to consolidate the TMAP effort into a comprehensive national policy to treat mental illness with expensive, patented medications of questionable benefit and deadly side effects." He also noted that officials with influence over the plan had received money from the drug companies who stand to gain from it, and members of the Freedom Commission have served on advisory boards for these same companies. Let's remember Eli-Lilly whose Olanzapine is one of the drugs specifically mentioned by the Freedom Commission once had H.W. Bush as a board member and W. Bush has appointed Lilly's CEO, Sidney Taurel, to the Homeland Security Council.

In November of 2004 a huge appropriations bill called the Labor, HHS, and Education Appropriations Act for FY 2005 passed with more than $20 million in funding for universal mental health screening. In September 2004, Representative Ron Paul (R-TX) tried in vein to put an amendment in the bill that would allow for parental consent prior to government psychological testing of children. The bill passed without this amendment.

Paul wrote to his colleagues "As you know, psychotropic drugs are increasingly prescribed for children who show nothing more than children's typical rambunctious behavior. Many children have suffered harmful effects from these drugs. Yet some parents have been charged with child abuse for refusing to drug their children. The federal government should not promote national mental health screening programs that will force the use of these psychotropic drugs."

Representative Ron Paul also warns against interpreting the small amount of money in the bill as insignificant. "Anyone who understands bureaucracies knows that they assume more and more power incrementally. A few scattered state programs [such as Texas] over time will be replaced by a federal program implemented in a few select cities. Once the limited federal program is accepted, it will be expanded nationwide. Once in place throughout the country, the screening program will become mandatory."

It is already happening in Illinois whose Children's Mental Health Act requires children be screened before entering kindergarten and during the transition to junior high and high school. Legislators in Minnesota have introduced a bill in that state similar to the one in effect in Illinois.

In Nazi Germany, anyone deemed to be "different" i.e.: Jew, gypsy, Slovak, homosexual etc...were persecuted. The Soviets classified dissidents or anyone who showed opposition to the state as mentally ill to be locked away. What will happen to people deemed to be different because they dissent or have different views? What about kids who express themselves differently through art or music. What about high school kids who express homosexual tendencies. Is it possible a segment of our society would consider them mentally ill? Should these people be required to medicate themselves, or should their parents be required to medicate them if they want to be able to attend school?

One of the proponents of the Texas program was the Department of Corrections. Just think of all the new "customers" for the pharmaceutical industry:

school children and state prisoners, a huge previously untapped market. The New Freedom Initiative report recommends that eventually screening should be expanded to include all Americans. Imagine that before obtaining a driver license, you have to submit to a mental screening with the results ending up at some Orwellian government agency.

Karen R. Effrem, M.D. who sits on the board of directors of EdWatch [11] said, "I am concerned, especially in the schools, that mental health could be used as a wedge for diagnosis based on attitudes, values, beliefs and political stances."

Anyone who has had a teenager knows that at times it is difficult, at best, to understand the things they do. You don't understand the music they listen to, the clothes they wear and the people they want to hang around with. They appear to reasoned adults at times to be completely insane and out of control. It's called adolescence and while sometimes the thought may cross our minds that it would be so much easier to deal with them with a few milligrams of Prozac coursing through their veins, or ours, the fact is very few require medication for this *condition*.

Some organizations that strongly oppose this screening program are Eagle Forum, the Association of American Physicians and Surgeons, Concerned Women of America, Freedom 21, the Alliance for Human Research Protection, the International Center for the Study of Psychiatry and Psychology and EdWatch. You might realize that a couple of these organizations are very conservative right wing groups. Apparently political ideology goes out the window when you start fucking with our kids. Every parent needs to know all they can about this and oppose it vehemently. Demand the government stay the hell out of our lives and our children's lives. The decision of what kinds of medication, if any, and how much should be prescribed to our children is a decision only parents and the pediatricians they choose should make.

8

Agri-business, Corporate Farming and the USDA

"Let the farmer forevermore be honored in his calling; for they who labor in the earth are the chosen people of God."
Thomas Jefferson

During the 2000, 2002 and 2004 election cycle's agribusiness donated $166 million to political campaigns in which almost 75% went to George W. Bush, the RNC and Republican candidates. [1] The agribusiness industry is huge, made up of mega corporations. The days of the mom & pop farms is rapidly becoming a thing of the past.

In the summer of 2002 the Farm Security and Rural Investment Act of 2002 (H.R. 2646) that authorized $180 billion in subsidies to the agribusiness industry over ten years, passed in both the House and the Senate. It was signed into law by President Bush on May 13, 2002. This was a complete reversal of the administration's previous position. Shortly after Bush took office in 2001, the administration released a 120 page policy report saying, "Subsidies stimulate excess production, inflate land rents and largely benefit a small number of large farms." H.R. 2646 replaced The Freedom to Farm Law of 1996 which was designed, in part, to wean farmers from government subsidies. The Freedom to Farm Act also ended a Depression era system of production controls and brought some control to farm spending and discouraged overproduction of surplus crops. Representative John Boehner (R-OH) said, "We're going back to what we know didn't work for 60 years." [2]

In May of 2002, on the floor of the Senate concerning H.R. 2646, Senator John McCain (R-AZ) said, "I oppose this new farm legislation because it is an appalling breach of our federal spending responsibility and could be damaging to our national integrity."

He seemed to agree with the administrations earlier view that large subsidies to agribusiness were not a responsible policy. He said, "A report by the General Accounting Office [now known as the Government Accountability Office, or GAO] highlighted the egregious disparity in farm benefits, demonstrating that over 80% of farm payments primarily benefited large farms. Other studies by the Environmental Working Group similarly found that, in evaluating U.S. Department of Agriculture data, the top ten percent of big farmers and agribusiness consumed about 80 percent of farm benefits, leaving small farmers out in the cold.

"…election year politics pressured conferees to reject any reasonable limitations. [To the farm subsidies in 2646. Was McCain referring to a payoff to big agribusiness corporations during the 2002 midterm election cycle?]. As a result, nothing in this bill will serve as a checks and balance system to prevent the bulk of payments to selected commodities such as cotton, wheat and corn growers and large farming conglomerates. The end result is a continuation of the disturbing trend of disproportionate payments to large farmers and agribusiness.

"Mr. President, all this new spending not only adds up to increased burdens for tax payers, it also may threaten U.S. commitments through various trade agreements.

"Our policy in this farm bill…sends the wrong message to developing countries for it says that no matter what our nation preaches about the free-market system and the need to promote free trade around the world, the United States Government will directly intervene in the market if it benefits politically powerful interests." [3]

Politically powerful interests? Say it ain't so John. The rhetoric of the Bush administration policy paper in early 2001 and subsequent statements made since then regarding the tearing down of barriers to trade, once again, doesn't equal the Bush administration's actions.

In 1999 in a speech at the Ronald Reagan Presidential Library, Bush said the case for trade "is not just monetary, but moral."

At the signing of the Farm Act of 2002, Bush said, "A completely free global market for agricultural products, for example, would result in gains of as much as $13 billion a year for American farmers and consumers. Lowering global trade barriers on all products and services by even one third could boost the U.S. economy by $177 billion a year,"

However as John McCain pointed out, the 80% increase in farm subsidies under the new law will in fact be an increased tax burden on tax payers. The only people profiting are, again, the corporate persons in the form of corporate welfare through tax payer dollars.

Bush goes on to say, "Free trade is also a proven strategy for global prosperity and adding to the momentum of political freedom. Trade is an engine of economic growth. It uses the power of markets to meet the needs of the poor. In our lifetime, trade has helped lift millions of people, and whole nations, and entire regions, out of poverty and put them on the path to prosperity." And "greater freedom for commerce across the borders eventually leads to greater freedom for citizens within the borders." [4]

But while the Bush administration pressures other countries to knock down their trade barriers thereby expanding the U.S. export market, they have made it increasingly more difficult for developing countries to access the U.S. markets. In an Oxfam International report to governments, institutions and multinational companies around the world, they state "In their rhetoric, governments of rich nations constantly stress their commitment to poverty reduction. Yet in practice rigged rules and double standards lock poor people out of the benefits of trade.

"Rich countries spend $1 billion every day on agricultural subsidies. The resulting surpluses are dumped on world markets, undermining the livelihoods of millions of smallholder farmers in poor countries.

"When developing countries export to rich country markets, they face tariff barriers that are four times higher than those encountered by rich countries. Those barriers cost them $100 billion a year—twice as much as they receive in aid." [5] Bush's version of free trade is very one sided to the extreme.

Because of the farm bill Bush signed into law the large agribusiness corporations are over-producing and "dumping" artificially lowered priced products in the developing nations Bush professes so much concern over. Because of the artificially lowered prices, farmers in developing countries can't afford to sell their products in their own countries, much less foreign markets. The big agribusiness corporations won't suffer from the lowered prices because the subsidies, paid for by us the tax payer, to the corporations will pick up the difference. On Oxfam's website they state the "WTO recently confirmed its rulings that rich countries subsidizing their farmers and dumping surplus crops on poor countries is illegal." Critics say this is not free trade and are calling for "fair" trade.

In the book *The President of Good and Evil* by Peter Singer, Singer writes that Bush "has supported one important initiative for some of the world's poorest nations, the African Growth and Opportunity Act (AGOA)…enacted during the Clinton administration, allows free market access for selected products from thirty eight African nations…Exports from AGOA nations to the United States were 'rising dramatically,' Bush said," Singer points out that while exports to the U.S. from AGOA nations were up in 2002 by 10% "more than three quarters of these imports were petroleum products, which do less to generate employment than more labor intensive products like textiles...Excluding petroleum products, all the thirty eight AGOA nations together exported only a modest $2.2 billion worth of goods to the U.S. (For comparison, Australia, with a population about one twentieth of the combined total of the AGOA nations, had exports to the U.S. of more than $6 billion.)" He concludes that "the growth in imports from AGOA nations was not enough to offset a more substantial decline in imports from other sub-Saharan African nations, which meant that overall U.S. imports from sub-Saharan Africa actually fell by more than 15% in 2002." The report Singer cites which documents the decline in imports from sub-Saharan Africa was a report submitted by the President of the United States to the U.S. Congress in May of 2003.

This is not about helping the family farmer, but it is all about garnering support from the corporate base during the 2002 midterm election cycle. 80% of the subsidies are going to the countries largest 10% of agri-corps. A report from Global Trade Negotiations Home Page says "The World Bank's Global Economic Prospects Report of 2002 estimated that over a ten year period, abolishing all trade barriers could increase global income by $2.8 trillion over half of which would accrue to developing countries reducing global poverty by 320 million people by 2015." [6]

If President Bush truly believes in eliminating, or at least alleviating poverty in the world as his past statements suggest, why the reversal in rhetoric from candidate Bush in 1999 and 2000 and the early policy paper of President Bush in 2001 to support for 80% increases in farm subsidies for big corporate agri-business which will continue to impoverish millions of people in developing countries (and a good number of people in this country). If the rhetoric is to be believed, Bush should not have signed the 2002 farm bill.

This hypocrisy is not lost on the rest of the world. While the U.S. is losing credibility daily in the world, it seems the only people in the dark are American's. One reason for this is because the main source of survival for people in developing countries is agriculture. They're paying attention.

When Bush says the case for free trade is "not just monetary, it's moral" he's right. However, it's more than just about money or morals, it's vital for our national security. And it's not necessarily free trade that's needed it is fair trade. The poorest countries on the planet that we are discussing in Africa are mostly Muslim. They're fertile recruitment grounds for radical Islamic extremists. They are increasingly aware of the policies of the rich countries in the western world that have created the conditions they endure. President Bush tells us over and over and over on almost a weekly basis that terrorists "hate our freedom" they "hate our way of life." In reality it's much more complex than that. They hate fifty years of policies which support puppet governments and oppressive regimes like Saddam Hussein, who we supported since he took power in 1979 all through the 80's during the Reagan Bush administration, and the Saudi Royal Family, arguably one of the most repressive governments on the planet and the Noriega's of the world and the list goes on. Most recently Bush has allied us with the most oppressive and brutal tyrant of the Middle East. Islam Karimov of Uzbekistan where they actually boil people alive as a form of torture. They hate policies like the one we're discussing that floods their markets with under priced goods which make it impossible for them to make a living.

The Oxfam report says "Large parts of the developing world are becoming enclaves of despair, increasingly marginalized and cut off from the rising wealth generated through trade. Shared prosperity cannot be built on such foundations. Like the economic forces which drive globalization, the anger and social tensions that accompany vast inequalities in wealth and opportunity will not respect national borders. *The instability that they will generate threatens us all.* In today's globalized world, our lives are more inextricably linked than ever before, and so is our prosperity. As a global community, we sink or swim together."

This generation has no choice but to fight terrorists who are bent on killing us, but if we don't do something about the inequalities and despair mentioned above we are creating a destiny where our children and grandchildren will face perpetual war.

So why are the cows so pissed?

In December of 2003, the first case of Bovine Spongiform Encephalopathy (BSE) was reported in the U.S by the USDA in the state of Washington. Better known as "Mad Cow Disease" Canada reported a case in May of the same year. BSE was identified in England in 1985 and spread across Europe leading to the slaughter of more than 3.7 million animals. To date more than 150 human deaths have been attributed to Mad Cow in Europe, mostly in Britain.

The disease is but one form of a family of diseases known as Transmissible Spongiform Encephalopathy's (TSE) caused by cannibalism not just in cow's but in other species as well. TSE's are caused by eating abnormal proteins known as prions. In deer and elk the lethal neurological condition is known as Chronic Wasting Disease. Cases have been found recently in Wisconsin and New York, among other states. [7] In sheep it's called Scrappie and in humans it's known as Kuru by ancient cultures who still practice ritualistic cannibalism. The most recent case of TSE in humans is in the Fore tribe in Papua New Guinea not discovered until the 20th century. Pathogenic prions are believed to trigger variant Creuzveldt-Jakob Disease (vCJD) as well as some forms of Alzheimer's as a result of contact with BSE or Mad Cow Disease. Prions accumulate in toxic quantities in brain and spinal tissue and have been found in blood and muscle tissue as well. Prions cannot be destroyed by irradiation, freezing, cooking, or by disinfectant methods used in hospitals.

Most disturbing is the evidence that prions can jump between species. In 1985 in five separate outbreaks in Stetsonville, Wisconsin, mink which were fed cattle derived remains developed a disease known as Transmissible Mink Encephalopathy (TME) which proved to be very similar to BSE. Experiments were done in which tissues from diseased mink were injected into Holstein cattle. The cattle developed spongiform encephalopathy. The remains of these cattle were fed to healthy mink which soon developed TME. Since everything from road kill to euthanized pets to poultry manure to human plate waste (left over garbage) to ground up carcasses go to rendering plants and end up as feed, the University of Wisconsin concluded, "if this is true, there must exist an unrecognized bovine spongiform encephalopathy like infection in American cattle." This Animal byproduct feed known as high protein total mixed ration (TMR) is produced by the large corporate agri-business because after injecting cows with growth hormones, antibiotics and other cocktails of drugs, the cows require more protein. The practice also cuts feed costs. By grinding up everything from bones and carcasses to organs and chicken shit and mixing it into the feed grain, the cost of feed is significantly reduced.

Animals that are treated like machines don't last as long on huge agri-business farms as they do at smaller free-range farms therefore standard practice on "factory farms" is the use of recombinant bovine growth hormone (rBGH) injections (The "r" in front of BGH indicates the bovine growth hormone is a laboratory copy of the natural hormone cows produce in the pituitary gland. The only company which makes rBGH is Monsanto, who claims it is completely safe for humans, however there is growing evidence linking rBGH to prostate cancer and breast cancer), TMR supplements in feed, which forces these cows to be cannibals, steroids and other supplements. Also dairy cows suffering from burn out have a high rate of mastitis or udder infection which requires antibiotics. Often calves are fed milk replacer or calf starter, as a supplement which contains cow blood, not only making them cannibals but vampires as well.

Some of these sick animals end up as "downer" cows. Downer cows are cattle that for whatever reason cannot walk and have to be dragged to slaughter and were identified as early as 1906. Chances are most of these cows have problems other than Mad Cow, but they are good candidates for inspection for Mad Cow. However by the time "downers" are tested, if they are at all, their meat has already been processed and distributed. Symptoms of BSE do not commonly manifest until after roughly five years of age, after the usual age of slaughter of about four years in the U.S. when a prion infected cow may still appear to be healthy. To date "downer" cows have not been ban from human consumption in the U.S.

The practice of turning animals that are not carnivores in the first place into cannibals has proved to be catastrophic in the U.K. The United States is following in the same footsteps as Britain in the 80's by ignoring the problem. Europe has put in place a full ban on livestock feed that has animal by-products in it and they require BSE testing on all animals over 30 months old. The U.S. still allows livestock feed to contain animal by-products. In 1997, the FDA issued a ruling that all livestock feed containing animal by-products such as meat and bone meal from ruminants must contain labeling saying, "do not feed to ruminants." But to date there are no policies in place to enforce the ruling. In 2002 the GAO reported the "FDA does not know the full extent of industry compliance." Furthermore, there is no ban on feed containing non-ruminant remains. If cow remains are fed to non-ruminants (horses, pigs etc...) and the non-ruminant remains are fed back to cows, and if the evidence that suggests prions can "jump" between species is correct, then there needs to be a full ban prohibiting all animal protein in cattle feed. The U.S. not only doesn't require testing of animals that are for human consumption, it has been made illegal (More on that in a moment). Japan requires testing on all animals slaughtered. With the discovery of BSE in Washington state 43 countries have imposed bans on U.S. beef. Of the top four beef importers which make up over 90% of U.S. export, only Canada does not have a full ban.

In 1997, John Stauber of prwatch.org and Sheldon Rampton authored a book called *Mad Cow U.S.A.* and in 1998 Howard Lyman, a former Montana rancher turned activist, published a book called Mad Cowboy warning of the potential problems with the U.S. governments complacency concerning the practices of large corporate farming over a decade after the crises in the U.K. Lyman created a fervor in 1996 as a guest on the Oprah Winfrey show when he outlined the conditions and practices in corporate slaughterhouses. After Oprah expressed her disgust, cattle futures dropped nearly 20% and the Texas Cattleman's Association promptly sued Oprah. Stauber, Rampton and Lyman were portrayed as kook's and alarmists. The corporate lobby went into high gear commissioning reports like the one done by the Harvard Center for Risk analysis which said, "We are *firmly confident* that BSE will not become an animal or public health problem in America. The United States is very resistant to BSE." And from the Cato Institute, the right wing conservative funded think tank of scientists whose only function it seems is to write reports supporting Bush's policies and dispute every other scientist's findings on the planet, are circulating reports disputing whether prions even exist or cause disease. [8] And then, after these expert assurances, the 2003 Washington cow was discovered.

As we've seen with the EPA and the FDA, it is commonplace in the Bush administration for former corporate executives and lobbyist's to be appointed to high level positions in the agencies whose function is to regulate the industry they have strong financial ties to. The USDA is no exception. USDA's BSE spokesperson is Lisa Harrison, former public relations director for the National Cattleman's Beef Association who has put out press releases with titles like "Mad Cow Disease Not a Problem in the U.S." Bush's choice to head the USDA was Ann Veneman, a beef and biotech industry shill whose 11 advisors are from the beef industry. Her chief of staff Dale Moore is a former lobbyist for the meat industry. She is an advocate of the 2002 farm bill Bush signed touting free trade that gives huge subsidies to large agri-business. Most American's believe, mistakenly, that our food supply comes from the family farmer and the subsidies are in place to protect rural families.

Veneman left at the end of Bush's first term. She'll probably end up back where she came from, an agri-business attorney or a lobbyist for big corporation.

Her replacement is Mike Johanns who is also an ardent supporter of Bush's 2002 farm bill. George Naylor, President of the National Family Farm Coalition [9] said, "This farm bill continues to tap taxpayers' hard earned money to keep the farm economy limping along while the giant food processors and exporters reap cheap commodities to expand their control of the world's food supply." [10]

As governor of Nebraska, Johanns tried to gut initiative 300, a 23 year old law which restricts large corporations from owning farmland and engaging in agricultural activities in the state. Robert Broom, an attorney who successfully defended I-300 in federal courts said, "There seems to be no useful purpose in modifying I-300 unless the purpose is to subject I-300 to legal attack." Nebraska's rural voters spoke and prevented Johanns's attacks on I-300. [11]

Before the discovery of BSE in this country the ex-corporate lobbyists, now in charge of government agencies, told us it couldn't happen here. Since the discovery of BSE in December of 2003 they have consistently told us everything is fine, not to worry, however, after almost two years, this administration has done very little to address the problem other than tell us not to worry. Because of that fact it shouldn't surprise anyone that Mad Cow has entered the United States.

The people in charge of the USDA, the regulatory body charged with protecting our food supply, is now heavily staffed by meat industry lobbyist's and former National Cattleman's Association employee's. They have a financial stake in how the nation's food supply is regulated, and they are telling us everything is great, nothing to worry about.

The Bush administration is treating this like it's a P.R. problem for big agribusiness and not a health problem that could potentially affect millions of us. While the USDA has taken some steps since December 2003, much more needs to be done. They have not ban animal by-products in cattle feed, there is no mandatory testing for BSE in cows over 30 months old, downer cows are not ban from human consumption and an attempt to ban milk from cows injected with rBGH from school's is dead.

While there is a moral argument to be made for changing the way corporate farms operate, we'll pass over that for now and focus on the practical argument. The main reason for change is the potential health risk to every man, woman and child in this country.

There is something those of us who do not wish to become vegetarians can do. There are still some farms and ranches producing "natural" beef and dairy products. Their cow's roam and graze freely and naturally, they receive no antibiotics, steroids, growth hormones or feed containing animal by-products such as blood, bone meal, meat and all the other slaughterhouse waste currently mixed into feed. There is no milk supplements containing cow's blood used to wean calves on these natural farms. Milk from these farms is rBGH free.

One such farm is Creekstone Farms, in Arkansas City, Kansas. [12] During 30 years in the cattle industry they have built a substantial business selling their products to the restaurant industry, and one of their largest clients, the Japanese. When BSE was found in the U.S. in December of 2003, the Japanese halted all imports from the U.S.

In an article by Edward Lotterman in Twin Cities Pioneer Press, Lotterman writes, "Creekstone understandably wants to resume this trade. Japan requires all cows slaughtered in that country be tested for BSE. Creekstone is willing, even eager, to do such testing. But the USDA has *prohibited even voluntary testing* of all cows at any U.S. packing house.

"USDA has maintained that 100% testing for BSE is not necessary for protecting public health and should not be mandatory." While Lotterman, an economist, agrees with the USDA he continues, "Not requiring testing, however, is a far cry from prohibiting voluntary testing…It is an axiom of economics that governments should not ban contractual agreements between a willing buyer and a willing seller when such agreements do not harm any third party."

The USDA's position is clear, the big meat packers and agri-business don't want testing to become mandatory. They view Creekstone's voluntary testing to be a slippery slope that would eventually lead to at least some level of industry wide mandatory testing.

Lotterman points out the irony of this by saying Creekstone "has identified niches where identity-preserved, high quality meat can earn more money not only for the firm, but also for the farmers and ranchers [the family farms] who sell their animals to Creekstone. Now the administration orders Creekstone to refuse to meet a legitimate preference of one of its best customers.

"A dynamic firm wants to expand U.S. farm exports but cannot because a Republican administration is squelching free enterprise to please a special interest group." [13]

Once again the Bush administration has shown their hypocrisy by going against their own rhetoric about free trade and helping family farmers. And have sided with corporations over the family farm that he professes so much concern about.

On June 9, 2005, in St. Paul Minnesota, Secretary of Agriculture Mike Johanns met with the big hitters from the agri-business industry and their lobbying groups to tell the world U.S. beef products are fine and mad cow is not a threat in North America. Their goal was to demand that Japan, Korea and other countries that still have a ban on U.S. meat imports open their markets. The group included the American Farm Bureau, the American Meat Institute, the National Cattleman's beef Association, the National Milk Producers and the National Renderers Association. No consumer groups were invited, nor were there any public interest groups or human health groups. And definitely no scientific groups that study mad cow disease. Only the media was invited.

What was not widely known at the time was that there was a second case of mad cow disease in the U.S., in Texas. The day after the St. Paul meeting, the USDA confirmed the cow had in fact tested positive. The animal was a downer cow that died in November of 2004. The Washington Post reported on June 11, "Although the first U.S. mad cow case involved an animal born and raised in Canada and then shipped to Washington state, USDA chief veterinarian John Clifford said the agency had 'no information' the possible second case was 'an imported animal.' He said the Texas animal was a beef cattle and was older but declined to give any more specifics." [14]

The Washington Post article also quotes Mike Johanns as saying the "result did not mean that people face a greater health risk from eating beef, because meat from the animal did not enter the human food chain or the beef feed chain."

Johanns' assurances should not comfort anyone since the Texas cow died before making it to the slaughterhouse. The fact the cow did not enter the food chain was not because of any firewall the government has in place to detect prion infected cows. The next logical question is, since there is no mandatory testing and there is no enforcement of the 1997 feed ban and there is no ban on downer cows being used for human consumption, how does anyone know how many BSE positive cow's have made it to slaughter and have become dinner?

The statement by USDA veterinarian John Clifford that the Texas cow was "older" is curious. Since the 1997 feed ban prohibiting the use of ruminant remains in ruminant feed, critics have raised concerns because there is no mechanism in place to enforce the ban. The FDA and USDA rely on industry compliance. It appears Clifford is trying to head off critics who say the 1997 ruling is ineffective by saying the cow was born before the ban. But Johanns' statement that there is no risk because the animal did not enter the "beef feed chain" implies animal by-products *are* used in cattle feed.

Johanns and the Bush administration had to know about the Texas cow, the second case of mad cow in the U.S., well before the June 9 St. Paul meeting, but still insist everything is fine. There is no reason to expect them to do anything differently with respect to how corporate farms operate since they haven't done much since the first case was reported in December of 2003. They will just continue to support their corporate donors and tell the rest of us to go eat a hamburger.

The Physicians Committee for Responsible Medicine would disagree. In a recent report by PCRM they state, "The conditions that led to the emergence of BSE in Britain have also been present in the U.S. The agent that causes BSE has already spread to at least one cow [Two now after the confirmation of BSE in the Texas cow] and other species of animals in the U.S. The extent to which BSE has entered the human food supply is unknown."

The report discusses Creutzfeldt-Jakob disease, a degenerative, fatal brain disease known as CJD and how BSE triggers a variant form of CJD in humans known as vCJD. The report goes on to address the failure of the Bush administration's policies in combating mad cow. Since doctors are not required to report deaths from CJD or Alzheimer's to the CDC, "Individuals showing signs of dementia due to such a condition may be misdiagnosed as suffering from Alzheimer's disease or stroke, and most dying with neurological illnesses are never autopsied." (The only way to confirm a diagnosis of CJD or vCJD is by brain biopsy or autopsy)

"There is simply no way of knowing whether vCJD has begun in the United States or not. Death certificates from 1979 to 1998 show that 4,751 people were identified with CJD in the United States. While the presumption is that they had the 'classical' form of the disease, rather than the new variant form which is believed to come from animal tissues, remains uncertain. While most victims were older (a sign of classical CJD), a small number were surprisingly young." [15]

The report concludes with recommendations for the government, most of which have been addressed above with the exception of one. Even if one were to swear off beef, pork and chicken that was not raised "naturally" on a free range farm, there are many other products containing animal by-products such as gelatin's, natural flavorings, cosmetics and certain drugs. Therefore the recommendations from groups like PCRM that feed containing animal by-products be ban for use in *all* livestock, not just cattle, the ban on downer cows for human consumption be implemented immediately and required testing of *all suspect* cows entering the human food chain and preventing the meat from such animals from being distributed until test results are known (which is also not currently done) is crucial to protect not only the population but the cattle industry and by extension the economy of the United States.

9

Banking and the Credit Card Industry

"The money power preys upon the nation in times of peace and conspires against it in times of war. It is more despotic than monarchy, more insolent than autocracy, more selfish than bureaucracy. It denounces, as public enemies, all that even question its methods or throw light upon its crimes. I have two great enemies, the Southern Army in front of me and the financial institutions at the rear. The latter is my greatest foe."
Abraham Lincoln

The bankruptcy bill Bush signed into law (written by the credit card industry) is but one more example of corporate pandering by this administration. The credit card industry lobby successfully convinced the American public people claiming bankruptcy were, for the most part, deadbeats and frauds. Anyone claiming bankruptcy, they said, were simply irresponsible and were the cause of huge losses to the industry. An industry that records record revenue's and charges as much as 39% interest on credit, not to mention late charges that are so exorbitant people sometimes pay over 100% more than the original debt. The credit card industry sends out almost *five billion* notices a year saying, "You are Pre-approved". Or transfer your outstanding credit to our card and pay 0% interest for the first six months. The fine print says if you're late with a payment you're interest rate could go as high as 39% in some instances. (Depending on the state you're in) This may be higher than the rate you were paying before you transferred you're balance to the new card. The credit card companies have been targeting high risk borrowers for years. They have at least helped in creating the problem of out-of-control borrowing. With 1.5 million bankruptcies a year, some changes are warranted. Unfortunately, the bill does nothing to address the predatory lending practices of the industry, but puts the total burden on the middle class person making it harder to get debt relief. But the bill does not affect the mega rich who use asset protection trusts to shelter assets like jewelry, automobile collections or mansions in different states.

With a little digging into the facts it becomes clear there are people who are irresponsible and decide to buy 60" plasma TV's, on credit, while they are unemployed, but the statistics show an overwhelming 90% of people who claim bankruptcy fall into one of four categories:

1.   Catastrophic illness and were either un-insured or under insured,

2.   Death in the family or divorce or

3.   Loss of their livelihood or career and

4.   Some combination of the above.

These people also tended to wait years to claim bankruptcy while trying to pay their debts. About ½ of the 90% were due to an unexpected medical crisis (How many of those cases resulted in un-employment?). Of that ½, just over 75% had at least some medical insurance. [1] This report shows the need to take a long hard look at the health care system in this country.

Bush speaks frequently about the "entrepreneurial spirit" of Americans and about his "ownership society." He speaks about his support for it. He made it a part of his campaign ads in 2004 and talked about it in the debates. Entrepreneurialism, by its definition, involves considerable risk. The bankruptcy bill will discourage the "entrepreneurial spirit" by removing an important safety net. People are not looking for a "bail-out," as the Presidents brother received during the savings and loan crisis in the 80's however, society has a vested interest in getting people solvent again, especially the ones with an entrepreneurial spirit.

As the bankruptcy bill moved through Congress, the Democrats tried to add a provision which would exempt people who found themselves in financial crisis due to a catastrophic medical condition. The Republicans in Congress rejected it. The bill passed without the provision. If, as the supporters of the bill claimed, they're goal was to rein in the irresponsible people who spent beyond their means, why oppose the medical provision.

Another provision introduced by the Democrats would have exempted military personnel serving in Iraq. Many of these people are National Guard that, to this day, still do not have the same full medical benefits as the regular Army, and whose deployments have been extended, which has resulted in many of them losing their stateside jobs. The provision was defeated. The bill was passed without it.

Yet another provision introduced was a cap on the interest rate credit card companies could charge. The thinking being, since they will no longer be losing huge amounts of their profits to "dead beats" they should no longer need to charge 39% interest. The provision was defeated. The bill was passed without it. Even the supporters of this bill admit the interest rates the credit card companies charge will not go down simply because of this bill's passage. Changing the law won't change the economic reality for the people who find themselves on hard times under this administration.

10

Cheney's Play

"Behind the ostensible government sits enthroned an invisible government owing no allegiance and acknowledging no responsibility to the people."
Theodore Roosevelt

It's interesting to look at how some of the corporations that have written the policies for this administration that we have been discussing and benefited the most from these policies have fared, and how everyone else may be doing. One way to do this is to look at how these companies have benefited financially. While some of the corporations we've been discussing are not publicly traded, it's easy to track the ones that are.

By using a subscription service that tracks approximately 7,000 stocks, I created two "baskets" of stocks, or portfolios. The first portfolio contains the Dow Jones Industrial Average, a basket of thirty stocks that are widely used as the barometer of how the overall stock market is doing, commonly referred to as the "blue chips," the Standard and Poor's index of the best 500 stocks on the planet and the NASDAQ, commonly referred to as the tech sector.

The second portfolio is a basket of seventeen stocks of the corporations that have been discussed here. They are mostly energy and drug companies and a couple of others, such as Caci, the corporation that has received no-bid contracts in Iraq and provides civilian contractor services to the Pentagon. They are as follows with their ticker symbols:

- Southern Company (SO)
- Dominion Resources (D)
- Cabot Corporation (CBT)
- Entergy Corp. (ETR)
- Exxon Mobil (XOM)

- Chevron (CVX)
- Caci International (CAI)
- Halliburton (HAL)
- Reliant Energy (RRI)
- Peabody Energy (BTU)
- Monsanto (MON)
- TXU Corporation (TXU)
- Eli-Lilly (LLY)
- Glaxo Smith Kline (GSK)
- Wyeth (WYE)
- Pfizer (PFE)
- Merck (MRK)

I tracked these two baskets of stocks beginning on Monday, January 22, 2001, the first business day after Bush's first inauguration.

There are many different ways to invest in the stock market. Some people invest on their own without a broker. Some make their own decisions and use a broker to buy and sell stock. The vast majority of investor's use a financial planer to manage their portfolio. There are stock portfolios, bond portfolios and a combination of both. There are mutual funds that pool monies from groups of investors. They all use the same benchmarks, how am I doing against the S&P, or the Dow. There are also investments that track the major indexes, the Dow, S&P and NASDAQ. If these indexes are doing well, your portfolio does well. These are very popular investments.

Since Bush's first inauguration in 2001, up to and including June 14, 2005, the Dow is down .29%. The S&P 500 is down 10.35% and the NASDAQ is down 24.98%. Cumulatively, they are down 11.87%.

In comparison, the basket of stocks above were up, cumulatively 58.35%. The pharmaceuticals in our basket above fared the worst. They were all down over the time frame covered with Merck being down 59.53% and Eli Lilly next worse at -29.9%, which isn't surprising since investor's tend to dump their holdings when a company's product is killing people and the company is forced to pull product off the market. However, a 58.35% total gain over the markets 11.87% total loss is a phenomenal return. Caci International was up an astonishing 405.24%. If we removed our stake in the pharmaceuticals as news broke their drugs were killing people and they were pulling their drugs off the market, our returns are much better. Without the five pharmaceutical companies in our portfolio, we are up a whopping 95.11% over the time frame of January 22, 2001 to June 14, 2005. (The 95.11% figure assumes we didn't have the drug companies in our portfolio at all, however, even with the losses from the drug companies, a 58.35% gain whollops a 10.35% loss if one were invested in the S&P). [1]

Corporate control of the government today is the worst it's been since the 1920's. Ex-corporate executives and former corporate lobbyists dominate every nook and cranny of the Bush administration from the EPA, FDA and USDA to Bush's cabinet up to and including the Vice President. The never ending supply of corporate cash has been used to buy the right to write legislation and dictate policy regarding regulation, or more accurately, de-regulation. Corporations are purely profit driven, period. There is no other force driving them. If feeding cows ground up animal parts can increase profit, then it's done. If dumping toxic waste upstream of a town in the Appalachians increases the bottom line, so be it. Even before this administration allowed them to write the policies protecting them from doing so, they did it anyway if they determined it was cheaper to pay the fines than it would have been to dispose of waste properly. This is precisely why this country needs people who are independent of the corporate world to write and enforce these policies. The problem is that all politicians, Republican and Democrat alike, are so dependent on corporate cash for their political survival, the interests of the people often take a distant second place to corporate interests. John Dean wrote, "For me, the line between bribes and contributions is only the label the parties place on the transaction."

History, i.e.: the Great Depression tells us the merging of pure unregulated capitalism with politics is dangerous. There is still debate today about the cause of the Great Depression. Most believe the stock market crash in October of 1929 caused the Great Depression, however the stock market crash is probably the result of many different factors. The consensus is the politicians of the time, who were bought and paid for by the corporate world, took the view that unregulated business was the key to economic growth which created huge disparities in the distribution of wealth. The top 0.1% of Americans had a combined income equal to the bottom 42% of America. Manufacturing output per worker from 1923 to 1929 grew 32% while wages increased only 8%. The increase in productivity went into corporate profits which rose 62% and resulted in supply outpacing demand; credit became hugely popular during the "roaring 20's" creating a "borrow against the future mentality." Prices rose and when the future arrived, the middle class couldn't pay up. The top 1%, whose income was almost 50 times the bottom half of the rest of the country, could not be expected to purchase 50 times more food or cars or houses to take up the slack. By the end of the 20's this economic instability resulted in an almost halt in spending and investing. During the 20's the Coolidge administration passed tax cuts that favored the rich and the Supreme Court held that minimum wage laws were unconstitutional which furthered the gap between the rich and the middle class. They also did the absolute wrong thing at the time with regards to trade by imposing high tariffs which protected industry, but hurt farming. And then the stock market crashed and the panic set in. It wasn't until Franklin Roosevelt's administration and the New Deal which reigned in out of control corporations and gave the middle class labor rights that the country slowly pulled itself out of the horrors of the previous thirty years.

This is a simplistic overview of the history of the Great Depression. Whole books have been written about the subject, but it illustrates the similarities of then and now. The Bush/Cheney administration holds the same view as the robber barons of the late 19th and early 20th century, that regulation of corporations of any kind is unconstitutional.

What is unconstitutional is the fact corporations are considered equal to living breathing human beings and they are allowed to participate in our political process. There is no lobby for poor people who have lost everything because of a medical catastrophe. But there is a huge lobby with unlimited cash who want to close "loopholes" which provide these people some protections and maintain the status quo with regards to the interest rate they can charge, or write a report which says mercury is not a toxic substance, or re-write legislation concerning pollution controls which affect their industry and at the same time shift the burden of cleaning up toxic sites to the tax payer.

In 1912, Teddy Roosevelt spoke of the robber barons of his time. He said, "We have permitted the growing up of a breed of politicians who, sometimes for improper political purposes, sometimes as a means of serving the great special interests of privilege which stand behind them, twist so-called representative institutions into a means of thwarting instead of expressing the deliberate and well thought out judgment of the people as a whole. This cannot be permitted.

"...largely under the influence of special privilege in the business world, there have arisen castes of politicians who not only do not represent the people, but who make their bread and butter by thwarting the wishes of the people. This is true of the bosses of both political parties."

This pertains today. The "special interests of privilege" are not standing behind the politicians anymore, they are the politicians. Every President in recent history, since Franklin Roosevelt, spent their lives as civil servants. Most had a law background or a military background, or both. There are three exceptions: Ronald Reagan was an actor before entering civil service, George H.W. Bush, after a distinguished record in World War II became an oil industry tycoon before entering civil service and George W. Bush followed in his father's footsteps by entering the corporate world of the energy industry before becoming Governor of Texas in 1994. Dick Cheney started in politics during the Nixon administration. After leaving politics during the Clinton years, Cheney spent most of the 90's as CEO of Halliburton.

The corporate neo-cons in control of the government don't view agencies such as the EPA or the FDA as necessary for the protection of the American public, but rather as a hindrance to the industries they are from. Given time they will render these agencies ineffective (like the Prescription Drug User Fee Act of 1992 which makes the FDA dependant on the drug companies for funding) or they will turn them over, along with the billions of dollars that go along with them, to the private sector they will undoubtedly return to. The beginnings of this are already apparent with the appointments of industry executives to these agencies, many who have been open critics of these agencies, and allowing the corporate donors to write and re-write policy. With control of the judicial branch, the Presidency and both House's of Congress, this "privatization" of government agencies and government programs such as Social Security and Medicare and Medicaid is coming dangerously close to becoming reality. Crucial for the neo-cons, to make this happen, is to remove the checks and balances on the executive branch that our three-branch system of government insures.

Cheney has held the position for years that the executive branch should not have to answer to Congress or anyone else for that matter. He has said he agrees with the view that the War Powers Act of 1973 is unconstitutional. The War Powers Act was enacted as a result of President Johnson's and President Nixon's aggression in Vietnam without Congressional approval. It was passed over Nixon's veto. Cheney obviously thinks Nixon's bombing of Cambodia without getting approval from Congress, or even telling Congress or the American people for that matter, is within a President's authority. He once said, "I don't think you should restrict the Presidents authority to deploy military forces because of the Vietnam experience." Even though the War Powers Act should be interpreted as the Congress, at that time, reasserting its Constitutional authority by reminding the executive branch only they had the authority to declare war as the Constitution clearly states.

When speaking about the first Gulf war Cheney said even if Congress had voted against using military force to remove Saddam from Kuwait "I firmly believe to this day even if Congress voted no we had no option but to proceed," showing complete contempt for the Congress of the United States.

Cheney also believes the Iran Contra scandal was nothing more than a Congressional attempt to "criminalize a policy difference" between President Reagan and Congress. Congress adamantly prohibited the funding of the Nicaraguan Contra's. Since they are the only body which can appropriate money for such an endeavor, the Reagan administration covertly sold weapons to Iran and used the proceeds to fund the Contra's behind the back of Congress, stepping all over constitutional checks and balances. This goes way beyond a "policy difference" to the point of high crimes and misdemeanor's. Cheney, while a Congressman from Wyoming, was critical of Reagan for allowing Congress to impose its will on the President giving the impression he believes the President has the authority to pick and choose the laws he wants to follow, even though the Constitution clearly states the Executive Branch has no legislative powers. That is solely a function of Congress.

On Watergate, Cheney said, "I'm not sure that [Watergate] justified reducing or restricting Presidential power or authority."

These extraordinary events in history illustrate the danger the country faces when a President assumes more power than is granted by the Constitution. It's precisely why the founders established the three-branch system of government to check the authority of each other, instead of a monarchy or a single branch form of Democratic rule. George Washington strongly opposed even a temporary king.

The founders also made Congress the most powerful of the three branches because they are the most representative of the people. This is probably why the duties of Congress are hammered out in Article 1 of the constitution. The Congress writes and passes laws. The President's job is to sign them or veto them, at which point the Congress can override, under certain circumstances, the President's veto. The Congress appropriates money to do the business of the country. This is why the President must go before Congress and ask for money for war in Iraq for example, or to fund the Contra's. The Constitution gives Congress oversight power of the Executive Branch in effect creating a co-equal branch of government under the Constitution of the United States.

When Bush and Cheney took office, they immediately began to "restore" the power they believed the presidency lost in the years after Watergate and to assume power they do not have under the Constitution. They walked away from the Anti-Ballistic Missile Treaty (ABM) of 1972 without any Congressional input at all. They walked away from the Kyoto Treaty the U.S. signed in 1997, reversing a campaign promise. Senator Russell Feingold (D-WI) said, "The Idea that Congress just sort of lets treaties expire without insisting on a vote...shows that not only is there a sense of people being a little intimidated, but also a lack of understanding of the historical role that Congress has played in the checks and balances scheme. What Congress is failing to do, almost in every instance, it seems-it's failing to take the power that the Constitution gives it."

Meanwhile, Cheney was laying out the coming agenda. "Even after we went through all of that [winning the electoral college, but losing the popular vote] he [Bush] never wanted to allow, correctly, the closeness of our election to in any way diminish the power of the presidency, lead him to make a decision that he needed to somehow trim his sails, and be less than a fully authorized, if you will, commander in chief."

Cheney's refusal to turn over documents to the Congress relating to his 2001 energy task force may have more than one motive. First, the goal of gutting regulation on the industry was achieved. Second, Cheney had to know that having closed door meetings with energy industry executives and then shortly afterwards announcing changes in policy that heavily favored these same corporations would prompt members of Congress to investigate. It's as if the confrontation was not only welcomed by the administration but planned to set the precedent that this administration would not be constrained by Congressional oversight.

During the debate about turning over the energy task force documents to Congress, Cheney said, "The GAO is a creature of Congress whose authority does not extend to the White House. I'm a constitutional officer, and the authority of the GAO does not extend in that case to my office." Translation: I'm above the law.

The conclusion could be drawn that the reason for withholding these documents is two-fold. They would incriminate Bush and Cheney, and other members of the administration, by disclosing that Cheney did in fact allow the energy industry to write policy which benefited them, in violation of the Federal Advisory Committee Act (FACA) discussed earlier, and to ultimately remove Congressional oversight of the Executive Branch.

This secrecy and arrogance began within days of Bush and Cheney taking office and has been prevalent in all of their decisions since. In the context of history, a President is only in power for a short period of time. Why then would Bush and Cheney make it a priority to create a presidency that has absolute power, a kind of tyranny, with the knowledge there may be a President that is not of their party in the future, possibly even the next one?

There is joint resolution being introduced in the House that was sponsored by Representative Steny Hoyer and co-sponsored by Representatives Howard Berman, Martin Sabo, Frank Pallone and F. James Sensenbrenner that seeks to repeal the 22nd Amendment to the Constitution. (HJ 24 IH) The 22nd Amendment is the law that limits a President to two terms of office. Could there be a connection between this resolution and the administrations "power play"? At the risk of sounding like a conspiracy theorist, I mention this because it is not simply a rumor in the blogosphere; the resolution was introduced in February 2005. It is important to note that Hoyer, a Democrat, said on the floor of the House of Representatives, on February 17, 2005, "Under the Constitution as altered by the 22nd Amendment, this must be President George W. Bush's last term even if the American people should want him to continue in office.

"Under the resolution I offer today, President Bush would not be eligible to run for a third term." Apparently saying the resolution would not include Presidents in office before the amendment has been ratified; however, this is not at all clear. The resolution is awaiting the House Judiciary Committee (whose chairman is F. James Sensenbrenner, one of the co-sponsors of the resolution) to schedule hearings. What the exact wording will be is not yet determined.

Hoyer also said, "We do not have to rely on rigid constitutional standards to hold our Presidents accountable. Sufficient power resides in the Congress and the Judiciary to protect our country from tyranny." The way this administration has usurped power and is increasingly making Congress the subordinate branch of government to the Executive Branch, this statement is also debatable. Not the Congress, nor the Judiciary, not even the press seems to have been able, or willing, to hold this administration accountable for anything during the past five years.

An Amendment to the Constitution could take years and would have to be ratified by two thirds of the states. At this point in time it is unlikely this amendment would find support from two thirds of the states, but we also don't know what the future will look like. If this amendment will not affect Bush's chance for a third term, then what is the motive of this administration's attempt to create a presidency that is not accountable to Congress or the American people?

Political historians tell us there is a shifting of power which flows from one end of Pennsylvania Avenue to the other in cycles. This administration seems to be bent on fixing the pendulum permanently to the far right. Hopefully the Congress will re-assert itself and perform their Constitutional duties by once again checking unbridled power of a runaway Executive Branch.

In Conclusion

While recognizing that large Corporations are vitally important to the economy of the United States, they also need to be regulated by the government and protected from each other and the people need to be protected from them, not they from us. When corporations become so powerful as to stifle competition and influence, and corrupt our government to the point that they are no longer accountable, corruption within the corporations runs rampant and the consumer looses. Case in point: Enron, MCI, World Com, Tyco, and Global Crossing to name a few. Without competition, product quality suffers while prices go up. Without sufficient regulation, worker safety, wages and worker benefits suffer resulting in a weakening of the middle class, not to mention the impact on the environment. There has always been a fight between large corporations and government regulators who, for the most part over the years have been working for our interests to protect the population. Until now that is. Not since the early part of the 20th century have we seen the merging of capitalism and politics like that which is going on now. The agencies charged with protecting the environment, our health and our food are being turned over to energy and timber industry lobbyists, drug company lobbyists, and agri-business lobbyists who are consistently undermining these agencies abilities to enforce regulatory laws in effect privatizing these agencies. The government is best suited to run these agencies, not the private sector through their proxies. This conflict of interest should end immediately and corporations should be stripped of "personhood" and not be allowed to participate in our political process.

Many people believe these large corporations deserve the big tax breaks and huge government subsidies because they employ the vast majority of the workforce. This is a common misconception and the facts do not support this line of reasoning. In 1995 there were 22.5 million independent enterprises. 16.4 million of those were non farm, sole proprietorships, 1.6 million were partnerships and 4.5 million were corporations. 99% of all independent enterprises in this country employ fewer than 500 people. Small business produced ¾ of the economy's new jobs between 1990 and 1995. [2]

In a 2000 report, Corp Watch reports that in the global context, the biggest of the big 200 mega corporations have combined sales bigger than the combined economies of every country on the planet minus the ten biggest. Topping the list of the largest 200 corporations in the world is the United States with 82 companies on the list followed by Japan with 41, Germany with 20 and France with 17.

The political influence of these corporations is staggering. In the U.S. the big corporations have successfully lobbied to prevent their international operations from becoming more transparent. For instance, they are not required to provide a breakdown of their employee's by country, their toxic emissions at overseas facilities, locations of overseas plants, wage rates at overseas facilities or any information regarding layoffs.

The report says that corporations, "when lobbying for policies to lift barriers to trade and investment [they] have promised that they will lead not only to improved consumer goods and services but also to significant job creation and an overall improvement in social welfare." So how are the mega corp.'s holding up to their end of the bargain. Not so great. "Between 1983 and 1999, the number of people employed by the top 200 firms grew 14.4%, an increase that is dwarfed by the firms' 362.4% profit growth over this period." To put it in perspective for the poorest people of the world, these firms combined sales are "18 times the combined annual income of the 1.2 *billion* people living in 'severe' poverty." Their sales are equivalent to "27.5% of world economic activity, while they employ only 0.78% of the world's workforce."

Many corporations in the U.S. will never pay their fair share of taxes at the corporate rate and many more will not pay any taxes at all due to rebates and government subsidies, or tax credits for research, oil drilling, accelerated depreciation write offs and a myriad of other techniques used by the mega corp.'s to reduce their federal income taxes, thereby shifting the tax burden elsewhere.

The Corp. Watch report concludes that "our analysis is that widespread trade and investment liberalization have contributed to a climate in which dominate corporations are enjoying increasing levels of economic and political clout that are out of balance with the tangible benefits they provide to society." [3]

We should re-visit Teddy Roosevelt's 1912 speech one more time here. He recognized the dangers of un-regulated out-of-control corporate abuse and at the same time the importance of their impact on a nation when he said, "Our aim is to control business not to strangle it" and "it is obvious that unless the business is prosperous the wage-workers employed therein will be badly paid and the consumer badly served. Therefore not merely as a matter of justice to the business, but from the standpoint of the self interest of the wage-worker and the consumer we desire that business shall prosper." He went on to say, "Through control by commission [regulation] we may secure freedom for fair competition, elimination of unfair practices, conservation of our natural resources, fair wages, good social conditions, and reasonable prices."

Bush and Cheney's compassionate conservatism could more accurately be called "compassionate corporatism."

11

Tax Cuts: It's Your Money, Right?

"When there is an income tax, the just man will pay more and the unjust less on the same amount of income."
Plato

Speaking in St. Louis, Missouri in February of 2001, newly elected President George W. Bush said, "I'm asking Congress to pass $1.6 trillion in tax relief, after we've met priorities. It's a plan that says, as opposed to pick and choose who the winners are, that everybody who pays taxes ought to get tax relief.

"It's your money." [1] But is it? While it is often difficult to look at our pay stubs each week to see what the government is taking and nobody enjoys the arrival of April 15th, most among us recognize the need for the government to collect taxes. We realize that as a society we must collectively pay for the things which benefit the common good. Everything from the roads we drive on to our police and fire departments which protect us, and a strong military. We need public schools to have an educated work force, public transportation, parks and libraries. Our form of representative government that makes laws, oversees regulations that protect business and tends to the everyday running of the country could not exist without sufficient taxes. And the list goes on. All we ask is that taxation be fair and that our government spends the money appropriately. Oliver Wendell Holmes said, "Taxes are the price we pay for civilization."

At the time of Bush's speech, according to government projections, there was a surplus in excess of $200 billion for the budget year that ended in September 2001. [2] Apparently Bush was saying the government owed us this money back. The only question then was how to divvy it up. Bush said, during the Presidential debates with Al Gore that "if you pay taxes, you're going to get a benefit. People who pay taxes will get tax relief." He reiterated that in the St. Louis speech above. He also said the plan would drop the rate at the top and the bottom. When the plan was signed, the top rate of 39.5% was dropped to 35% and the bottom rate was dropped from 15% to 10%. The rates were dropped by approximately the same amount of percentage points. A close look at the results shows the cuts are not proportionate. If Bush's plan only cut the bottom rate the wealthy still would have benefited because they pay that rate on that portion of their income also. Why then an across the board cut? Also the 2001 tax cut will phase out the estate tax, or as Bush calls it, the "death tax." (More on that in a moment).

In 2003, Bush pushed through another round of tax cuts which are estimated to cost in the neighborhood of $600 billion on top of the 2001 cuts, totaling over $2.2 trillion (over the full 10 years the tax cuts are scheduled to be fully phased in). The 2003 package is designed largely to eliminate personal income tax on dividends and reduce capital gains taxes on sales of stocks. The following is from a CBO report released in August of 2004 and is their analysis of the combined distributional effects of the 2001, 2002 and 2003 tax bills.

- The bottom 20% of households with an average income of $16,000 would realize an average tax cut of $230 which is approximately 2.8% of the total share of the tax cuts.

- The middle 20% of households with an average income of $57,400 would realize an average tax cut of $980 which is approximately 11.5% of the total share of the tax cuts.

- The top 20 % of households with an average income of $203,700 would realize an average tax cut of $4,890 which is approximately 60% of the total share of the tax cuts.

I know it takes time to digest the numbers. Mull them over for a moment because there are more. This is the definition of disproportionate. But what is more telling about the Bush tax cuts is the after tax income percent change. Regarded as the best way to determine who will benefit the most from proposed tax legislation. The less one pays in taxes proportionately affects the more one keeps. Duh! The bottom 20% of earners will realize an after tax income increases of a mere 1.5% while the top 20 % of income earners will realize an after tax income increase of 3.3%. And because of Bush's tax cuts the top 1% of earners will realize an after tax income increase of 5.3% more than three times that of the bottom 20%. [3]

If the above numbers don't convince you as to who benefits the most from Bush's tax cuts, the following should. The above statistics compiled from CBO data only reflect 2001 through 2003. Most of the provisions do not really kick in until after 2005. Currently the top 1% of the population, the wealthiest of the wealthy receives almost 25% of the tax cuts. By 2009 they will receive over 45% of the cuts and in 2010 they will receive approximately 52% of the $234 billion scheduled for that year. In comparison, the middle 20% will receive 9.6% of the total cuts in that year and the bottom 20% will receive only 1.2%. *The top 1% will receive as much as the bottom 60% does.*

Bush's tax cuts do not adequately address the Alternative Minimum Tax (AMT). The AMT was designed to close "loopholes" that very high income earners use to reduce or in some cases completely eliminate their tax bill. The AMT would apply if a person's regular income tax is less, (because of deductions most of us have never heard of), than the AMT. Using the AMT, deductions and exemptions are calculated differently. The higher of the two is the tax due. Critics have charged the AMT does not do what it was intended, but the major problem is the AMT threshold is not indexed for inflation or income growth but is simply changed periodically by Congress. The Bush tax package of 2001 temporarily solved this problem by raising the threshold from $45,000 to $49,000. However the relief sunsets, or expires, after the 2004 tax year. As more and more middle class people attain this threshold, more will be hit by the AMT. That will result in millions of middle class people being snared by the AMT. Many won't realize this until they start doing their taxes in early 2006. In 1999 the AMT only affected about a million tax payers, the vast majority of them being the mega-rich, by the time Bush's tax cuts are fully realized, in 2010, 36 million families will be affected and will pay in excess of $140 billion on top of their regular taxes which will mean the cuts they enjoyed from 2001 to 2004 will in effect be wiped out. [4] This is not what the AMT was designed to do.

Bush's 2001 tax cuts seek to eliminate the Estate Tax, or as Bush calls it the "Death Tax" by 2009. Proponents for the repeal of the estate tax claim that it hurts family business and family farms whose heirs have to liquidate to pay the taxes when the owner dies. A report by the Center for Budget and Policy Priorities shows, "Fewer than 1.9 percent of the 2.3 million people that died [in 1997] had to pay any estate tax." That translates to just two out of every 100 people. The number of family businesses or farms affected is even less, only six of every 10,000. Professor of Economics and International Affairs at Princeton University, Paul Krugman Ph.D, has said, "Tales of family farms and businesses broken up to pay the estate tax are basically rural legends; hardly any real examples have been found, despite diligent searching." In 2001, to be subject to the tax, an estate would have had to be worth $675,000 or more. That threshold is being raised to $1 million in 2006 (if it's not eliminated by Bush's tax plan). A married couple could leave $2 million to their heirs ($1 million each) without being subject to the estate tax. Currently the law allows for special breaks in the cases of family farms or businesses such as higher exemptions and deferral of tax payments for up to 14 years if the value of the family business or farm exceeds 35% of the total estate.

During the Presidential debates in 2000 Bush said the estate tax should be eliminated because "people shouldn't be taxed twice on their assets." This is misleading in two ways. First, there is nothing anywhere that says income can't be taxed twice. Taxes are taken from your paycheck and the money that's left is taxed when you spend it at the grocery store, or buy a T.V. or an airline ticket or that cute little handbag you saw at the mall. Is Bush saying sales tax should be abolished? Secondly a vast majority of the estates that would be subject to the "death tax" include stock portfolios. When one sells stock is when they realize a tax in the form of capital gains. However if one dies and passes on the stock, no taxes have been paid on those assets. Data from the Survey of Consumer Finances state capital gains make up 37% of the values of estates worth more than $1 million and about *56% of estates worth more than $10 million.* If the estate tax is repealed, no taxes will ever be paid on such assets because even if the heir sells the stock it won't be taxed because it was an inheritance and no longer subject to the estate tax.

The cost in lost revenue to the country would be $294 billion over the ten years from 2002 to 2011. Once the effect is fully in place in 2011 the cost would be over $60 billion a year, so from 2012 to 2021 the cost could soar to roughly three-quarters of *a trillion dollars.* [4]

Where will this money come from? The answer is obviously you will, I will and our children and our grandchildren will pay for it. Everybody who pays taxes will have to pick up the tab for what the wealthiest of the wealthy, the 1.9% used to pay. The hardest hit will be the people who are unfortunate enough to be born into the middle class or worse the lower middle class. The estate tax only reduces the amount an heir receives for doing nothing, while the elimination of the estate tax will reduce the earned income that hard working middle America gets to keep. As Warren Buffet puts it, "The DuPonts might believe themselves perceptive in observing the debilitating effects of food stamps for the poor, but were themselves living off a boundless supply of privately funded food stamps...The idea that you get a lifetime of food stamps based on coming out of the right womb strikes at my idea of fairness."

It's interesting to look at some of the people against the repeal of the estate tax. The list reads like a who's who of great American capitalists and is a bit surprising. There is Theodore Roosevelt who formally proposed an inheritance tax in

1906. He believed the person who benefited the most simply from living in the greatest country with the greatest opportunities, owed the most. Besides heir's of the Roosevelt family, there's William Gates, Sr., George Soros, Ted Turner, Steven Rockefeller and, as we've seen, Warren Buffet to name a few. Unlike Roosevelt who believed the estate tax was an obligation, Andrew Carnegie saw it as a moral issue. He said, "Why should men leave great fortunes to their children…great sums bequeathed often work more for the injury than the good of the recipients." And the "instances of public servants that live off their wealth in order to devote themselves to community service are rare." There are different ways to deal with wealth at the end of one's life. It can be left to heirs, left for public interest or spent during one's life. Carnegie preferred the last two options. He wrote, "The man who dies rich dies disgraced." Carnegie not only talked the talk, but walked the walk. He gave away 90% of his estate *before he died* and left a trust fund for Teddy Roosevelt's wife because the government at the time did not provide for the widow's of former Presidents.

President Bush has urged Americans to be charitable. Charitable contributions help the less fortunate among us so that some tax dollars can be used elsewhere. Carnegie would have been proud. In the forward to Melvin Olasky's book *Compassionate Conservatism* Bush wrote "Share our resources, both material and spiritual with those who need them most." Tax payers who don't have enough deductions to itemize currently have to take a standard deduction that does not allow them to deduct contributions to charity. Therefore lower income people do not contribute as much because they cannot lower their tax burden by charitable contributions. Candidate Bush pledged, in 2000, to allow people who do not itemize to deduct charitable contributions to spur charitable giving as per his philosophical beliefs described in *Compassionate Conservatism*. However the deficits created by his tax cuts have forced him to renege on that promise.

If Bush wanted to fulfill his campaign pledge, he would not advocate the repeal of the estate tax. Current estate tax law provides for unlimited charitable deductions. No estate tax is due on funds bequeathed to charities. Charitable deductions are used mostly by the largest estates to reduce their tax burdens. In the late 90's the largest estates gave approximately $7.5 billion to charity. Without the "death tax" what motivation is there for the continuation of this practice? As Carnegie said people who use their wealth to "devote themselves to community service is rare." The loss to charities will increase when one factors in the fact that some give away a large portion of their estates before they die to reduce their assets on which estate tax will be levied. Studies show that eliminating the estate tax would significantly reduce charitable bequests. [5] With programs being cut due to huge deficits and the potential for charities that would pick up the slack to suffer, the repeal of the estate tax would mean the poorest among us loose again.

The tax cuts are deficit financed in that currently they are being funded largely from the Social Security trust fund. When the treasury bonds Bush is "borrowing" from the Social Security surplus come due, all of us will pay. (Social Security is the subject of the next chapter).

Bush's 2003 tax cut package that will reduce taxes on capital gains and eliminate taxes on dividend income also benefits the wealthiest among us. The mega-rich make money off of their money, i.e.: capital income. Bush's plan to cut or eliminate taxes on this income further shifts the burden from capital earners to wage earners, the bottom 80% of the population.

Bush claims his tax cuts will stimulate the economy thereby creating new jobs, and has urged Congress to make the cuts permanent. The thinking here is the shortfall in revenues collected will be made up when more people are working. In September of 2003 in Indianapolis Bush said, "If Congress is really interested in job creation, they will make every one of the tax relief measures we passed permanent." The Bush administration predicted the cuts would produce 4.3 million new jobs in the first year; however as of August of 2004 there had been only 1.6 million new jobs created. 2.7 million short of their prediction. [6] Economists are not optimistic this will change over the longer term.

According to experts, a better way to stimulate the economy immediately would have been to put the money in the hands of the people more likely to spend it. The middle and lower middle class spend money immediately upon receiving it jump starting the economy, while the wealthy tend to invest and save "extra" income or move it to foreign investments. What if there were no tax cut at all and instead of giving the surplus Bush inherited to the wealthiest 1% of the population he had increased government spending on programs that benefit the working poor, putting money in the hands of the people who would spend it. Instead, the deficits the tax cuts have caused have forced states to cut programs and increase taxes.

Bush has spoken frequently about education, but has been forced to cut federal funding to states for his own "No Child Left Behind" initiative because of the revenue deficit his tax cuts created. The No Child Left Behind law requires every school's standardized test scores to increase yearly or face sanctions including school closings. Eight school districts in three states, Texas, Michigan and Vermont and the nations largest teachers union, the National Education Association are bringing law suits against the federal government. Wording in the law requires the federal government to fund the program and the states are suing because they are being forced to spend their own budget's to meet federal require-ments. They are basically saying NCLB is an unfunded mandate by the federal government. More states are expected to file suits. Many teachers have criticized No Child Left Behind because they say they are no longer "teaching" children, rather they are simply preparing them for tests required by NCLB.

Most Countries in the industrialized world fund education through their trea-suries. The education system in the U.S. relies mostly on property tax for funding which means schools in lower income districts are less equipped to meet the needs of students. In his inaugural address on January 20, 2001, Bush spoke of education and the less fortunate among us and compassion. He said, "While many of our citizens prosper, others doubt the promise, even the justice, of our own country. The ambitions of some Americans are limited by failing schools and hidden prejudice and the circumstances of their birth. And sometimes our differences run so deep, it seems we share a continent, but not a country.

"We do not accept this, and we will not allow it…And this is my solemn pledge; I will work to build a single nation of justice and opportunity."

Instead of tax cuts that benefited the top 1%, would it not have been better to spend some of the budget surplus on education? That would seem to have been a better way to fulfill his pledge of a nation of opportunity. Education is the only way to create the opportunity to rise above poverty.

In the first paragraph of this chapter is a comment made by Bush in St. Louis in which he said he was asking for the tax cuts *"after we've met priorities."* Giving back a surplus to tax payers is a good thing, but not if it creates the biggest deficits in history. The Chairman of the Federal Reserve, Allen Greenspan, speaking about Bush's second round of proposed tax cuts at his semi-annual Congressional testimony in February of 2003, warned about the effect of the "growing budget deficit" on the economy and stressed the need for "budget discipline." He also questioned whether any stimulus package was needed at all at a time of uncer-tainty about Iraq.

Bush's first Secretary of the Treasury, Paul O'Neill agreed with Bush that all priorities needed to be met before proceeding with the tax cuts. In the book *The Price of Loyalty, George W. Bush, the White House, and the Education of Paul O'Neill* by Ron Suskind, Greenspan and O'Neill identified what they considered to be a top priority. Suskind writes, "Greenspan felt the surplus needed to be cleared away. There was currently $3.2 billion in national debt that required interest payments and created a drag on the economy." Vice President Al Gore had also proposed paying down the national debt with the surplus during the campaign in 2000.

"Fine-reduction of debt is a priority-but what happens to the big item, the tax cut, if the surpluses evaporate? [Greenspan] asked.

"Triggers,' O'Neill said…It would be a statutory enforcement of fiscal prudence. Balance sheet behavior common to most companies and households-whereby spending is linked to availability of funds.

"If, however, a combination of tax cuts and depressed tax receipts from an economic slow down caused the surplus to evaporate-and if there were not spending cuts to avoid slipping into deficit-the tax cut would be reined in.

"And so it was hatched: a secret pact…Two men with nearly ninety years of experience in and around Washington, colluding to prevent an elected President-with virtually no experience in setting national economic policy-from acting in a way that they were convinced was ill-considered. He'd thank them later." [7]

They were not against tax cuts; they were against squandering away a surplus that could have solved so many different problems, strengthening the economy for years to come. They wanted to create a fiscally responsible policy where tax cuts would be given only after all other priorities were met as the President himself had alluded to. That would mean not making the tax cuts permanent, but making them conditional to paying down the debt in a given year. The tax cuts may or may not be what the President wants year over year. Contrary to his rhetoric, making sure all priorities are met, Bush is opposed to this. Paul O'Neill was fired for not getting on board with Bush's economic policies.

Besides education and paying down the national debt, what other priorities were not met that the surpluses could better have been spent on. Because of the astronomical deficits caused by some of the largest tax cuts ever seen (*The* largest in absolute dollars and, inflation adjusted, second only to Reagan's cuts by a couple of percentage points) and Bush's refusal to roll some of them back, or make them *conditional* as Paul O'Neill proposed, almost all domestic programs have, and will continue to suffer drastic cuts. The FY06 budget includes $214 billion in cuts to discretionary programs over the next five years alone. The budget also includes cuts to mandatory programs such as Medicaid, the food stamp program and child care assistance to low income working families. That needs to be reiterated, low income *working* families. Child care assistance will end for 300,000 low income children by 2009 and food stamp cuts will affect almost the same number of low income *working* families with children. $45 billion in Medicaid cuts to the states over the next ten years will cause states to have to cut their Medicaid programs increasing the number of uninsured currently numbered at around 45 million people. [8]

This budget does not include the cost of the war in Iraq and Afghanistan which are considered supplemental appropriations and therefore are not figured into the deficits.

Two of the provisions in Bush's 2001 tax cuts which he refuses to put on the table for roll back are a repeal of provisions his father negotiated with Congress when he was President as part of a deficit reduction program. Those provisions phased out certain personal exemptions and some itemized deductions for taxpayers at the highest income levels. Bush's tax plan will repeal these provisions, again benefiting only the wealthiest among us.

One of the most disturbing targets of the budget cuts are military veterans. The Bush administration points out the budget for the VA has increased every year since Bush took office, as pointed out by Factcheck.org. [9] This is true. The budget request for the VA for FY06 total is about 65 billion, which is approximately a 20% or so increase. The budget for the VA also increased every year that Clinton was in office, the difference being that during the Clinton administration there weren't thousands of Americans coming home with severe wounds from fighting in a foreign war. But let's concentrate on the so called discretionary programs, not the funds Congress is required by law to provide, such as funds for compensation and pension payments, but the funds that a soldier coming home from Iraq with his or her arm or leg blown off, or with severe mental distress would be concerned with. The portion of the VA budget proposed by the Bush administration for veteran's *healthcare* for FY06 is $28.1 billion, an increase of approximately 1% over FY05. That 1% increase goes down significantly when one factors in the fee vet's will now have to pay, under Bush's budget, for services. The fee would only affect "higher" income veterans, those making around $26,000 to $40,000 a year. Apparently the Bush administration considers a veteran with a wife and a couple of kids who makes over $26,001 a year high income. Also those same veterans' drug co-pays would increase over 100%, from an average of $7 to about $15. The budget would also cut long term care for veteran's and reduce funds for nursing home care, which would lead to the elimination of about 5,000 nursing home beds and force hospital closures. [10]

The VA's Under Secretary testified the VA health care system needs a 13-14% increase annually to maintain the services they provide now. Bills have been introduced in both the House and the Senate to make funding for VA *health benefits* mandatory (H.R. 2318 and S. 50) but have yet to come up for a vote. The house bill was introduced by Rep. Lane Evans in 2003 and has 188 co-sponsors. The 13 or 14% annual increase the VA is seeking is obviously more than the rate of inflation. This is because, not only will the VA be caring for veteran's of Vietnam and the first Gulf war and veteran's injured while on active duty in peace time, but now there is a huge increase of veteran's who will need care due to the wars in Afghanistan and Iraq. The 1% increase in health benefits is insufficient to deal with this influx and is therefore actually a cut no matter how many Bush administration supporters spin the numbers.

An independent budget policy report written by AMVETS, Disabled American Veterans (DAV), Paralyzed Veterans of American (PVA) and the Veterans of Foreign Wars (VFW) recommended $31.2 billion in funding for veterans *health care* for FY06. The $3.1 billion more than the Bush administration is asking for would, according to them, "meet realistic inflation and health care demand increases." This recommendation is put out by the above groups for policy makers to provide a perspective on actual needs by veterans. The report only suggests funding for discretionary programs such as health care, benefits delivery, medical facility construction etc...and not on funds which Congress is required by law to provide. Until a bill is passed that requires mandatory funding of veteran's health care, we will continue to see the DAV, PVA and the VFW struggle for funding for the VA. Since Bush's tax cut have stretched our treasury to the breaking point, theirs will be a loosing battle. [11]

Congressman Lane Evans (D-IL) asked, "Who deserves to receive the benefits of the national treasury-America's disabled veterans or America's millionaires?" I ask again, were all the priorities met before the tax cuts were given, mostly to this countries wealthiest? No President in history has given a tax cut in a time of war, not only *a* tax cut but two of the three largest ever given and at a time when this countries veterans are desperately in need. Putting a yellow ribbon on your bumper does not equate to supporting the troops. A few million phone calls and E-mails to Congress is the least we can do.

Did everyone who pays taxes benefit as Bush promised? The short answer is yes, the more complex answer is no.

First the short answer. As the study above shows, the poorest among us received a benefit of $230 and a benefit is a benefit no matter how disproportionate it may be. Would the $230 multiplied by the millions of low income earners who received the benefit been better spent by the government on social programs to help alleviate poverty? Author Peter Singer, in his book *The President of Good and Evil, the Ethics of George W. Bush* points out that "Studies of national tax and spending policies have shown that societies in which governments tax more, as a proportion of gross domestic product [GDP], are also societies with lower income inequality. Higher welfare spending does work. And since among the richer nations (for example, the twenty-three higher-income members of the

Organization for Economic Development and Cooperation) the more equal ones have, on average, a higher income per capita, more redistribution by the state leads to a lower rate of absolute poverty, as well as to greater equality and a lower rate of relative poverty." [12]

The longer more complex answer is that eventually the tax cuts will have to be paid for. To date the tax cuts have eroded the budget surplus to the point where we have the largest deficit in the history of the U.S. The Center for Budget and Policy Priorities said the "Data in the administration's own Mid-Session Budget Review indicates that the tax cuts have played a larger role than all other legislation enacted since the start of 2001 in the emergence of the current sizable budget deficit, and that the tax cuts account for the majority of the current deficit." This has resulted in the cuts being financed with borrowing. Eventually the tax cuts will have to be paid for by spending cuts to essential programs and/or a tax increase. Either way the middle class looses, again.

The Center for Budget and Policy Priorities has produced two different scenarios on the future effects of Bush's tax cuts. The two scenarios are because the Bush administration has not addressed how the tax cuts will be paid for so CBPP had to. The first scenario shows the average net effect of financing the tax cuts with equal dollar burden per household. "Households in the middle quintile would, on net, lose an average of about $870 per household per year." Their report shows the top 20% of earners would end up ahead by about $3,934 per year.

In the second scenario, households would pay for the tax cuts in proportion to their incomes. Middle America would lose an average of $230 per year while the top 20% would still come out ahead by about $1,000 per year.

So, the answer to the question, "have all the priorities been met?" is no. The answer to the other question asked in this chapter, "is the money yours?" is also no because of the simple reason that all the priorities of this country have not been met. There was a surplus not because there was too much taxes and the money should have been returned to us, or more accurately the most affluent among us, but because there was too little government spending. The surplus should have been spent on health care for veterans and programs that would help low income working families with child day care so they can continue to work and food stamp programs for the poor. It should have been spent to lower the national debt to bolster the economy; it should have been spent to help the weakest among us. It could have been spent to fund a war on terrorism. Unless one was born with the name Rockefeller, or Dupont, or Vanderbilt, or Kennedy one has probably needed help at some point or another in ones life. Whether that help has come from family or friends or the government, it was none the less needed. Our society is not going to be judged on the number of strip-malls we build but rather on how we treat the less fortunate among us.

For those who subscribe to the idea that people who receive government help in the form of subsidized housing or child care or food stamps are lazy bums that want to live off of welfare, here's a short story about one recipient of government help. There are probably millions of similar stories.

In 1999 the space shuttle Columbia lifted off with the first female commander in the history of the U.S. space program. USAF Col. Eileen Collins had previously flown as a mission specialist and as the first female shuttle pilot. More than two years after the shuttle Columbia disintegrated over the Texas skies in 2003, NASA is ready to return to space. The astronaut selected to command America's return to space is Eileen Collins. Collins grew up in the small town of Elmira, N.Y. After a major flood in 1972 the family was forced to move creating a financial burden. Shortly after that her parents separated and Eileen and her mother and three siblings found themselves needing government help. They lived for a time in government subsidized housing and received welfare and food stamps. She attributes everything she is to her parents who she witnessed struggling but never giving up and keeping the family intact. "We were poor, but we weren't disadvantaged" she once said.

What would have happened to her and her family if they hadn't received the help they needed during hard times? Who knows? Collins was determined to fly and worked odd jobs to pay for flying lessons. The point is two fold, first they got the help they needed allowing them to help themselves out of the hard times they were experiencing and secondly, they weren't lazy people taking advantage of government handouts which is the perception some have of people receiving welfare.

During the eight years Reagan was President and the four George H.W. Bush was President the huge tax cuts they gave resulted in a huge budget deficit, quadrupled the national debt, forced huge cuts to social programs, income inequality rose significantly and poverty rose by 6.5 million people. By contrast, during the eight years of the Clinton administration there was a record 22 million jobs created, median income rose twice as fast as the previous twelve years and the deficit turned into a budget surplus for the first time in almost a quarter century. Over 7 million people rose above the poverty line. Clinton accomplished this by raising income taxes on the wealthy, (but also cut some taxes on the long term capital gains from 28% to 20% which benefited the wealthy) expanding breaks for the working poor and balancing the budget. Deficit reduction spurred investor confidence, interest rates came down and growth was the by-product. The lesson is fiscal responsibility is a better economic stimulus package than tax cuts and the study of countries that spend higher amounts on welfare programs result in a higher income per capita and lower rates of poverty is accurate.

This is the economic environment Bush inherited when he was sworn in on January 20, 2001. Since then the deficit has soared to record levels, unemployment has risen dramatically and Americans living in poverty has risen every year since 2001. Bush is the first President since Herbert Hoover who's economic policies did not create one new job by the end of his first term. In all fairness the economy was showing signs of slowing at the end of 2000, the internet bubble burst wiping out billions of paper gains and manufacturing jobs were going overseas at an increasing rate. But all of these were manageable problems that were poorly managed, or mismanaged, by the Bush administration. Then there was September 11th which is probably the best argument against the Bush tax cuts of 2003 and for rolling back at least some of the 2001 cuts.

Bush's tax cuts are widening the gap between the have's and the have not's. The old adage the rich get richer and the poor get poorer is alive and well when we should be striving for the rich getting richer and the poor getting richer, as was the case during the 90's

The argument is out there that the rich deserve the majority of the breaks because when the money is placed in their hands it will "trickle down" through the economy. This has proven to be a flawed concept as we have previously discussed and as the Reagan tax cuts proved. As we've seen, there are much better ways to stimulate the economy and as Teddy Roosevelt pointed out, the issue is more about obligation. He is not alone in that belief. The philosophers of ancient Athens, the cradle of civilization, recognized this 2500 years ago. The Athenian tax structure initially was a flat tax that burdened everyone by the same amount. The less one had, the heavier the burden. They realized this was an unfair system and argued those who received the greatest benefits from being Athenians should bear the greatest burden of maintaining the system that allowed them to prosper. This was the invention of a progressive tax, based on ones ability to pay and the creation of the world's first democracy. Bush has said his tax cuts will be "revenue neutral," in other words, the revenue needed for the country to operate will not suffer because of his tax cut. That's code speak for the tax burden will have to be shifted from the wealthy to the middle class, from the capital earner to the wage earner, from our generation to our children's generation.

The Bush administration continually reminds us there is a strong economic recovery taking place due largely to Bush's tax cuts. However, they have been talking about a recovery for almost five years. This would make it the longest recovery after the smallest recession, (which began and ended in 2001), in history. Corporate profits are at a record high due to increased productivity from workers, while in 2004 wages lagged behind inflation for the first time in over 15 years, and wage earners are making less, adjusted for inflation, than they were in 1970. Health care costs are through the roof preventing smaller employers from giving raises and requiring employee's to pick up more of the cost of premiums, if they even have the option of health care. More of the gains of this "recovery" are going to corporate profits rather than to the wage earner. This phenomenon has not occurred during any other recovery in history, meaning the recovery taking place, due to Bush's tax cuts, are not trickling down to the middle class but are benefiting the "other" persons, Bush's favorite, the corporate kind.

12

Social Security Crises?
A Solution in search of a Problem

*"The test of our progress is not whether we add more to the abundance of those who
have much; it is whether we provide enough for those who have little."*
Franklin D. Roosevelt

The Social Security Act was signed into law on August 14, 1935 by President Franklin D. Roosevelt. The law was only part of the New Deal which was designed to help American's during the Great Depression. Social Security was designed to help America's senior citizens whose poverty rate exceeded 50% at the time. It was an insurance program referred to by Roosevelt as "social insurance" and was not designed to be a savings or an investment program. The original 1935 law only paid benefits to the primary worker. In 1939 the law was changed to include survivors' benefits for a worker's spouse and minor children if that worker should die. In 1956 disability benefits were added and Medicare was added in 1965 by the Social Security Act of 1965.

Roosevelt's New Deal called for sweeping changes designed to prop up the working class. Under Roosevelt child labor laws were enacted, unions were protected and the right to collectively bargain gave them power to represent the worker, overtime rules were put in place and an eight hour work day was established. Until 1935, most middle class people simply worked until they either died or couldn't work anymore. Roosevelt believed that by setting a retirement age more people could enter the work force as the elderly left, but to do this he recognized the need for an insurance program that would insure people would not retire into poverty. Social Security was the solution. An insurance program funded by current workers, not the government, to pay retiree's benefits. When you retire, the next generation pays your benefits and so on, and so on. It was a brilliant plan that has worked, and worked well, for seventy years. The very nature of the program has kept administration costs below 1% historically.

In 1935 an employee paid 2% of the first $3,000 of their income into Social Security. That amount was matched by the employer for a total of 4%. Those figures have been adjusted over the years to where currently, (2005) an employee pays 6.2% of the first $90,000 of their income matched by the same amount by the employer for a total of 12.4%. This is where the benefits that are paid out to current retiree's come from as per the Federal Insurance Contributions Act (FICA). The employee also pays 1.45% to Medicare also matched by the employer for a total of 2.9%. The grand total paid to Social Security, therefore, is 15.3% (12.4 +2.9) half coming from the employee and half paid by the employer.

Many people mistakenly believe the FICA tax taken from their paycheck is pooled into a kind of interest bearing account somewhere awaiting their retirement. If they die before they retire, the money is simply gone, taken by the government. In reality the FICA taxes you and I and everyone else pays goes directly to pay the benefits of current retiree's, eligible dependants and the disabled. The excess revenue left over goes into the Social Security Trust fund. As per the law, these funds are invested in U.S. Treasury bonds. These bonds are the absolute safest investment on the planet backed by the full faith and credit of the United States. The same bonds many of us received from our grandparents for our birthdays when we were kids and many people still give to their grandchildren now. If you buy a $1,000 T-bond, for example, you are loaning the government $1,000. When the bond matures, ten, twenty or thirty years out, you receive your $1,000 plus the pre determined interest at that future date. Billions of dollars of T-bonds are purchased by the private sector for their portfolios and by foreign countries. China is the largest purchaser of U.S. bonds, "loaning" the U.S. billions that is financing deficit spending.

At the end of 2004, the amount of FICA receipts that exceeded benefits paid was $1.7 trillion. In 2004 alone the surplus was $1.56 billion. [1] This is exactly what Roosevelt envisioned, an eventual surplus that would weather any unforeseen shortfalls in Social Security, however many administrations over the years have used the Social Security surplus to fund spending programs. In the 2000 Presidential race, Al Gore proposed putting the Social Security surplus in a "lock box" making it untouchable to government spending. He was ridiculed for the suggestion.

Why is Social Security so important? In 1936 most of the nation's elderly lived in poverty. By 1973 the elderly living in poverty had dropped to 16.3% and in the thirty year period from 1973 to 2004 poverty among the elderly fell 37% to 10.2% because of Social Security. [2] Right now 21% of the aged population rely on Social Security for 100% of their income and 13% rely on Social Security for 90-99% of their income. Social Security makes up over half of income for 31% of the elderly. That's fully two thirds of the elderly in America relying on Social Security for either all or the vast majority of their income. [3] Without Social Security millions of seniors would live below the poverty line taking us right back to 1936. Social Security is also disability insurance. In a speech on the Senate floor in January of 2005, Tom Harkin (D-IA) spoke about how the FICA tax provides a very good disability insurance policy. Citing Social Security statistics he said, "For the average wage earner with a family, Social Security benefits are equivalent to a $322,000 life insurance policy or a $233,000 disability insurance policy. I had my staff look into how much it would cost to replace those benefits in the private market…the cost of a modest $100,000 term life insurance policy varies from $140 per year for a healthy 25 year old to $3,815 a year for a not so healthy 45 year old.

"The more shocking news is that you cannot accurately price a policy that would make up for disability. The vast majority of currently available disability policies are group policies…and these policies are not stand alone policies; they are supplemental policies.

"More to the point, this kind of disability policy would not be available to just anyone. For instance, according to Patricia Owen, the former Associate Commissioner of the Social Security Administration, private insurance generally will not cover blue-collar occupations. And long term disability insurance for workers is the least offered. With Social Security disability insurance, all are covered." [4] The cost to replace the benefits Social Security guarantees workers would far exceed the 6.2% paid to FICA.

President Bush has been telling the American people for more than five years that Social Security is in crisis. He has made it a major focus of his presidency. After the 2004 election it became the top priority. In a November 4, 2004 press conference he said, "I earned capital in the campaign, political capital, and now I intend to spend it. It is my style. That's what happened in the-after the 2000 election, I earned some capital. I've earned capital in this election-and I'm going to spend it for what I told the people I'd spend it on, which is-you've heard the agenda: Social Security and tax reform…" Apparently, in his view, winning by the smallest margin of any incumbent President in history has somehow earned him a mandate to turn Social Security on its head.

So what is the "crisis?" According to President Bush, the Social Security system will not be able to handle the large number of baby boomers moving into retirement, and "in 2041, the system goes bankrupt." [5] He has mistakenly said this numerous times throughout his presidency. His plan is to partially privatize the system by allowing younger workers to divert a portion of their money, currently going to FICA, into their own private accounts which will be invested in the stock market. (The administration doesn't use the words "crisis" or "privatize" any more because they didn't play well with their focus groups. The new words are "problem" and "personal accounts.") While the baby boomer generation is expected to cause problems for Social Security it does not rise to the level of "crisis" and there are major problems with the President's plan.

According to the Social Security Administration (SSA), sometime around 2018 or 2019 there will no longer be enough FICA tax coming into Social Security to pay full benefits, forcing Social Security to begin drawing on the trust fund surplus (currently at $1.7 trillion) sometime around 2022 or 2025. The SSA predicts the trust fund will be depleted in 2042. The Congressional Budget Office (CBO) predicts this will happen in 2052. (6) This is the approximate date the President claims that Social Security will be "bankrupt" implying there will be no more Social Security. In a speech in Maryland in June of 2005 while responding to a question from a younger worker about benefits for older people nearing retirement Bush said, "When they start hearing people talking about reforming the system, they're really thinking, well, maybe my check is going to go away. And people have got to know it's not...*but I'm not so sure you're going to have a check.*" This is so misleading that it seems specifically designed to scare people.

First, in 2042, or 2052 depending on which report you use, Social Security will still be taking in enough FICA taxes to pay almost 79% of benefits until almost the end of the century [6] even if nothing is done to "fix" Social Security. Right now the U.S. Government does not take in nearly enough revenues, after Bush's tax cuts, to pay anywhere close to 80% of its bills. So, by the end of the century, Social Security will be doing better than the U.S. Government is doing right now today. Social Security is not even close to being bankrupt. Also the growth numbers for the economy the SSA bases its assumption the trust fund will be depleted in 2042 is 1.6% and the CBO uses 1.9% to arrive at their 2052 prediction. However the Bureau of Labor Statistics shows that since the end of W.W. II the nation's economy has grown an average of 2.1% annually and in no twenty year period, including the Great Depression has the U.S. economy grown as slowly as either projection by the SSA or the CBO. [7] Each year the Social Security trust fund is supposed to be depleted moves farther and farther into the future. For example, in 1996 the date the trust fund was projected to dry up was 2030, in 2000 that date was 2036 and now its 2042 because the economic growth rate used by the SSA and the CBO tends to be on the pessimistic side. If the economy grows at 2.4%, lower than the sluggish period during the 1980's, the trust fund never runs out.

Secondly, Bush's plan calls for diverting a portion of younger workers FICA into private accounts. At the same time Bush is using the pessimistic economic numbers from the SSA and the CBO above to project when Social Security will go "bankrupt," he paints a rosy picture of economic health to persuade people to put their Social Security into private accounts and invest it in the stock market. He can't have his economic cake and eat it too. The administration has yet to lay out a concise plan that can be examined, but the President has made reference to "younger" workers being people born after 1950 and the portion of the money they can put into a private account at "about a third of your payroll taxes." [8] Other administration officials have said two thirds of the 6.2% currently paid to FICA. Remember, the revenue from the FICA tax we pay goes right out to pay current retirees, survivor benefits and the disabled. If a bill were to go through both houses of Congress and was signed by the President today that diverted 4% of FICA taxes (this amount is referred to in the President's Commission to Strengthen Social Security report of March 2002) multiplied by every worker born after 1950 to private accounts, it would create a shortfall of almost $2 trillion over the coming decade. The money to pay current retirees has to come from somewhere. Social Security would have to tap the trust fund surplus, not starting in 2019, but tomorrow to pay current benefits. Even proponents of Bush's Social Security "reform" admit that private accounts do nothing to solve the solvency problem nearly a half century out. Even Bush's supporters, in this case, can't be accused of not being able to add and subtract.

In the Maryland speech in June Bush said, "Social Security is not a trust. It's a pay-as-you-go system…the federal government spends your payroll taxes on retirees, and with the money left over, it goes for government programs. And all that's left is a file cabinet of IOU's." [9] In West Virginia in April, the President said, "There is no 'trust fund,' just IOU's I saw first hand, that future generations will pay-will pay for either in higher taxes, or reduced benefits, or cuts to other critical government programs.

"The office here in Parkersburg stores those IOU's. They're stacked in a filing cabinet. Imagine-the retirement security for future generations is sitting in a filing cabinet." This is a huge problem for this administration. As the President said, when the Social Security trust fund buys government bonds it is in effect loaning the government money to fund various programs. It has been so since the beginning of the Social Security program. The government has to put this money back at some point in the future, however this administration has used the Social Security trust fund to fund the largest tax cuts in history, mostly going to the wealthiest among us at a time of war, creating the largest deficits in history. (See the previous chapter on the tax cuts) Privatizing the system will dramatically increase the already out-of-control debt. China and Japan are buying most of that debt and as Bill Spriggs of the Economic Policy Institute said, "At this rate, the board of directors of the ownership society will have to meet in Beijing." When the President says that future generations will pay for the shortfall in Social Security, he's saying that future generations will pay for the tax cuts to the rich that he's giving away today wiping out any tax cut realized in the 2001 and the 2003 tax package. Enjoy your $400 now.

For the President to say there is no trust fund is simply absurd. On the one hand he says there is no trust fund and on the other hand he says that this nonexistent fund will go bankrupt in 2042. Is there a trust fund or isn't there. Currently there is in excess of $1.7 trillion in the trust fund in the form of government bonds. By implying the "IOU's sitting in a filing cabinet" are nothing more than worthless paper is also absurd. If intentionally designed to imply that Social Security is going to somehow evaporate in 2018 or 2019, instead of 2042 which isn't going to happen either, then the statement is a blatant lie. Again, the "IOU's" in the trust fund are government bonds backed by the full faith and credit of the United States. And while raising taxes and/or cutting benefits and programs is, as the President said, one way to pay for these bonds when they come due, it is not the only way. They can be paid for out of a budget surplus, like the one this country had when George W. Bush was elected in 2000, or the government can simply issue more bonds. During World War II the government waged a very successful campaign to raise billions of dollars to fight the Nazi's in Europe. There were posters on every street corner in America with a picture of Uncle Sam pointing out with a caption saying "Buy Bonds." It was considered a patriotic duty. Millions of people bought bonds, in effect "loaning" the government money to fight World War II and every one of those people got their money back with interest. Why? Because they are the safest investment known to man.

The filing cabinet references made by Bush dozens of times as he traveled around the country on a sixty day tour to sell this plan to the American people shortly after the 2004 election is one of the most irresponsible things an American President has ever done. The President's job is to create a strong and stable economy and to portray it to the world as such to help calm often volatile world markets. If the largest holders of U.S. treasuries (China, Japan, Germany, France, Russia, etc…) were to suddenly cash them in while they're still worth something, the world economy would be plunged into chaos creating a real crisis far greater than the health of Social Security nearly half a century out. Fortunately, the holders of T-Bills don't believe they're worthless IOU's and therefore don't believe the President's claim that Social Security is in crisis because there has not been a rush to cash them in. It also seems the President doesn't even believe it. He has talked about where private accounts should and should not be invested. He believes the options should be limited presumably for the sake of safety. One place he specifically has mentioned is government bonds. That's right, the same bonds he's been saying are nothing but IOU's sitting in a filing cabinet somewhere and the $1.7 trillion Social Security trust fund surplus (the one that doesn't exist) is invested in by law. Also the President holds almost $5 million in Treasury notes in his personal portfolio according to his financial disclosures that are made public when running for President. [10] It seems investors holding government treasuries should watch closely to see when Bush sells off his bond holdings. If the government is going to default on them he'll know. It wouldn't be the first time Bush has been suspected of insider trading.

The Bush administration has said Social Security reform would also mean the way benefits are calculated will have to change. (Again, since there is no real plan, only rhetoric, one can only go by statements made to date). He also says he is adamant nothing will change for current retirees or those close to retirement, but read on, we'll see the slight of hand the Bush administration has become known for. Currently, benefits are based on wages. Every year your earnings are restated to the current year level by indexing pre-retirement earnings to wage growth, but the administrations plan would calculate benefits based on the consumer price index (CPI), simply a measure of inflation. Since inflation does not rise as fast as wages, benefits over time will be less than they would have if they were left alone. A study by the Center for Retirement Research at Boston College in January 2005 says, "Price indexing produces annual benefits, [for the average worker] in current dollars, equal to $12,558 for the indefinite future. Since real wages are rising, this benefit amount replaces a declining portion of pre-retirement earnings." In essence this is an over time cut in benefits.

- In 2025, under the current system, the average worker would receive $16,205 (in 2005 dollars). If Bush's plan becomes a reality the 2025 worker would receive $12,558 (in 2005 dollars).

- In 2045, under the current system, the average worker would receive $20,050. Under the price indexing system the 2045 worker would receive $12,558.

- In 2065, under the current system, the average worker would receive $24,805. Under the price indexing system the 2065 worker would receive $12,558. and

- In 2085, under the current system, the average worker would receive $30,689. Under the price indexing system the 2085 worker would receive $12,558.

The report concludes, "Price indexing does more than simply cut benefits below the amounts scheduled under current law; it cuts them more each year. Eventually benefits will become trivial relative to workers' [pre-retirement] earnings. If the goal is to restore balance to the Social Security program by cutting benefits, an across the board cut of 20 percent for those under age 55 or an increase in the normal retirement age to 70 would achieve the same result over the next 75 years without putting the system on a downward trajectory." [11]

By 2025 Social Security benefits stand to be cut by almost 40% if benefits are indexed to inflation as the President proposes. Bush has said people are going to receive 100% of their benefits as promised, and they will. They will receive 100% of benefits that are indexed to inflation, so even current retirees will feel the effects over time, as illustrated above. And there's the deception.

All Social Security benefits are calculated in basically the same manner, so if retirement benefits are cut by almost 40% disability benefits and survivor benefits will also be cut by roughly the same amount. No one in the administration is talking about the disability side of Social Security. In its final 256 page report, the President's Commission to Strengthen Social Security used all of two pages to address the Social Security Disability Insurance Program. On page 149 the report states, "In absence of fully developed proposals, the calculations carried out for the commission and included in this report assume that defined benefits will be changed in similar ways for the two [retirement and disability] programs." [12] The sixteen member commission put together to recommend ways to strengthen Social Security was specifically instructed to only consider how to incorporate private accounts. Nobody plans to become disabled, but younger workers with 30 or 40 years of their working lives ahead of them should seriously consider what the implications of Bush's plan to "reform" Social Security are for them, and their families, if they find themselves partially or totally disabled some day.

Another argument the President uses over and over is the average life expectancy is so much greater now than it was in 1935 or 1940. Speaking from Pease International Tradeport Airport in Portsmouth, New Hampshire on February 16, 2005, Bush said, "things have changed since the 1950's…instead of living to about 60 years, which was the life expectancy early in the Social Security calculations, we're now living to 77 years." [13] And in West Virginia in April of 2005 he said, "Life expectancy has increased. They're collecting benefits for longer periods of time. In other words, if you've retired and you're living longer, the system must pay for your benefits longer." Listening to these simplistic statements one could conclude that Social Security is indeed in a "crisis." If most people in the 1950's didn't even make it to retirement and now there are millions living for 12 years in retirement, the system must be going broke. This is exactly the response the administration is banking on. But, according to the CDC, the average life expectancy in 1950, the decade referenced by the President, was 68.2 for all races and both sexes. African American's, both sexes had a life expectancy of 60.8 in 1950, but it's doubtful the President was referring to just African American's. In fairness to the President he also referred to the "life expectancy early" in Social Security. So, back to the CDC statistics. In 1940 the life expectancy for all races both sexes was 62.9 which is very close to the number the President used. And in 2002 the life expectancy for all races both sexes was 77.3, again very close to the number used by the President. However, the President is again being very misleading, and not by mistake. He has used these numbers time and time again. The problem is the use of the *average* life expectancy. In the 1930's and 1940's the rate of infant and young child mortality was high. Injuries and diseases that killed millions in the 1920's, 30's and 40's are very survivable today and are considered routine due to the incredible advances in medical technology. Workplace and industrial accidents in the 1930's, by todays standards, were horrendous. All of these factors contributed to the skewing down of the *average* life expectancy. The more accurate number to use is the life expectancy of a person who managed to make it to the age of 65. In 1940 a person that attained the age of 65 could expect to live for 13.7 more years or to the ripe old age of 78.7. In 2002 a person making it to the age of 65 could expect to live for another 18.2 years or until the age of 83.2. [14] That's just a little over 4 years in difference from 1940 to 2002, not the 17 years the President implies. *Average* life spans have increased in the 20th century due largely to medical technology that has prevented death early in life but has not significantly added years to the human life span. By using the 60 year life span in the 1940's and the 77 year life span today, one can reasonably assume the President is using the CDC and the SSA data. It is un-imaginable that someone in the administration has not simply scrolled down a half a page to the data that shows how long a person can be expected to live after reaching the age of 65. It is therefore reasonable to suspect that since the President continues to use the wrong data to make the argument for Social Security privatization, over and over; that he is intentionally misleading the American public and the real intention is to turn Social Security over to the private sector.

Bush has used this identical argument to try and sell his plan for privatization to the African American community pointing out the life expectancy for an African American male is 68.8 and a white American male's life expectancy is 75.1. It's these figures he cites when he claims that Social Security is "inherently unfair to many blacks." But once again the President is using the misleading number. The CDC statistics show that an African American male that lives to be 65 can expect to live for another 14.6 years or until 79.6 and a white male that lives to 65 can expect to live another 16.6 years or until the age of 81.6, a difference of a mere two years. [15] (Females of both races tend to live longer than males do). Under the President's plan, African Americans would actually come out worse off than other demographic groups. African American's wages are lower than white's and because of the way Social Security benefits are calculated lower income earners receive a higher return on their payroll taxes. The benefit formula is progressive in that the factor applied to the first dollars of earnings is higher than those applied to additional amounts. Therefore, the formula replaces a larger percentage of a low income workers pre-retirement wages than that of higher income workers. [16] While dollar for dollar, African Americans receive less than white's in their monthly Social Security checks, due to wage inequality, the amount represents a larger percentage of their pre-retirement earnings. It is this reason that not just African American's, but all low income earners would be negatively affected by Bush's plan. Wage inequality is the reason that more African American's (on a percentage basis) are below the poverty line and have a higher rate of uninsured resulting in less access to preventative health care which brings us full circle to the reason that an African American's *average* life expectancy is less than that of white's. If Bush really was concerned about the well being of African American's, he would not use the "race card" to sell his privatization scheme but rather do something about the wage inequality between African American's and white American's that cause higher rates of poverty among African American's and also do something to make sure the 45 million American's, of all races, living without access to health care get the access they need. The numbers Bush uses, the *average* life expectancy, is precisely why this is more an inequality and health care issue than it is a Social Security issue.

African American's also benefit from the current system in terms of disability and survivor benefits. 73% of benefits paid to white's are retirement benefits while 46% of African American's rely on Social Security for its disability and death benefits. Almost 70% of African American's are kept out of poverty by

Social Security's disability benefits. [17] Under the Bush plan, as we've seen, survivor and disability benefits would be cut by roughly the same amount as retirement benefits over time resulting in the minority communities suffering disproportionately.

Bush focuses on the fact that in "1950, there were 16 workers for every beneficiary. Today there are 3.3 workers for every beneficiary. Soon there will be two workers for every beneficiary." [18] He makes this argument in conjunction with the number of baby boomers getting ready to retire. These numbers are again misleading because Social Security does not only pay retirement benefits, it also pays survivor and disability benefits. Doug Orr, professor of economics at Eastern Washington University and speaker on private sector pensions and Social Security issues writes, "The logic is appealingly simple, but wrong...No amount of financial manipulation can change this fact: all current consumption must come from current physical output. The consumption of all dependants (non-workers) must come from the output produced by current workers. It's the *overall* dependency ratio-the number of *workers* relative to *all non-workers* that determines whether society can 'afford' the baby boomers retirement years." Because Orr is talking about *all non-workers*, not just retiree's the real numbers are "in the 1960's we had 1.05 workers for each dependant...In 2030, we will have 1.27 workers per dependant." Orr also writes that Bush's "demographic imperative' ignores productivity growth. Average worker productivity has grown about 2% per year, adjusted for inflation, for the last half century. That means real worker output doubles every 36 years. This productivity growth is expected to continue, so by 2040, each worker will produce twice as much as today. Suppose each of three workers today produce $1,000 per week and one retiree is allocated $500, then each worker gets $833. [And the retiree gets $500] In 2040, two such workers will produce $2000 per week (after adjusting for inflation) and the retiree gets $1,000, then each worker still gets $1,500. The income of both the workers and the retirees go up."

The Fix

While there is, as we've seen, credible evidence that absolutely nothing needs to be done to Social Security, most people and law makers believe that Social Security faces some problems in the not too distant future and therefore changes should occur sooner rather than later. By funneling tax receipts meant for Social Security into private accounts, Bush's plan for privatization would create a $2 trillion shortfall almost immediately, while doing nothing to solve the solvency situation predicted to happen in 2042 (or 2052). That coupled with the benefit cuts in the Presidents plan would, over the next twenty or thirty years, make Social Security so ineffective that future neo-cons will be able to make the argument the whole system should be scrapped. This is actually the end game, conservative Republicans have been trying to dismantle not just Social Security, but all of Roosevelt's New Deal programs for most of the last 70 years. Barring this radical approach, the following proposals are alternatives to the President's privatization plan:

- We only pay 6.2% in FICA tax on the first $90,000 of income, so a person making $90,000 pays $5,580 per year in FICA. A person making $2.5 million still only pays $5,580 per year. Congress could simply raise the cap to maybe $140,000 or $150,000. This "revenue raising fix" would not affect anyone making under $90,000 per year. Some have suggested removing the cap all together.

- Congress could approve a hike in the 6.2% to maybe 7% or 7.5%. Remember the employer matches what we pay into FICA so the total into Social Security would go from 12.4% to 14% or 15%. This would be phased in over time. The downside to this is it affects all tax payers including those making less than $90,000 per year.

- Bring in certain workers who are not currently part of the Social Security system. They would start paying FICA at the current rate of 6.2% of the first $90,000 of income. They could include federal employees hired before 1984 who are not currently in the system and certain state and local government workers.

- Increase the retirement age to maybe 68 or 69. An increase in the retirement age is already phasing in from 65 to 67; however the phase in to 67 is very gradual. It is currently 65.5 years of age and could possibly be sped up and/or increased.

- There could be a slight increase in taxes on benefits.

There could be a blend of any or all of the above proposals. With the exception of raising the retirement age, Bush is opposed to all of them. He has made it clear he won't even consider raising taxes by raising the $90,000 cap for example. [19] Most of the proposals that include some tax increases do not affect low and middle income earners; however in a televised news conference on April 28, 2005 he did endorse reducing benefits.

1983 was one of the few years Social Security took in less than it paid out prompting concern about future generations, specifically the baby boomers. President Reagan appointed Alan Greenspan to chair a commission to address the problem. Those recommendations became the 1983 Amendments to Social Security and were signed into law by Reagan. The new law increased the payroll tax to 12.4%, where it is currently, it raised the cap to $90,000, where it is currently, it brought additional employees into the system, made some of Social Security benefits taxable income and raised the retirement age. Some of these very same things are being proposed today as stated above. It's been almost a quarter century since some of these things have been adjusted. As a result of the 1983 amendment, Social Security began generating huge surpluses and has not looked back. Reagan's minor "fixes" insured Social Security solvency from 1983 to approximately 2042 (or 2052) or roughly sixty to seventy years. (The SSA is required by law to make projections 75 years out. Considered impossible by some experts, but is the goal they try to achieve. Under the guidance of the Greenspan commission, Reagan's fix came damn close). The extreme radical changes Bush is proposing are irresponsible and dangerous for Social Security for both current and future retirees, and are not necessary unless the goal is to dismantle Social Security.

In 1978, during a failed attempt at a House seat in Texas, then Congressional candidate George W. Bush told the USA Today and the Texas Observer that unless it was privatized "Social Security will go bust in ten years." [1988] He has been advocating turning over Social Security to the private sector for over twenty years now. So what does this really mean?

Who Benefits?

"They want the federal government controlling Social Security like it's some kind of federal program." That was George W. Bush in St. Charles, Montana on November 2, 2000. He obviously didn't know that Social Security is and always has been a federal program or he was making clear that if he had anything to do with it, that it would change. He is now trying to make that change and turn over $2 trillion to the private sector.

As has been done throughout this book the key to understanding what drives Bush administration policy is to examine who benefits, since it's certainly not the American people.

Large coalitions of industry backed lobbies have been set up to push for the privatization of Social Security. One is the Alliance for Workers Retirement Security (AWRS) set up in 1998. Members of AWRS include the Securities Industry Association (SIA), which represents 600 securities firms, the American Bankers Association (ABA), Charles Schwab and Wachovia. G. Kennedy

Thompson, the CEO of Wachovia is the chairman of SIA. The Executive Vice President of Wachovia, Betsy Duke is the chairman of ABA.

Another coalition of industry lobbyists is the Coalition for the Modernization and Protection of America's Social Security (COMPASS) set up by AWRS to promote the privatization of Social Security through a public relations blitz. COMPASS boasts a membership of 116 industry associations and advocacy groups including high powered financial lobbies such as the American Bankers Association, the American Insurance Association, America's Community Bankers, the Bond Market Association, the Financial Services Roundtable and the Securities Industry Association. The Financial Services Roundtable put together a "Blue Ribbon Commission on Retirement Security" that among other things pushed for *mandatory* private accounts and Social Security benefit cuts and allowing people to invest their FICA tax into an "array of private investment options from a broad range of *financial service providers.*"

Many financial firms do not make their ties to front groups like AWRS and COMPASS public and there are no laws requiring them to disclose many contributions to these groups. The investment banking industry also backs a number of other groups pushing for privatization such as the conservative think tanks Cato Institute and the Heritage Foundation and numerous 527 groups. In 1983 the Cato Institute published an article in the *Cato Journal* titled *Achieving a Leninist Strategy* in which they urged the waging of "guerrilla warfare" against Social Security and noted "financial institutions that stood to benefit would be an obvious element in a pro-privatization constituency." Cato Institute contributors have included the Securities Industry Association, the Bond Market Association, American Express, AIG, Amerisure, Chase Manhattan, Charles Schwab, Citigroup, E-Trade, Fidelity, Prudential, Bank of America subsidiary Quick & Reilly, Sun Trust and USAA. [20]

The American Council of Life Insurers (ACLI) while claiming to be neutral on the privatization issue is none the less keeping their iron in the fire in case the privatization of Social Security goes forward. Private Accounts would be paid to retiree's in the form of annuities. Life insurance companies are the main providers of annuities. ACLI is headed by Frank Keating, the former governor of Oklahoma. Keating has recently taken a page out of President Bush's play book by utilizing the "race card" in an advertising campaign targeting African American's claiming that Social Security constitutes "reverse reparations" because it benefits whites at the expense of blacks. Unbelievable!

COMPASS is spending almost $20 million on ads supporting Social Security private accounts and AWRS is planning to spend "multiples" of $5 million to push it. When it's all said and done groups with ties to Wall Street plan to spend upwards of *$70 million* to lobby for Social Security privatization. [21]

The Wall Street investment banking industry is not spending this kind of money for nothing. Heavy corporate Contributors to the RNC and to the Bush/ Cheney campaign such as the energy, timber and logging, defense contractors, credit and pharmaceutical industries have, as we've seen, reaped huge returns on their "investments" during the five years of the Bush administration. Wall Street corporations have contributed heavily and now they're dipping their oar into the money lake. Make no mistake; this industry cares nothing about your retirement status or mine. Their motive in pushing for the privatization of Social Security is the billions upon billions of dollars to be had by managing the trillions of dollars that will be held in private accounts. Rob Mills, Vice President of SIA, in a report published in December of 2004, concluded that privatization is "hardly likely to be a bonanza for Wall Street." [22] It's not surprising that a lobbyist would take that position, however that statement seems hollow when one considers the billions of dollars at stake.

A report by Austan Goolsbee of the University of Chicago in September of 2004 found that "Creating individual accounts in the Social Security system would lead to a massive increase in payments of financial fees to private financial management companies...the net present value of such payments would be $940 billion [over 75 years]."

Since the G.A.O. cites studies that indicate expenses would range anywhere from 32 to 150 basis points (.32 to 1.5 percent) and the C.B.O. puts expenses at anywhere from 80 to 109 basis points Goolsbee tested three assumptions erring "on the side of being conservative." The midrange number for fees of 80 basis points that would "likely correspond to limited customer service and a limited number of investment choices" and applied to Model II of the Presidential Commission to Strengthen Social Security (the most likely of the three scenarios in the CSSS report) results in the $940 billion figure. (Goolsbee also applies the three different possible fees to Model I and Model III in the CSSS report).

Goolsbee concludes that "the fees would be the largest windfall gain in American financial history [and] would be an increase more than 8 times larger than the decrease in revenue from the 2000-2002 collapse of the bubble...the fees amount to about 25% of the NPV of the revenue of the entire financial sector for the next 75 years.

"For a worker at the average income level, the fees in privately managed accounts are likely to reduce the ultimate retirement value of their individual accounts by 20% for the intermediate case." [23]

The Cato Institute, which has been pushing for private accounts, agrees. Michael Tanner, a Cato analyst said Goolsbee's administrative cost estimate is only slightly higher than Cato's, which put management fees at 65 basis points, but "not unrealistic." [24]

Social Security Hits Home

The neo-cons in office today, given their way, will destroy Social Security. The far right wing of the Republican Party has had it out for Roosevelt's New Deal social programs for seventy years, but no administration has come as close to achieving the goal as this one has. Poll numbers show the American public is opposed to Bush's plan to privatize Social Security nearly 2 to 1 and that there is little support in Congress to make it happen. The reason it needs to be discussed is that even though it seems to be dead now, this President has made the program easier to attack. It is no longer the "third rail" of politics. Millions of people have relied on Social Security over the years. Something this President, who hasn't had to work a day in his life, couldn't possibly understand. This is the story of just one.

In 1963, there was a woman who found herself divorced with a three year old son. She had a high school education, but no higher education. In an era when women stayed home and cooked, she had to make a decision. She went to work as a receptionist or secretary or whatever work she could find. The only family she had was her mother, father and brother all of whom were middle to lower middle class citizens, all hard working. Over the years they helped this woman the best they could as any family would do, but they weren't capable of providing much help. Never the less, this woman worked, sometimes two jobs, to make ends meet. Her son always had clothes for school, always had dinner, a birthday gift every year and a Christmas tree and Christmas presents every year. Even though there was no insurance, he went to the doctor and dentist regularly. She never once received government subsidized housing or welfare or food stamps. It probably never occurred to her. She never received child support from her ex-husband and never really knew where he was or even tried to find him. Her father died in 1971 leaving her nothing material, but more than one could imagine in other ways. Her mother died in the mid-80's, again leaving no assets other than memories and lessons about life. She was never able to save much money although she worked hard for over forty years. She never owned her own home, only able to rent over the years. This woman is retirement age today and without Social Security she would live in poverty. The twist to this story is in1996 a tragic event occurred that would actually help her. Her brother died at the young age of

56. Unlike her mother and father, her brother had some modest assets in the form of a little property and a small portfolio of stocks. With these assets she was able to buy a house for the first time in her life and put some savings into a retirement account although trying to start saving for retirement in her mid 50's did not present too many opportunities. Ideally one would prefer to start a retirement plan much earlier. But even with these modest investments made in her mid 50's, without Social Security, she would retire very close to the poverty line. Social Security is not a government handout or an entitlement program. It is an insurance program that insures that this woman, who worked all her life and paid her FICA taxes for more than 40 years, to insure the generation before her did not live in poverty, won't live in poverty. This woman was not lazy or looking for a handout from the government, in fact if you ask her she would probably say she had a good life. She is not the minority, she is Jane Q. Public, and she is my mother.

The President's proposal to take two thirds of every workers FICA and give it to Wall Street adding trillions more to an already out-of-control debt is bleeding this country dry. Why don't they just say what they really want to do; do away with Social Security and give all of the FICA tax to Wall Street and completely privatize the system instead of deceptively selling partial privatization as a "fix" for Social Security? What's another couple of trillion.

If a person with a three year old son or daughter wanted to make sure their child could get an education and go to college if something were to happen to them, first of all they can know that under the current system Social Security will provide a monthly check for fifteen years or until their child is 18. If that check were about $1,200 per month that would total approximately $200,000 over the fifteen year period. They could also go out and purchase a term life insurance policy for $200,000, for a term of fifteen years, which would pay a lump sum on top of Social Security for more peace of mind. That person can go to sleep at night knowing if something happened to them that their wife, or husband, and their child will be O.K. The life insurance will pay off the mortgage and the Social Security check will provide a level of support. If at the end of the fifteen years that person is fortunate enough to be alive on their child's 18th birthday, what happens to the term policy they purchased and fifteen years of premiums they paid? Nothing, the term is up, they paid for peace of mind, they paid for insurance. Social Security is similar to the term policy in that if you die your dependant receives benefits but unlike the term policy if you make it to 65 you will, under the current system, receive a check until you die. What about the millions of people who can't afford life insurance? Social Security insures everybody that works.

Social Security was never meant to be a retirement savings account or an investment account. It was and is meant to do exactly what it's been doing for 70 years. As Roosevelt said, it's a social insurance program and it is the best government program ever devised that has kept millions upon millions of people out of poverty at a very low cost. We already have personal investment accounts, they're called 401(k), 403(b), IRA's and Roth IRA's, SEP's and more. Large numbers of people don't take advantage of these personal retirement accounts now, even though they have access to them. Social Security may need to be adjusted and there are many things that can be done that will insure its strength for many decades to come, but the one thing it does not need is to be turned over to the private sector as the extreme right wing of the Republican party would have us believe.

13

The Morals of Compassionate Conservatism

"The hottest place in Hell is reserved for those who remain neutral in times of great moral conflict."
Dr. Martin Luther King

After the 2004 Presidential elections, the media focused on the fact that the Republican Party and George W. Bush were able to mobilize their base more effectively than the Democrats. That base, they claim, are the "moral value" voters. They would more accurately be called the "single issue" voters or the people who voted for Bush because he is pro-life, against gay and lesbian marriage, for school prayer and he invokes God. All of these are, for them, a single "moral value" issue. Almost one quarter of people polled said they turned out to vote for "moral values." The media has simply accepted and passed it along as fact that nearly one quarter of the electorate turned out to vote for the above "moral values" and George Bush. But isn't lying about weapons of mass destruction a moral value? What about pulling the U.S. out of nuclear and environmental agreements, cutting veterans benefits, turning over the environment to industry and deregulating mercury and other pollutants, depleting the treasury to give tax cuts that go mostly to the wealthy, preserving pharmaceutical industry profits at the expense of the elderly, deceiving people about the state of Social Security, outing CIA agents to settle political vendetta's? Could all of these things, and more, be considered moral value issues? It's more than likely that when people were asked about "moral values" that a large number of them were talking about a myriad of issues and not just the single issue voter's interpretation of "moral values" and that many of them did not vote for George W. Bush. For the media to assume otherwise is just plain laziness or worse incompetence. In case you haven't realized it by now, everything in this book has been about moral values.

After graduating from Harvard in 1975, George W. Bush's ambition seemed to be to follow in his father's footsteps and pursue a career in the oil industry, not politics. In 1975, Bush raised over $3 million to start his first company; Arbusto. Investors included his uncle Jonathan Bush and his grandmother Dorothy Bush. Besides family, there were powerful Bush family friends and prominent Republican Party fund raisers such William Draper who would become the head of the Export-Import Bank in 1984 while H.W. Bush was Vice President. Under pressure from H.W., Draper reversed bank policy and guaranteed loans to Saddam Hussein. There was Russell Reynolds who was a George H.W. Bush fund raiser and Lewis Lehrman. Lehrman is a board member for the Project for the New American Century (PNAC). Another investor in Arbusto was a friend of W's, from his days in the National Guard, James Bath, who became an aircraft broker in Houston, Texas and a middle man for business deals for many Saudi Royal family members. Bath sold planes to Salem bin Laden one of Osama bin Laden's half brothers.

Arbusto was a miserable failure that drilled one dry hole after another. After Arbusto became known in the oil industry as Ar-"bust"-o, Bush changed the name to Bush Exploration Oil Co. in 1982. As Bush Exploration was sinking an unlikely investor stepped forward. A Princeton classmate and friend of James Baker III, (who in 1982 was Reagan's Chief of Staff and later became H.W. Bush's Secretary of State), Philip Uzielli bought 10% of Bush Exploration for $1 million when at the time the whole company was valued at only $382,376 according to an article in *Time Magazine* published in 1999. This infusion of cash did little to help Bush's company. But by now his father was Vice President of the United States and a pretty good bet to be the front runner for President in 1988 and there was no way for him to fail, simply because of who he was. In 1984 the Bush name attracted the attention of the heads of another oil exploration company, Spectrum 7. Ohio investors William DeWitt and Mercer Reynolds III merged with Bush's failing company giving Bush 1.16 million shares of Spectrum 7 and naming him CEO with a salary of $75,000 a year and consulting fee's of approximately $120,000 a year.

By 1985 there was a banking crisis and the oil market was experiencing tough times. Even the large oil companies were struggling. The little guys like Spectrum were faring even worse. Spectrum was hemorrhaging money and was more than $3 million in debt. During this rough period for oil companies where investors were nowhere to be found and while Spectrum continued to drill dry holes in the Earth Bush's name once again attracted the attention of fresh money. In 1986 Dallas based Harken Energy Corporation bought Spectrum 7. George W. Bush was paid over a half million dollars in stocks, given a seat on Harken's board and on its three member audit committee and a salary of up to $120,000 a year.

Investors in Harken included people with close ties to the Bank of Credit and Commerce International (BCCI) including Abdullah Taha Bakhsh, a Saudi with close ties to the Saudi Royal family and Khalid bin Mahfouz, the largest shareholder of BCCI. [1] The Saudi's often used third parties to mask their investments and business deals in U.S. corporations. Khalid bin Mahfouz is the son of the founder of Saudi Arabia's first bank who became the personal banker of the Saudi Royal family. Mahfouz inherited numerous assets from the Saudi bin Laded Group (SBG) when Salem bin Laden died in a plane crash in 1988. Among these assets was an interest in Arbusto. Mahfouz's holdings were managed by James Bath. Mahfouz's charity organization, Muwaffaq Foundation, was named as an al-Qaeda front by the U.S. Treasury Department in 1999 and the Saudi named to run the charity by Mahfouz was named a supporter of terrorism. [2] It has also been suggested that Mahfouz is the owner of Harken Energy. [3] Bush has denied any knowledge of Mahfouz's involvement in Harken Energy even though he held a position on the board and the audit committee.

By 1989 Harkin was nearly bankrupt. But instead of reporting $13.4 million in losses for the year, Harken arranged to sell 80% of one of its subsidiaries, Aloha Petroleum, to a group of Harken insiders for $7.9 million. The money came in the form of loans from Harken to the group and the whole deal was approved by the board of directors. With this "profit," Harken reported just $3.3 million in losses. [4] It's interesting to note that Harken's accountant at the time was Arthur Andersen & Co. The same Arthur Andersen & Co. of Enron fame who helped "cook" the books for the Enron insiders. They are also the accounting firm of choice for Dick Cheney's Halliburton. The SEC would later find the Aloha deal bogus and force Harken to restate 1989 losses to reflect the real loss of over $13 million.

Were any laws broken in 1989 at Harken? No one on the board of directors was indicted, the SEC simply required Harken to restate earnings; however the whole incident was very Enron-esk. But the issue, for this chapter is not the law but rather morals. It's a little more than ironic that George W. Bush has campaigned partly on a platform of corporate responsibility especially after the Enron debacle. On July 9, 2002 he said the SEC should "put an end to all company loans to corporate officers." Yet Bush received $180,000 in loans, while he was a board member of Harken, to buy stock not to mention the Aloha deal.

Also in 1989, George W. Bush borrowed $500,000 from a Midland, Texas bank, he was a director at, to purchase a 1.8% share of the Texas Rangers baseball team. SEC records show that in April of 1990 Harken's board of directors was notified by Harken's President, Mikel Faulkner, the company faced a "liquidity crisis." [5] In May the board was told they would run out of money in three days. In June Bush asked Harken's legal department for advice. In a nine page memo dated June 15th they advised "The act of trading, particularly if close in time to the receipt of the inside information, is strong evidence that the insider's investment decision was based on the inside information...The insider should be advised not to sell." [6] One week later on June 22, Bush sold 212,140 of his 317,512 shares at $4 for a total of $848,560 to pay off his bank loan according to him. His timing for paying off his bank loan was impeccable because three weeks later Harken would report losses of $23.2 million for the quarter ending June 30, 1990. [5] Harken stock would plummet to $2.37 later to bottom at just 22 cents a share.

By law, an insider must report the sale of stock to the SEC by the 10th of the month following the sale. Bush would not report the sale for eight months. This would ultimately draw the attention of the SEC. Investigators soon discovered the June 22 sale was not the only sale of stock Bush failed to disclose. SEC documents showed there were four separate sales totaling $1,028,935, however the investigation went nowhere. By now Bush simply walked away from Harken and the oil business to go to Washington to help with his father's re-election campaign. He was still a member of the board, but apparently decided politics is where he belonged after all.

During the SEC investigation of Bush's insider trading his father was President of the United States and the Secretary of State was James A. Baker III of the law firm Baker Botts. The chairman of the SEC, appointed by H.W., was Richard Breeden, a close Bush family friend and former lawyer at Baker Botts. Another SEC lawyer on the case was James Doty, also a Baker Botts attorney who represented Bush in the Texas Rangers deal. Bush was being represented by Robert Jordan, yet another former Baker Botts attorney who would later become George W. Bush's ambassador to Saudi Arabia. [7] It seems conflict of interest has followed George W. Bush his entire adult life up to and including his presidency.

So, were any laws broken? This time the answer is probably yes. Martha Stewart went to prison for six months for a lot less than what George W. apparently did. But once again this is a chapter about morals. While Harken was downplaying its financial problems keeping its stock price stable, the small investor suffered. A person trying to decide whether or not to buy stock in a company for his or her personal portfolio has nothing more to go by than the financial statements put out by that corporation. By the time the individual investor realizes there's a problem insider's like Bush have long since dumped their stock and have moved on before the companies news is made public, while the small investor watches their holdings get cut in half or worse. Not all corporate insiders would do something like this, but too many will.

The issue would not come up again until Bush's run for governor of Texas in 1994. By then few cared, and Bush simply claimed vindication. "The SEC fully investigated the stock deal. [Although they had not, Bush was never questioned] I was exonerated." However, a top SEC official, Bruce Hiler said, "it [the investigation] must in no way be construed as indicating that the party has been exonerated or that no action may ultimately result from the staff's investigation." [8]

Bush, who had been bailed out of tough situations by powerful friends and acquaintances of his father time and time again would finally strike it big, not in the oil industry or politics, but in his investment in the Texas Rangers.

Base-a-bol Been Bedy Bedy Goo to Me [9]

In 1989 George W. Bush, son of the soon to be President of the United States, was invited to invest in the Texas Ranger's baseball franchise. With $600,000 (He could only muster $100,000 at the time and had to borrow $500,000 which he eventually paid off with the sale of his Harken stocks) he became a 1.8% owner. By the time the deal, that included politically connected millionaire and billionaire investors, tax increases, shady land deals and corporate welfare, was finished, Bush would net over $15 million.

In 1989 the Rangers wanted out of Arlington Stadium, the stadium they called home since leaving Washington D.C. As a lot of sport franchises do, they threatened to leave Texas unless the local municipality built them a new state of the art stadium funded by tax payers. In a deal solidified by the Ranger's investors and Mayor Richard Greene a ½ cent sales tax was put on a referendum and approved by Arlington voters. The tax increase would raise $135 million in tax payer monies for corporate millionaire's to build a new stadium.

But there was a small obstacle to the stadium plan. The site needed was owned by private individuals, so the Rangers investors pushed a bill, with the help of Republican State Representative Kent Grusendorf, through the Texas legislature that would create a government entity (known as the Arlington Sports Facility Development Authority or, ASFDA) that could issue bonds and was given the power of eminent domain. The ASFDA offered $1.5 million for a parcel of land owned by the heirs of T.V. magnate Curtis Mathes who rejected the offer and countered with a price of $2.8 million. The ASFDA then offered $817,220 which was promptly rejected by the Mathes family. The ASFDA then condemned the land and seized it under eminent domain paying just $817,220.

The seizure of private property by the government is covered under the 5th amendment of the Constitution. It requires that just compensation be paid and that "public use" of the property be demonstrated. Is the property going to be used to build an industrial complex that will bring in outside investment that will revitalize and benefit the community? Is it going to be used to build road access to bring in tax dollars from tourism thereby benefiting the community? In essence does the seizure of private property benefit the community? In this case it does not. An attorney for the Mathes family said, "It was the first time in Texas history that the power of eminent domain was used to assist a private organization like a baseball team." An Arlington jury has agreed. In 1996 they awarded the Mathes heirs $4.98 million saying the ASFDA's offer was unfair.

The deal the Ranger's, a private entity, made through their high powered political investors including George W. Bush would allow them to take title to the stadium that cost tax payers $191 million to build for the cost of rent and upkeep paid to the city of Arlington for 12 years, a total of $60 million. The Ranger's would also receive all revenue's generated by the seized land the stadium was on including, but not limited to, all concessions, parking, sublease revenues, naming allowances and all other revenues produced within the facility.

While it's not clear what role Bush played in the plan to condemn the Mathes land, it is clear that he had a vested interest in seeing the team prospered. According to a 1994 article in the *Houston Chronicle* under the terms of his agreement with the Rangers, once his partners recoup their investment, Bush's share of the club will jump from [1.8%] to more than 11%. [10] The investors that bought the Rangers paid $89 million in 1989; by 1996 the team was valued at $138 million.

If Bush had argued the seizure of the Mathes land was in the best interest of the Arlington community and the tax increase to the community was necessary to further the benefit to the community, there would not be a moral issue here. He would have been arguing for what he believed to be right. However, not only has he not made that argument, he has made the exact opposite argument. A private entity took private land to benefit private individuals and received corporate welfare to build a private facility while Bush vigorously campaigned against such practices. In 1993 while running for governor of Texas Bush campaigned against all the things the consortium of investors he was part of in the Rangers Stadium deal did, thereby creating a moral dilemma.

On big government Bush, in November of 1993 said, "…the best way to allocate resources in our society is through the market place. Not through a governing elite…not through some central bureaucracy." [11] But it was this very government elite that pushed the tax subsidy and the land seizure that allowed the Rangers to build their stadium that directly benefited Bush among others. In October of 1994 he said, "I understand full well the value of private property, and its importance not only in our state but in capitalism in general, and I will do everything I can to defend the power of private property and private property rights when I am the governor of this state." And "We must change a welfare system that has created dependency on government." [12] Bush must be talking about removing low income families from welfare and not the corporate entities that depend heavily on government subsidies and tax dollars to build stadiums like the one that benefited him and the other investors in the Ranger Stadium deal.

By the time his father was elected President of the United States George W. was nearing his mid forties and had accomplished nothing. The Texas Rangers deal was the first success he had in business and seemed to happen in spite of everything he claimed to be against. While claiming no knowledge of the Mathes land seizure he would readily point to the new stadium to show how successful he was in business during his gubernatorial campaign. He was quoted as saying, "It solved my biggest political problem in Texas. There's no question about it and I knew it all along. My problem was 'What's the boy ever done?'" [13]

A Culture of Death

Bush speaks frequently about the "culture of life." The phrase was coined by Pope John Paul II during a visit to the United States in 1993 while speaking about abortion and euthanasia. "The culture of life" he said, "means respect for nature and protection of God's work of creation. In a special way, it means respect for human life from the first moment of conception until its *natural end.*" The phrase "until its natural end" reinforced the Catholic Church's opposition to war and the death penalty.

Bush first used the term during the Presidential debates in October of 2000. Since then Bush and others on the far right of the Republican Party have bastardized the term "culture of life" to simply refer to abortion and stem cell research solidifying their single issue voter base since it's obvious that Bush is not opposed to war or the death penalty. By the 2004 Presidential race the term was incorporated into the Republican Party platform and became synonymous with anti-abortion.

During his six years as governor Bush signed 152 death warrants, more than any other governor in recent history. From 1976, when the death penalty was reinstated, to 2000, the year Bush left Texas, there were 206 executions, which means that in the 18 years before Bush became governor there were only 54 executions in Texas. He signed off on every single death warrant that came before him over his six years as governor with the exception of one.

It has been widely reported that Bush never spent more than roughly one half hour reviewing clemency cases and usually on the day the executions were to take place. According to freelance journalist Alan Berlow who spoke with then Governor Bush's legal council Alberto Gonzales, Bush didn't even read the clemency petitions but relied solely on Gonzales's short summaries. [14] In one case, an attorney, representing a death row inmate where there were serious questions regarding the mans guilt, told Berlow that he "received a phone call from Gonzales's office about a week to ten days before the execution, advising him there would be no reprieve." Berlow writes, "The timing is significant because Gonzales's execution summary is dated June 16, 1997, the day of Stoker's execution. If that decision had been made a week or more before Bush even read the summary, it is fair to ask whether Bush was actually in the loop or-as many suspected-had simply made clear to both Gonzales and the BPP [Board of Pardons and Paroles] that he wasn't interested in commutations." [15]

In another case, Bush signed off on the execution of a severely retarded man, named Terry Washington, on the day of his execution. The information he received was a three page Gonzales memo. The memo does not mention that the condemned man's mental condition was not presented to the jury. While there is no question of the man's guilt there is question as to the mitigating circumstances of the case. [16]

Bush, as have many others, has argued the death penalty is consistent with their "culture of life" position claiming the difference between the death penalty and abortion is a matter of guilt. Bush also argues the death penalty has a deterrent effect thereby saving innocent lives, however studies show that states without the death penalty have not realized any significant increase in homicides and states with the death penalty have not realized and significant decrease in homicides, in fact, in some cases states with the death penalty have a higher homicide rate than do a neighboring state without the death penalty.

Author Peter Singer, professor of bioethics at Princeton University's Center for Human Values has noted that a severely retarded person "is likely to be incapable of understanding right and wrong, and thus to be morally innocent...[A position that the United States Supreme Court has accepted].

"If Bush supports the death penalty because he believes that it saves lives by deterring potential murderers, and if mentally retarded people are morally innocent, then in signing the death warrant for Terry Washington, Bush was deliberately causing the death of a morally innocent human as a means of saving the lives of others. That is, of course, exactly what he refuses to support in the case of human embryos." [17]

Since the death penalty was reinstated in 1976 through February 2005 *one hundred twenty one* death row inmates have been exonerated in 25 states. [18] Texas is third on the list with eight innocent men freed from death row, at least one during Bush's term as governor. Over a 25 year period from 1973 to 1998, there was an average of 2.96 exonerations per year. In the five year period from 1998 to 2003 exonerations jumped to 7.6 per year. [19] The jump in exonerations per year coincides with the science and subsequent acceptance of DNA technology beginning around the early to mid 90's. It also suggests there are serious problems within the system. How many innocent people were put to death before the use of DNA technology?

In the late 90's, a group of Northwestern University journalism students began investigating the case of death row inmate Anthony Porter. Their investigation produced evidence that cleared Porter after 17 years on death row. Illinois governor George Ryan ordered an investigation into the states death row system. Ultimately 13 more death row inmates were exonerated prompting a shocked Ryan to issue an immediate moratorium on executions in Illinois. In January of 2003, as Ryan was leaving office, he commuted the sentences on all 156 inmates on Illinois death row to life in prison. Four inmates were pardoned because of evidence they were tortured into confessing to murders they didn't commit. In his statement he said, "Our capital system is haunted by the demon of error; error in determining guilt and error in determining who among the guilty deserves to die. What effect was race having? What effect was poverty having? Because of all these reasons, today I am commuting the sentences of all death row inmates." [20] George Ryan is no bleeding heart liberal pacifist. He is a Republican politician who headed George W. Bush's 2000 Presidential campaign in Illinois and an ardent death penalty supporter who simply felt the need to rethink his position on the death penalty based on the preponderance of evidence presented to him. Granted the vast majority of the inmates who had their death sentences commuted by Ryan were guilty of heinous crimes and probably deserve to be removed from our planet, and while only the most extreme death penalty opponent would argue that someone like a Ted Bundy or a Timothy McVeigh does not deserve to die, there is a point where the cost of the death penalty is too high. That cost, for Ryan, appears to be the risk of executing just one innocent person.

When Ryan spoke about the effects of race and poverty on the death penalty, he could have been citing a 1999 justice department report prepared for President Clinton that says, in part, "U.S. Attorneys were almost twice as likely to recommend seeking the death penalty for a black defendant when the victim was non-black as when the victim was black. In comparison, U.S. Attorneys were slightly less likely to recommend the death penalty for a white defendant when the victim was non-white rather than white." [21] Or he could have been citing numerous other reports that have raised questions about indigent defendant's legal representation, violations of defendant's legal rights and other serious questions that could ultimately lead to wrongful convictions.

With all this evidence available to him, and as many death penalty supporters were beginning to realize there may be serious problems with the death penalty, that the system may be broken, Bush continued to sign death warrants at a pace unmatched by any other governor in the country. In fact Bush has made the system even worse in Texas. Alan Berlow writes, "Only three of Texas's 254 counties have full time public defender offices...the Texas legislature unanimously approved a bill that would have encouraged the creation of more public defender offices. But it was vetoed by [Governor] Bush."

He also points out that "in 1995, Bush championed and signed legislation designed to limit appeals by death row inmates and to shorten the time between conviction and execution, despite overwhelming national evidence that a sizable number of people including several in Texas, one during Bush's first term would have been wrongly executed had that time been narrowed." [22]

Berlow has examined in detail many Texas death row cases and has found disturbing evidence that more than one innocent person in Texas may have been convicted of capital offenses. [23] It is possible, even probable, that more than one innocent person was put to death during Bush's term as governor.

Compassionate Conservative? You decide.

Our Captain Ahab

Torture has been used throughout all of human history, in every culture, and throughout history attempts have been made to limit wartime behavior with respect to the treatment of prisoners and civilians alike. In the sixth century BC, Chinese warrior Sun Tzu advocated for "rules" of war and around 200 BC the concept of war crimes appeared in the Hindu code of Manu.

The first treaties of the Geneva Conventions inspired by Henri Dunant, the founder of the Red Cross, were signed in 1864. Since then numerous treaties have been signed by virtually all of the industrialized nations of the world. The treaties of concern here are the four Geneva Convention treaties signed in 1949, specifically Convention III which addresses the treatment of POW's and Convention IV which addresses the civilian population during armed conflict, and the Torture Convention of 1994, ratified by the U.S. in that year, and the War Crimes Act of 1996, all of which have been violated by the Bush/Cheney administration.

Since the invasions of Afghanistan and Iraq thousands of people have been rounded up by U.S. forces and held in various prisons throughout the world, the most infamous being Abu-Ghraib, Bagram Airbase in Afghanistan and Guantonimo Cuba, but there are dozens more in places like Egypt, Saudi Arabia, Jordan, Syria and Pakistan. It's unknown how many have been tortured while in U.S. custody, but according to Human Rights First, "28 to 31 detainees died in U.S. custody due to suspected or confirmed criminal homicides. A total of 108 detainees have died while in U.S. custody in Iraq and Afghanistan." [24] In May of 2004, citing a U.S. Army report, the *New York Times* reports, "Citing previously unknown incidents are the abuse of detainees by Army interrogators from a National Guard unit attached to the Third Infantry Division, who are described in a document obtained by the New York Times as having 'forced into asphyxiation numerous detainees in an attempt to obtain information' during a ten week period last spring." And in the same article, "In one of the oldest cases, involving the death of a prisoner in Afghanistan in December of 2002, enlisted personnel from an active duty military intelligence unit at Fort Bragg, N.C., and an Army Reserve military police unit from Ohio are believed to have been 'involved at various times in assaulting and mistreating the detainee.'" [25]

A 2005 Army report confirmed the beating death of two Afghan detainees at Bagram Airbase in December of 2002. According to the report a Mr. Habibullah was chained to the ceiling in his cell and was subjected to repeated severe blows to the side of the legs above the knees, known as "peroneal strikes" which incapacitates the legs by hitting the common peroneal nerve. By the time doctors were summoned, he was dead. [26] The other detainee named Dilawar, a 22 year old cab driver, was picked up for simply passing a checkpoint at the wrong time. Dilawar was hung by his wrists for almost four days and according to one MP, every time he was struck he would scream "Allah." He also said, "People kept showing up to give [him] common peroneal strikes just to hear him scream out 'Allah.'" At one point a guard tried to force Dilawar to his knees, but his legs would no longer bend, so they hung him back up. By the time medical care was summoned, rigor had set in. [27]

In August of 2002 a man named M. Sayari was killed by four U.S. military personnel *after* being detained for tracking their movements. In November 2002, a detainee died at a site known as the "Salt Pit," a secret U.S. run prison north of Kabul when, according to a Washington Post article, the man was left chained to the concrete floor of his cell naked by Afghan guards paid by and under the supervision of the CIA. An autopsy determined the cause of death to be hypothermia. [28]

These incidents, and many more that are slowly beginning to come to light show a pattern of abuse extending back to the beginning of the war on "terra," long before the images of Abu-Ghraib, long before the invasion of Iraq. Contrary to the Bush administration's assertion that Abu-Ghraib was the result of "a few bad apples," it's clear that torture has, sadly, been U.S. policy since at least early 2002. A fact alluded to by Cofer Black, former director of the CIA's counterterrorism unit, in testimony to Congress in 2002 when he said, "There was a before 9-11 and an after 9-11. After 9-11 the gloves came off." Also, the photo's of Abu-Ghraib display a knowledge of Arab culture that "a few bad apples" on the night shift probably didn't posses such as groups of naked men piled on top of each other and detainees shown in simulated acts of homosexuality. These acts are not only offensive to Arab men but are against Islamic law. There are reports that more than one detainee tried to commit suicide after being forced to do these things. This is indicative of a psychological operation (psy-op) well known to military intelligence and explicitly forbidden by the Geneva Conventions. Geneva Convention III, Article 13: "…prisoners of war must at all times be protected, particularly against attacks of violence or *intimidation and against insults* [emphasis added] and public curiosity." Article 14: "Prisoners of war are entitled in all circumstances to respect for their persons and their honour." Convention III also says "Although one of the powers in conflict may not be a party to the present convention, the powers who are parties thereto shall remain bound by it…"

Geneva IV affords vast protections for civilians in areas of armed conflict. The fact that thousands of people are being detained by U.S. forces in Afghanistan, Iraq and elsewhere would suggest that a percentage of them are civilian since reports show that many people are picked up in military sweeps and at check points and that in Afghanistan warring factions are simply turning in their enemies to U.S. forces as Taliban and al-Qaeda fighters and accepting bounties. Geneva IV places the burden of responsibility on identifying prisoners on the detaining power. The likelihood that civilians are being illegally detained and tortured is problematic to say the least.

So problematic, in fact, that Bush, Cheney and Rumsfeld have taken steps to minimize the chance of prosecution for war crimes in the future. It began with a January 9, 2002 memo from John Yoo, an attorney for the Justice Departments Office of Legal Counsel (OLC). At this time, over a year before the war in Iraq began, the U.S was holding thousands of prisoners captured during the Afghan operations in Cuba and Afghanistan. Yoo examined the possibilities of prosecutions under the War Crimes Act and how they might apply to the military. It seems the administration was more concerned about how the War Crimes Act would apply to senior administration officials, including Bush. (We'll get to that)

The memo concluded the Geneva Conventions, specifically Geneva III, did not apply to al-Qaeda or Taliban fighters in Afghanistan. Shortly after learning of the Yoo memo, Secretary of State Colin Powell sent a memo to the President urging him to reconsider the administrations position.

On January 25, 2002 then White House Counsel Alberto Gonzales sent a memo to the President which said, "On Jan. 18, I advised you that the Department of Justice had issued a *formal legal opinion* concluding that the Geneva Conventions III (GPW) does not apply to the conflict with al-Qaeda…I understand that you decided that GPW does not apply.

"The Secretary of State has requested that you reconsider that decision…I understand, however, that he would agree that al-Qaeda and Taliban fighters could be determined not to be POW's but only a case-by-case basis following individual hearings before a military board." Powell's argument here is consistent with the rules of Geneva Convention IV; however Gonzales says, "As you have said the war on terrorism is a new kind of war…In my judgment, this new paradigm renders obsolete Geneva's strict limitations on questioning of enemy prisoners and renders quaint some of its provisions." He then makes the main argument for not affording detainees coverage under GPW. The decision, he writes, "Substantially reduces the threat of domestic criminal prosecution under the War Crimes Act (18 U.S.C. 2441).

"That statute, enacted in 1996, prohibits the commission of a 'war crime' by or against a U.S. person, including U.S. officials. 'War crime' for these purposes is defined to include any grave breach of GPW or any violation of common Article 3 thereof. Some of these provisions apply (if the GPW applies) regardless of whether the individual being detained qualifies as a POW. Punishments for violations of Section 2441 include the death penalty. A determination that the GPW is not applicable would mean that Section 2441 would not apply…" He goes on to advise the President that, "it is difficult to predict the motives of prosecutors and independent counsels who may in the future decide to pursue unwarranted charges based on Section 2441. Your determination would create a reasonable basis in law that Section 2441 does not apply, which would provide a solid defense to any future prosecution." [29]

On August 1, 2002 a memo prepared by Jay Bybee, then Assistant Attorney General for the Office of Legal Counsel (OLC), and John Yoo, Bybee's deputy, for then White House legal counsel Alberto Gonzales defined torture in such broad terms that under their interpretation not even Saddam Hussein, in cases that did not result in death or "major organ failure," would be guilty of torture. The memo has come to be known simply as the "torture memo." [30] In it, they create a new term, "unlawful combatant," that is not defined by the Geneva Conventions. They also make the argument the President is not bound by law because, in their view, anything Bush authorizes while executing the "war on 'terra'" cannot be unlawful because he is the Commander-in-Chief during wartime, therefore he *is* the law. The argument they make that torture may be legally defensible is a weak attempt to remove the President, and other top officials, from operating outside the law and placing them above the law. Nixon tried a similar argument to get out from under Watergate that was ultimately rejected by the courts.

On March 6, 2003 a Pentagon working group convened by Secretary of Defense Donald Rumsfeld also came to the same conclusions as OLC that compliance with international treaties and U.S. laws on torture could be circumnavigated because of legal technicalities and national security. [31]

Many military lawyers and many in the State Department are appalled at the legal opinions of OLC and the Pentagon. In his memo to the President urging him to reconsider his policy, Colin Powell wrote that by not recognizing the Geneva Conventions, "It will reverse over a century of U.S. policy and...*undermine the protections of the law of war for our troops*, both in this specific conflict and in general.

"It has a high cost in terms of negative international reaction...

"It will undermine public support among critical allies, making military cooperation more difficult to sustain.

"Europeans and others will likely have legal problems with extradition or other forms of cooperation in law enforcement, *including in bringing terrorists to justice.*

"It may provoke some individual foreign prosecutors to investigate and prosecute our officials and troops.

And "We will be challenged in international fora (UN Commission on Human Rights; World Court; etc.)."

Ignoring the only member of his Cabinet to have served in the military and experienced combat, George W. Bush, on February 7, 2002 signed an order stating, "Pursuant to my authority as commander in chief and chief executive of the United States...I accept the legal conclusion of the Department of Justice and determine that none of the provisions of Geneva apply to our conflict with al-Qaida in Afghanistan or elsewhere.

"I also accept the legal conclusion of the Department of Justice and determine that Article 3 of Geneva does not apply to either al-Qaida or Taliban detainees."

All the ass covering going on in these memos is the result of men who knew they were guilty of serious crimes that were being committed shortly after 9-11, long before the invasion of Iraq. The common thread throughout these memos is not an administration asking the Justice Department "what's legal and what's not" but rather "make the case for us to do this and not be held accountable in the future." The knowledge that they were committing crimes is what generated the memos. This knowledge makes it clear there was a policy in place to *extract* information by any means necessary and they needed to protect themselves from any possible fallout.

Contrary to popular belief, the dozen or so photo's of naked detainees piled on top of each other at Abu-Ghraib are not equivalent to a college fraternity hazing as Rush Limbaugh has said. At least one photo shows a dead Iraqi wrapped in plastic and packed in ice, his face beaten and bloody with a U.S. soldier standing over him smiling. [32] As discussed previously, there are over 100 deaths of detainees that have occurred since early 2002, some of which may turn out to include completely innocent victims. It's interesting to note that of the deaths being investigated only one of those occurred at Abu-Ghraib. The rest have taken place elsewhere in the world. The implication is that Abu-Ghraib is not the story but merely the tip of the iceberg.

Pulitzer Prize winning journalist and author, Seymour Hersh, who broke the Abu-Ghraib story, has said the 12 or so photo's from Abu-Ghraib pale in comparison to the dozens of photo's and at least four video's that, in one case, shows the torture of children, including sodomy with a broom handle, in front of their parents, to extract intelligence from the parents. He has not written about this yet but claims he has seen them and the government is in possession of them. Through a freedom of information act request (FOIA) by the ACLU, a judge has ordered that these new photo's be released. The Bush administration has refused claiming they would only enrage Muslims and provoke violence against troops in

Iraq. Here's a news flash for the Bush administration; The Muslim community and most of the rest of the world already know these events have taken place. The only reason to withhold them is to keep the American public from becoming enraged.

Information obtained through torture is not reliable. This has been an accepted fact for almost 70 years in the United States. Harvard law professor and former deputy U.S. attorney general Philip Heymann said, "About 70 years ago, the Supreme Court stopped the use of evidence produced by third-degree tactics largely on the theory that it was totally unreliable." [33] The Bush administration is seeking to change that. During a December 2004 U.S. District Court hearing to determine the status of detainees being held in Cuba without charges, U.S. District Judge Richard J. Leon asked if detention would be illegal if it were based solely on evidence obtained by torture. Deputy Associate Attorney General Brian Boyle answered that "if the military's combatant status review tribunals (CSRT) determine that evidence of questionable provenance were reliable, nothing in the due process clause prohibits them from relying on it." [34]

Two months after 9-11, a Canadian man named Ahmad Abou El-Maati was arrested in Damascus and accused of being a terrorist. After two years of being tortured, he named every Muslim he knew. In May of 2002, one of the men named by El-Maati, Abdullah Almalki, also a Canadian was arrested while visiting his parents in Damascus. He too would spend the next two years in a Syrian prison being tortured. Almalki named another Canadian named Arward Al-Bousha who was arrested in July of 2002 while visiting his dying father. All three of these men named Maher Arar, a Canadian computer scientist, who was arrested in September of 2002 at JFK Airport in New York. Arar was flown, (or "rendered") to Syria via Washington, Rome, and Amman, Jordan where he spent the next 12 months being tortured, [35] which violates at least two of the Geneva Conventions. Convention IV regarding the treatment of civilians and Convention III, Article 12:

> Prisoners of war may only be transferred by the Detaining Power to a Power which is a party to the Convention and after the detaining Power has satisfied itself of the willingness and ability of such transferee Power to apply the Convention. When prisoners of war are transferred under such circumstances, responsibility for the application of the Convention rests on the Power accepting them while they are in its custody.
>
> Nevertheless, if that Power fails to carry out the provisions of the Convention in any important respect, the Power by whom the prisoners of war were trans-

ferred shall, upon being notified by the Protecting Power, take effective measures to correct the situation or shall request the return of the prisoners of war. Such requests must be complied with.

But as we've seen, the United States no longer recognizes the Geneva Conventions, or the War Crimes Act of 1996 for that matter. The only reason the men mentioned above are note worthy is because all of them were detained on information gathered through the use of torture and all of them have been released without charge or explanation. It is highly unlikely the Bush administration would release terrorists given the fact they are holding thousands of detainees for almost four years now, many without being charged with anything.

The stories of people being arrested and "rendered" to third party countries could fill volumes. The above are but a couple of examples. Intelligence is hard enough to decipher without having to weed through erroneous information acquired through torture. And how many hard working intelligence officers are running around the world on wild goose chases vetting claims made by people trying to stop a broom stick from being shoved up their ass, again.

Torture is never justifiable or defensible either legally or morally. Nothing good can come from torture. Innocents will suffer, our troops will suffer, and the United States will suffer. We are losing our standing and credibility in the world as it is under the leadership of this administration, and that was before the Abu-Ghraib scandal broke. Torture represents nothing more than revenge and hatred and should not be tolerated by any true American. These memos show these are not the actions of moral men. The results of Bush's pursuit of his white whale will not be fully realized for years, and the effects will not be good.

Abortion, Abstinence, and Education

A discussion about morals is impossible, given the current political atmosphere, without bringing up abortion. The spiritual and philosophical arguments surrounding pro-life and pro-choice issues run deep and it is beyond the scope of this book to attempt to defend one side or the other on this issue. It is not beyond the scope of this book to examine the results of the Bush administration's policies regarding these matters.

The main policy of the Bush administration and in fact the only policy, to combat unwanted pregnancy, sexually transmitted diseases (STD) and abortion is Bush's faith based abstinence-only education. Shortly after taking office in January of 2001, Bush signed an executive order, without any Congressional approval or support, creating faith based initiatives and allowing federal funding to go directly to organizations that teach abstinence only without going through the states. In December of 2002, again with no support, or approval, from Congress, Bush signed another executive order expanding faith based initiatives into other departments of the federal government allowing religious organizations to compete for federal dollars. Meanwhile funding for comprehensive sex education programs has been drastically cut or eliminated entirely. The problem is that studies show abstinence only education is not working. While we don't want our kids to be promiscuous and practice irresponsible sex the fact is sex, for every species on the planet, including humans, is a natural behavior, therefore comprehensive sex education that is age appropriate is an essential part of our children's education and wellbeing.

Under the Bush administration, an organization applying for federal funds must meet all of the following definitions of abstinence education, known as AH (A through H):

a. Has as its *exclusive purpose*, teaching the social, psychological, and health gains to be realized by abstaining from sexual activity;

b. Teaches abstinence from sexual activity outside marriage as the expected standard for all school age children;

c. Teaches that abstinence from sexual activity is the only certain way to avoid out-of-wedlock pregnancy, sexually transmitted diseases, and other associated health problems;

d. Teaches that a mutually faithful monogamous relationship in the context of marriage is the expected standard of human sexually activity;

e. Teaches that sexual activity outside of the context of marriage is likely to have harmful psychological and physical effects;

f. Teaches that bearing children out-of-wedlock is likely to have harmful consequences for the child, the child's parents, and society;

g. Teaches young people how to reject sexual advances and how alcohol and drug use increases vulnerability to sexual advances; and

h. Teaches the importance of attaining self-sufficiency before engaging in sexual activity.

Aside from pushing their moral standards on people, we have a policy that prohibits federal funding of any organization that teaches the proper use of condoms to prevent sexually transmitted disease or unwanted pregnancy and falls right in line with the religious right's opposition to any form of birth control. The only time that abstinence only programs are allowed to discuss condoms is when they are discussing them in the context of failure rates even though many of the claims are either misleading or even false. There is no evidence that abstinence only programs significantly reduce sexual activity among teen's; Moreover teens who do pledge abstinence only eventually have sex often engaging in other forms of sexual activity such as oral and anal sex to *preserve* their status as virgins and their abstinence only vows. [36] And when they do become sexually active and practice intercourse, as many of them do, without the proper education, many of them do not use condoms. The reason is some abstinence only programs provide scientifically inaccurate information such as condoms fail to prevent HIV 31% of the time, so why bother. Also, when they do contract an STD, because of the lack of sexual health education, they tend to seek medical help less often than non-pledges putting future partners at risk. [37] And what about teens who are already sexually active; how does abstinence only education address them? The answer is it doesn't.

A report prepared for Representative Henry Waxman (D-Ca.) found that of the 13 most commonly used curricula for abstinence only education, 11 used by 69 organizations in 25 states contain unproved claims, subjective conclusions or outright falsehoods. The federal government does not review or approve the accuracy of the information presented in abstinence only programs. There is no oversight of your tax dollars for these programs. One inaccuracy is the claim above that condoms fail to prevent HIV 31% of the time when in actuality a *New England Journal of Medicine* study failed to find one single case of HIV transmission between HIV-positive individuals and their HIV-negative partners who used condoms *consistently*, despite a total of 15,000 acts of intercourse. [38]

Another falsehood identified in the Waxman report is that many abstinence only programs teach that *½ of all gay male teenagers have tested positive for HIV*. The CDC shows that 59% of HIV infected male's ages 13 to 19 contracted the virus through homosexual activity. It's easy to see how the abstinence only groups could twist this to say half of gay male teenager's are HIV positive. The CDC says *½ of those infected*, not ½ of *all* gay males. We don't know what the number infected gay male teens is but, for example, if there is 100 gay male's and 10 of them have HIV, then the CDC statistics are saying that 6 of them (59% of the 10) got HIV through homosexual activity, 6 out of the 100, not 50 out of the 100 as the abstinence only programs are leading teens to believe. The variable the abstinence only advocates leave out of the equation is how many gay males are actually HIV positive. There are many more distortions and falsehoods, to numerous to go into in detail here, in the Waxman report.

Yet another inaccuracy the Waxman report found is that AIDS can be transmitted through sweat and tears. On ABC's *This Week with George Stephanopoulos* on December 5th, 2004, Senator Bill Frist (R-Tenn.) created an uproar when he seemed unable to dispute the claim. Stephanopoulos quoted from the Waxman report and asked:

> "You're a doctor. Do you believe that tears and sweat can transmit HIV?"
> Frist: "I don't know. I can tell you…"
> Stephanopoulos: "You don't know?"
> Frist: "I can tell you things like, like…"
> Stephanopoulos: "Well wait, let me stop you, you don't know that, you believe that tears and sweat might be able to transmit AIDS?"

Stephanopoulos seemed shocked and after a brief discussion in which Frist incorrectly talked about a 15% failure rate in condoms, Stephanopoulos steered the conversation back to tears and sweat.

> Stephanopoulos: "Let me just, I wanted to move on to another subject, let me just clear this up, though. Do you or do you not believe that tears and sweat can transmit HIV?"
> Frist: "It would be very hard. It would be very hard for tears and sweat, I mean, you can get virus in tears and sweat but in terms of the degree of infecting somebody, it would be very hard."

The political dance by Frist was laughable. The fact that, as a doctor, he was unwilling to dispute a major inaccuracy in one of the White House's abstinence only programs is shameful. Not only would it be "very hard" but the CDC reports that "HIV has not been recovered from the sweat of HIV infected persons" and there has never, ever, been one single case in which HIV was transmitted through saliva, sweat or tears. [39] A simple no should have been First's answer instead of perpetuating myth's about AIDS. As to Frist's other claim that condoms fail 15% of the time, the CDC finds that if condoms are used inconsistently or incorrectly they can have a failure rate of up to 13% however when used consistently and correctly the failure rate is "less than 2%." [40] Another CDC study found that epidemiological examination of STD rates in populations rather than individuals "demonstrated that when condom use increases within population groups, rates of STD's decline in these groups. Other studies have examined the relationship between condom use and the complications of sexually transmitted infections. For example, condom use has been associated with a decreased risk of cervical cancer-an HPV [Human Papillomavirus] associated disease." [41]

Abstinence only advocates claim the only 100% sure way to avoid STD's, HIV, and unwanted pregnancies is abstinence and that is absolutely correct, however is it realistic to expect people to abstain from sex? This is not the 1950's when women stayed home and cooked and the man went out and earned a living. Many women today put off marriage into their 30's and even 40's as they pursue careers. Some want children but don't necessarily want a husband. The point is while abstinence should be taught, it should not be taught exclusively.

Abstinence only education does not work and it becomes apparent when one examines abortion rates. In a *Houston Chronicle* article in October of 2004, Glen Harold Stassen wrote, "I am a Christian ethicist, and trained in statistical analysis…Abortion was decreasing. When President Bush took office, the nation's abortion rates were at a 24 year low, after a 17.4% decline during the 1990's." Stassen cites data from the Alan Guttmacher Institute (AGI) highly respected for their data by both sides of the abortion issue.

While there is no data regarding abortion rates by either the CDC or AGI since 2000, Stassen did his own studies and "found four states that have posted three year statistics: Kentucky's [abortions] increased by 3.2% from 2000 to 2003. Michigan's increased by 11.3% from 2000 to 2003. Pennsylvania's increased by 1.9% from 1999 to 2002. Colorado's skyrocketed 111%. We found 12 additional states that reported statistics from 2001 and 2002. Eight states saw an increase in abortion rates (14.6% average increase), and four saw a decrease (4.3% average)."

Stassen's report indicates that "Given the trends of the 1990's, 52,000 more abortions occurred in the United States in 2002 than would have been expected before this change of direction. [Change of policy from the 1990's]" [42]

Stassen does not address the shortfalls in abstinence only programs, but does cite economic concerns for the increase in abortion rates. He found "First, two thirds of women who abort say they cannot afford a child (Minnesota Citizens Concerned for Life Web Site). In the past three years, unemployment rates increased…Not since Hoover had there been a net loss of jobs during a presidency until the current administration. Average real incomes decreased, and for seven years [Eight as of this writing] the minimum wage has not been raised to match inflation.

"Second, half of all women who abort say they do not have a reliable mate. Men who are jobless usually do not marry...As male unemployment increases, marriages fall and abortion rises.

"Third, women worry about health care for themselves and their children. Since 5.2 million more people have no health insurance now than before this presidency-with women of childbearing age overrepresented in those 5.2 million-abortion increases.

"Economic policy and abortion are not separate issues; they form one moral imperative." [43]

Stassen's research has been disputed. In an article on factcheck.org titled *The biography of a bad statistic*, while not addressing the impact of the economy on women that Stassen identified they write, under the heading of *Cherrypicking data*, "A close reading of Stassen's article makes clear that he didn't even pretend to have comprehensive national data on abortion rates. He said he looked at data from 16 states only...So Stassen was projecting findings onto the entire country from 12 states that he said had showed an increase and [4] that he said had shown a decrease." [44] They correctly point out that Stassen, at the time, *didn't pretend to have full data* because there wasn't any as Stassen himself points out. However, using data from roughly 35% of the country, that was available, and extrapolating that to a conclusion is valid.

Because of this controversy, the Alan Guttmacher Institute (AGI), again highly respected by both sides of the abortion debate, has put out a report on abortion for 2001 and 2002. Their findings do, in fact, show a decrease in abortions in 2001 and 2002. "The declines in abortion incidents seen in 2001 and 2002 were continuations of the declines seen in the 1990's. Between 1992 and 1996, the annualized declined was 3.4% per year...The annualized decline between 2000 and 2002 was 0.9% per year, suggesting that the last two years reflect a continuation of the trend of the late 1990's, albeit at a slightly slower rate of decline."

Stassen, who wrote his findings before AGI looked at 2001 and 2002, has publicly stated he has no reason to dispute the AGI numbers. But, the AGI numbers show a significant slow down in the decrease in the rate of abortions in this country which can be interpreted as the beginning of a reversal in the trend. We'll have to wait until someone such as AGI or the CDC crunches the numbers for 2003, 2004, and 2005 to see, but it appears the decrease in abortion rates are, at the very least bottoming out, and probably reversing to the upside.

Shouldn't it be expected the rate of decrease in abortions under the leadership of a pro-life President at least match if not exceed those of a pro-choice President?

No matter whether one is pro-life or pro-choice, isn't the ultimate goal to see fewer abortions occurring in the United States? The difference is education. This administrations goal as we've seen with other policies seems to be to undo everything Clinton. If abortion and unwanted pregnancies is in fact on the rise shouldn't the President re-examine the policies he has instituted to determine if abstinence only is working and does he need to restore funding to comprehensive sex education programs that have shown to be effective in the past.

The teen pregnancy rate in California in 1991 was higher than the national average and 11th in the nation. Over the following ten years, California's teen pregnancy rate dropped by 40% and in Berkeley the rate dropped by 50%. [45] They accomplished this through a comprehensive health education course that includes overall health, mental health counseling, HIV testing, pregnancy counseling, birth control methods, and sexual health education. Because these programs have worked so well, California is the only state in the nation that has turned down federal funds for abstinence only education that prohibits the teaching of birth control methods. This policy has allowed Berkeley to offer accurate, comprehensive sex education curricula that includes *both abstinence and birth control.* [46] The results have been a sharp decrease in unwanted teen pregnancies and abortions. While hundreds of millions of tax dollars go to abstinence only programs, Berkeley has had to fund their programs through other means, some of which come from the local and state government. However because of state budget cuts the programs are in jeopardy. Without these programs, the California Department of Finance predicts the decline in teen pregnancy rates will reverse-increasing an estimated 23% by 2008. [47]

The dumbing down of America's teens is not a sustainable policy. Kid's need honest answers to extremely difficult questions and the tools to make educated decisions. The pandering to the extreme right of the Republican Party in the face of overwhelming evidence that his policies are not working is once again evidence that Bush's "stay the course" attitude is not a sign of strength, but rather a sign of weakness, a lack of courage. Rational people who strongly believe in something, when confronted with overwhelming evidence to the contrary will re-evaluate their stance. That's true strength. If the evidence supports their belief then, and only then, will they stay the course. Bush is once again showing the evidence is not what motivates his decisions but rather his base, in this case the extreme religious right wing of the Republican Party.

According to Mickey Herskowitz who was to ghost write George W. Bush's book *A Charge to Keep* (yes W. didn't even write his own biography) "He told me that as a leader, you can never admit to a mistake. That was one of the keys to being a leader."

The Bush administration is not only "staying the course" of a failed policy in this country, but are exporting these same failed policies around the world by cutting funding for programs in countries that have been the hardest hit by the HIV/AIDS pandemic and by:

- Pushing for language promoting sexual abstinence for adolescents instead of comprehensive sexuality education and lobbying against language referring to reproductive health care at the United Nations Special Session on Children in May of 2002

- Rescinding U.S. support for the 1994 U.N. International Conference on Population and Development (ICPD) agreement. The U.S. delegation challenged the use of the terms "reproductive health" and "reproductive rights" [pro-choice language] and *opposed* the inclusion of a paragraph on adolescent reproductive health, particularly its promotion of "consistent condom use" as a central HIV/AIDS prevention strategy.

- Increasing funding for foreign abstinence only until marriage programs and decreasing funding for prevention efforts. A bill known as the Global Aids Bill allows faith based groups who receive funds to exclude information about contraceptive methods, including condoms.

- Reinstating the Global Gag Rule, prohibiting foreign organizations receiving U.S. funding from providing abortion information, counseling, or services. In August of 2003, the Bush administration expanded the Global Gag Rule to reach groups receiving family planning funds from the United States Agency for International Development (USAID). They have used this policy to restrict the activity of groups focused on sexuality education, HIV/AIDS prevention, violence against women, and reproductive health.

- Cutting off a total of $34million in funding for the United Nations Population Fund (UNFPA) which provides family planning, maternal and child health care, and sexually transmitted disease prevention and treatment to millions of people in over 160 countries. UNFPA has estimated the funding cut by the U.S. could have prevented as many as 2 million unwanted pregnancies, 800,000 induced abortions, 4,700 maternal deaths and 77,000 infant and child deaths. The

U.S. is the only country ever to deny funding to UNFPA for non-budgetary reasons. [48]

Poor countries like Uganda that have, up until now, had success in reversing their rate of HIV transmission by promoting prevention programs such as the use of condoms along with abstinence will likely see a reversal in those statistics.

The only explanation for the adamant support of abstinence only policies that are not effective in reducing unwanted pregnancy and abortion is that Bush views this as a political issue and not a moral one. Bush supporters should assess whether political pandering to the "single issue voter" base, at the expense of proven comprehensive education programs, is consistent with their moral values.

14

Where Are We Going?

"The liberties of our country, the freedom of our civil Constitution, are worth defending at all hazards; and it is our duty to defend them against all attacks...It will bring an everlasting mark of infamy...if we should suffer them to be wrested from us by violence without a struggle, or to be cheated out of them by the artifices of false and designing men."
Samuel Adams

In the second chapter the question was asked "How did we end up here?" It seems appropriate to conclude by trying to determine where we are headed. We have an administration run by the ultra-right wing of the Republican Party, with a Republican Congress, a Republican Senate, a conservative Supreme Court that will soon be conservative to the extreme, and a Judicial branch becoming more and more conservative through political appointments.

This administration has, as we've seen throughout this book, sold this country to corporate interest. Or more accurately, they sold their takeover to us and we've paid dearly. Nearly every appointment this President has made has been a payoff in one way or another to party supporters or lobbyists with corporate interests. Agencies like the EPA are now being run, by proxy, by the energy industry, in effect they have been privatized. Even our voting system has been turned over to the private sector. While the Republican Party has historically run on a platform of smaller government and fiscal responsibility, and accused Democrats as the tax and spend party, we've seen the privatization of government agencies, tax breaks for the most affluent among us resulting in record deficits and a stagnating economy and an ever widening gap in income evidenced by the fastest rise in poverty in years as middle class people sink further into debt and the gutting of federal programs designed to help the middle and lower class. We've seen corporate tax breaks and corporate welfare on a scale unmatched since the early part of the 20th century. Exxon Mobile earned *$8.4 BILLION* for the forth quarter 2004, ($25 Billion for the year) the single largest quarterly earnings report in history while gas prices are at record levels. The President's response to energy costs was to ask Americans not to take unnecessary trips and ordered his staff to turn off lights and computers at night. More Americans are living without health insurance while the FDA has been turned over to the drug companies and is now staffed by former drug company lobbyists and Social Security and Medicare are under attack.

We've been lied into a war through the manipulation, and fabrication, of evidence by a small group of militaristic neo-cons and the cost has been funded by "emergency appropriations" that are not reflected in the budget making the deficits worse than the figures released suggest.

Terms like "tax and spend" and "liberal" have been vilified while a "borrow and spend" policy resulting in the worst deficits in history, which will adversely affect our children and grandchildren, has been accepted as responsible policy. This has been sold through bumper sticker slogans and by talking points distributed to conservative media hacks, who will spew the party line over and over and over until it is repeated by their followers as fact, by an administration that has campaigned on a platform of personal responsibility and of not leaving problems for future generations. So much for fiscal responsibility! Government should neither be too big nor too small, but rather as big as it needs to be to meet its obligations and not be gutted simply because extremists of one party say it's too big. (Chapter 11 discusses how the obligations of government, currently, have not been met).

We have a rubber stamp Congress that has continually blocked investigations into everything from vote fraud to the Downing Street memo's to the widespread corruption in the Republican Party leadership. This is by far the most corrupt executive and legislative branch in the history of our country, and people are paying with their lives. With all due respect to John W. Dean, the title of his book, *Worse Than Watergate,* is a gross understatement. (The book, however, is an excellent read)

This administration does not seem to understand the culture of the Muslim world, nor do most people in this country. This is a repeat of the mistake made during the Vietnam War. A 111 page report titled *Report of the Defense Science Board Task Force on Strategic Communication* [1] commissioned by Deputy Secretary of Defense Paul Wolfowitz discusses the enormous opposition in the Middle East to U.S. policies. The report says, "We call it a war on terrorism-but Muslims in contrast see a history-shaking movement of Islamic restoration. This is not simply a religious revival, however, but also a renewal of the Muslim World itself.

"If there is one overarching goal they [moderate and radical Islamists] share, it is the overthrow of what Islamists call the 'apostate' regimes: the tyrannies of Egypt, Saudi Arabia, Pakistan, Jordan, and the Gulf states. The United States finds itself in the strategically awkward-and potentially dangerous-situation of being the longstanding prop and alliance partner of these authoritarian regimes. Without the U.S. these regimes could not survive." [2] This is why, as the report states they hate our policies, and not our freedom [3] as Bush insists continually. The populations of the Muslim world view their governments as puppets of the U.S. and therefore view the U.S. as their oppressors. What the vast majority of Muslims really want, to varying degrees, is an Islamic government based on Islamic law, not democracy. The report recognizes this fact. While discussing the difference between the Cold War and the war on "terra" it says, "in stark contrast to the Cold War, the United States today is not seeking to contain a threatening state/empire, but rather seeking to convert a broad movement within Islamic civilization to accept the value structure of Western Modernity-an agenda hidden within the official rubric of a 'War on Terrorism'...[The Cold War emphasized] Dissemination of information to 'huddled masses yearning to be free.' Today we reflexively compare Muslim 'masses' to those oppressed under Soviet rule. This is a strategic mistake. There is no yearning-to-be-liberated-by-the-U.S. groundswell among Muslim societies-*except to be liberated perhaps from what they see as apostate tyrannies that the U.S. so determinedly promotes and defends."* [Emphasis in original] [4]

The report discusses the result of our Iraq adventure. "American direct intervention in the Muslim World has paradoxically elevated the stature of and support for radical Islamists, while diminishing support for the United States to single digits in some Arab societies...the dramatic narrative since 9-11 has essentially borne out the entire radical Islamist bill of particulars. American actions and the flow of events have elevated the authority of the Jihadi insurgents and tended to ratify their legitimacy among Muslims...What was a marginal network is now an Ummah-wide [the entire Muslim community] movement of fighting groups: the unifying context of a shared cause creates a sense of affiliation across the many cultural and sectarian boundaries that divide Islam." [5] The report makes clear what many have been saying all along: The invasion of Iraq has created more extremist fighters than it has eliminated and has legitimized them in the eyes of the moderate Muslim world. We are experiencing a rise in global terrorism while the President tells us we are safer because of the Iraq war. Their own report doesn't agree.

The Bush administration has entered into a war in Iraq and as was pointed out in chapter three there is no exit strategy because they don't plan to leave and in fact are very likely planning more military action in the region as per their quest for global domination. (Chapter's three and four). How did they convince millions of people of things that are not true? First, reports like the one above are virtually ignored by the press the last few years and have been replaced with bumper sticker slogans like, "They hate our freedom," "We're bringing democracy," "Freedom's on the march," and "We have to fight them over there so we don't have to fight them here."

We have a press that is asleep at the wheel, the proof being the majority of voters who voted for George W. Bush in 2004 still believe that Saddam Hussein was complicit in the September 11ᵗʰ attacks on the World Trade Center and the Pentagon and had WMD, even though the final report of the Iraq Survey Group (ISG), presented to Congress by Charles Duelfer (the Duelfer report) concluded the opposite. Also a Senate intelligence Committee report and an earlier ISG report by David Kay came to the same conclusion and the 9-11 Commission found Saddam offered no support for al-Qaeda. These same people, when polled, said that if Iraq did not have WMD and did not provide support to al-Qaeda, the U.S. should not have gone to war. [6] The press has done a great job of taking dictation, simply passing on this administration's "talking points" without investigation or fact checking.

The case of Armstrong Williams, a prominent newspaper columnist and talk show host, shows this administration is not above using state run propaganda by manipulating our "free press" in violation of federal laws. Williams was paid $240,000 to promote Bush's No Child Left Behind plan under the guise of legitimate news. Since then it has been discovered the government has been producing many prepackaged "video news releases" touting support for NCLB, Bush's prescription drug plan, and his Social Security privatization plan and distributing them to news organizations for release during news programs purposely designed to look like news. In one a woman "acting" as a reporter inserts commentary supporting NCLB and ends her report saying, "In Washington, I'm Karen Ryan reporting."

Government Accountability Office (GAO) auditors, in a recent report, found the Bush administration violated the law by "disseminating covert propaganda" in the United States. The report also says, "The failure of an agency to identify itself as the source of a prepackaged news story misleads the viewing public by encouraging the audience to believe that the broadcasting news organization developed the information. The prepackaged news stories are purposefully designed to be indistinguishable from news segments. When the television viewing public does not know that the stories they watched on television news programs about the government were in fact prepared by the government, the stories are, in this sense, no longer purely factual. The essential fact of attribution is missing." [7]

The disturbing point is that news rooms will accept these video releases and run them as news and facts, without edit, and allow people to believe they are watching news instead of what they really are, prepaid government info-mercials, state propaganda.

While propaganda is an effective and necessary tool to be used against an enemy, it should cause concern when the government interferes with the free press and uses it against the people of the United States. It should also cause great concern to find out the Bush administration is engaged in a policy of propaganda designed to gain support for future military conflict against countries that pose no threat to the United States. The propaganda used by the neo-cons in the Bush administration to gain support for the invasion of Iraq by manipulating and fabricating evidence (see chapter 3 and 4), which has led to disaster in Iraq, is not slowing their plans for global domination but rather is being used as a lesson for future media manipulation and militaristic endeavors.

Contrary to the Bush administrations rhetoric that everything is going as planned in Iraq, the report commissioned by chief neo-con Paul Wolfowitz (the strategic communication report cited above) is the result of the Defense Departments recognition of their failures in Iraq and their desire to have a better outcome for their next militaristic adventure.

Completed in September of 2004, the report was withheld until after the November Presidential elections. In the memo creating the task force dated May 20, 2004 titled *Terms of Reference-Defense Science Board 2004 Summer Study on the Transition to and from Hostilities,* Wolfowitz writes, "Our military expeditions to Afghanistan and Iraq are unlikely to be the last such excursion in the global war on terrorism." He discusses the need for "intelligence preparation of the battlefield in the years-not weeks or months-preceding hostilities."

While Wolfowitz points out the need to ensure "democracy, and human rights," which we have seen the majority of the people in that region don't want the former and the U.S. has not provided the latter, he also speaks to the failure to bring stability to Iraq after the fall of Baghdad. All of these things, he believes, "would be facilitated by successfully shaping activities *in the years before the outbreak of hostilities.*"

Wolfowitz then instructs the task force to focus on "The gathering of long-lead intelligence and effective preparation of the battlefield-in absence of an immediate threat [which will] require diligence, foresight and preparation." [8] The "long-lead" intelligence is necessary to provide the time it takes to cherry-pick and manipulate it as we saw in the run-up to the invasion of Iraq. The phrase "in absence of an immediate threat" should cause great concern, because we now know Iraq did not pose an immediate threat and look at where we are. Moreover the fact that they still have the same mindset regarding future conflicts is troubling.

Besides pointing out the problems faced in Iraq, as discussed above, the report extensively studies ways to "shape" and influence perception among the "target audiences" by, among other things, utilizing private sector media.

"The new U.S. strategic communications effort should utilize the same media as do the private sector marketing and political campaigns." The report says. "Their deployment tactics should be adapted to government needs. Channels include classic broadcast media such as television, film, newspaper, radio, periodicals and e-magazines. *Interactive channels, as described above, permit a sustained conversation. Country by country, target audience by target audience, the most credible channels and the most promising techniques need to be identified and used to deliver appropriate messages.*" [9] Simply stated, the report is suggesting the government use the free press to disseminate one sided information, or propaganda (the appropriate message), to create a "sustained conversation," which would begin, if necessary, years before hostilities begin. Dictator X has weapons of mass destruction and is a threat to the U.S will be repeated over and over.

The authors of the report suggest ways to utilize the private sector. "These observers see value not only in leveraging private sector competencies but in new structures and a *degree of distance* [emphasis in original] that attracts credible messengers with non-government resumes, creative thinkers and talented communicator's uncomfortable working with government agencies." [10]

Translated; credible messengers with no apparent connection to the government having a degree of distance, means it will be *intentionally* impossible to determine the difference between news and government propaganda.

If this all sounds like a conspiracy theory by the black helicopter crowd, just remember the Government Accountability Office has already found this government has been distributing pre-packaged news, otherwise known as propaganda, illegally in this country, as discussed above, and we know the evidence for the invasion of Iraq was manipulated and passed to the media as fact for public consumption. The report recommends ways to build on "factors that motivate human behavior" and "create message authority." [11] This is happening. This administration has become very adept at "staying on message" to the point that they don't argue their position or facts when disputed by people like Richard Clarke, Paul O'Neill, Joe Wilson and others, but rather attack the messenger and provide the bumper sticker slogans for their followers to repeat. The vast majority of Bush supporters that still believe these fabrications are testimony that propaganda works.

When Paul Wolfowitz says, "our military expeditions to Afghanistan and Iraq are unlikely to be the last," believe him!

Over the last twenty years or so television news has gone from being a public service to being a for-profit part of the corporation that owns the network. Pressured to get ratings which bring in advertising dollars, news has been relegated to tabloid status. Due to de-regulation of the industry an ever smaller number of large corporations now controls everything we see, hear and read. Anyone who thinks these mega-corporations don't influence their news rooms, thereby influencing what we get to see or not see, would be mistaken. Corporations like General Electric that have billions of dollars in government military contracts and owns NBC, CNBC, MSNBC, 28 local television stations in the U.S., Universal Pictures and a 30% share of Paxson Communications. [12] Ultra-conservative Rupert Murdoch's News Corp owns 35 local television stations in the U.S. alone, many in the same markets, 18 DBS and cable stations, 4 film studio's, over 25 newspapers around the world, 5 magazines and 38 publishing companies. [13] Clear Channel, whose vice chairman bought the Texas Rangers making George W. Bush a multi-millionaire, owns 1,225 radio stations and 39 television stations many in the same markets in the U.S. [14]

The Founding Fathers considered a free press fundamental to the success of our democracy. A "Market Place of Ideas" where the people would be the ultimate check on the government and where the people would hold the government accountable. The press would be independent from and beyond the authority of the government and would be responsible for keeping the public well informed and provide a clearing house, if you will, of ideas to be debated. However, in the current day and age of television the flow of ideas has become a one-way street. It is impossible for individuals to be a part of the national debate. We can't simply walk into a television studio and ask to let our voice be heard. Therefore it is more important than ever for the media to do their job as it was envisioned by the Founding Fathers. Unfortunately this has not been the case. During the 2004 Presidential campaign MoveOn.org, while representing individual's voices, collectively, attempted to run paid ads critical of Bush administration policies. Chief

Counsel to the Republican National Committee, Jill Vogel, sent a letter to 250 stations across the country accusing them of being in violation of federal laws. "As a broadcaster licensed by the Federal Communications Commission, you have a responsibility to the viewing public, and to your licensing agency, to refrain from complicity in any illegal activity…Now that you have been apprised of the law, to prevent further violations of federal law, we urge you to remove these advertisements from your station's broadcast rotation." [15] They were. This was happening at a time when the Bush administration was illegally disseminating propaganda through "pre-packaged news" releases and paying commentators for favorable coverage of their policies. Whether one agrees with Move On's message or not, the fact that the media was coerced into censoring it should cause concern.

On February 3, 2005, Fox News' Brit Hume "reported" "It turns out that FDR himself planned to include private investment accounts in the Social Security program when he proposed it. In a written statement to Congress in 1935, Roosevelt said that any Social Security plans should include, quote, 'Voluntary contributory annuities, by which individual initiative can increase the annual amounts received in old age,' adding that government funding, quote, 'ought to ultimately be supplanted by self-supporting annuity plans.'" Hume was implying that Roosevelt said Social Security should be privatized as Bush was proposing.

The speech Roosevelt gave in 1935 actuality had three parts to it. The first part addressed the elderly who would retire in 1935 who never paid into Social Security, because Social Security was just beginning. Their retirement would have to be funded by the government.

The second part of the speech referred to the mandatory or compulsory contributions through the FICA tax which eventually would become a self supporting system whereby the government could phase out their role of paying for people to old to contribute in 1935. This is what we currently have today, the current generation paying for the elderly moving into retirement and what Roosevelt meant by "self supporting annuities."

The third part of Roosevelt's speech referred to a voluntary annuity that would *supplement* the mandatory part of the program.

Hume picks two sentences out of Roosevelt's speech, the second being only a partial sentence, which effectively distorts the entire theme of the speech. After the first sentence quoted by Hume, the second sentence reads in full, "It is proposed that the federal government assume one-half of the *old pension plan,* which [and here is where Hume picks up] ought to ultimately be supplanted by self-supporting annuities." This is important because what Roosevelt was saying is not that Social Security should be replaced with private accounts but that the *old pension plan,* ½ of which was funded by the government to people too old to contribute at the beginning, would eventually be replaced by Social Security FICA tax relieving the government of the burden, referring to the first part of the speech which Hume ignores altogether. [16] Hume also ignores the second part of the speech in which Roosevelt talks about the mandatory contributions which we know today and that Roosevelt in no way shape or form mentions going away. Hume also neglects to mention the voluntary contributory annuities would be a *supplement* to Social Security, not a replacement for.

He did this not as an editorial or a commentary piece but as a factual piece of news reporting. Hume's capacity at Fox "News" (which is owned by Rupert Murdoch's News Corp) is managing editor and anchor. These inaccuracies and distortions happen on a daily basis on Fox "News." [17] This is not news, but the definition of *Strategic Communication meant to shape the message and influence the target audience.* It works amazingly well. In the weeks after Hume's piece aired on Fox, one only had to listen to the call in talk shows to hear the *target audience* authoritatively repeat that Roosevelt himself wanted private accounts for Social Security. The President himself evoked Roosevelt's name in his State of the Union Address regarding Social Security privatization. James Roosevelt Jr., former associate commissioner of Social Security and Grandson of Franklin D. Roosevelt said, "The implication that FDR would support privatization of America's greatest national program is an attempt to deceive the American people and an outrage." [18] He has also called for Brit Hume's apology and resignation. Like that's going to happen. Can anyone say revisionist history?

When you're watching an interview with a journalist who's risking his life in Baghdad discussing the latest wave of violence and the interviewer interrupts to say, "Sorry, we have to cut away for breaking news in California" and they cut to the Michael Jackson trial, you know there's something very wrong with the media in this country.

The average citizen probably can't discuss the details of the indictment against Jack Abramoff, even if they know who he is, or his connection to Congressional leaders, because the media is not covering it effectively. They probably don't know who Tom DeLay is or the indictments against him, because the media is not covering it. Few probably know how the Medi-Care prescription drug bill got passed through Congress or the fact that DeLay was reprimanded for his role in the bill's passage by the Ethics Committee, because the media didn't report it. Very few people know that since Representative John Conyers couldn't get a hearing in the Republican controlled Congress to look into voter fraud, after the

2004 elections, he held his own hearings and the report was published in book form in January 2005 titled *What Went Wrong In Ohio*, and fewer have read it, because the media didn't report it. Why hasn't the media reported on the legitimate question of why the "terra" alert bounced from yellow to orange and back like a ping-pong ball all throughout 2004, but since the election there's been no mention of the alerts. The ever-changing alerts would often take up at least the first segment on the evening news broadcasts upstaging either bad news for the Bush administration or a Kerry event leaving the impression they were politically motivated. Former Homeland Security Director, Tom Ridge said, "More often than not we were the least inclined to raise it. Sometimes we disagreed with the intelligence assessment…There were times when some people were really aggressive about raising it, and we said, *'For that?'*" [19]

We hear about the deficits, but how many know what the number is and its impact on the economy? Why doesn't that story get any coverage? Why hasn't the media reported the Davis-Bacon Act of 1931 was suspended by Bush on September 7, 2005 in the wake of Hurricane Katrina? The Davis-Bacon act requires construction workers be paid "no less than the locally prevailing wage" on government public works contracts. And that Halliburton has received a no-bid contract in the region at the exclusion of local contractors and because of the suspension of the Davis-Bacon Act they can employ outside workers for less than the prevailing wage thereby increasing their profit margin.

Why doesn't the majority of the American public know about the *Report of the Select Committee on Intelligence on the U.S. Intelligence Community's Prewar Intelligence Assessments on Iraq,* released on July 9, 2004? [20] This Senate report confirms all the other independent reports that have said Iraq had no WMD, no links to al-Qaeda, and no involvement in the September 11th attacks. The report cited the Presidential Daily brief given to the President ten days after 9-11, on September 21, 2001. (Not to be confused with the September 6, 2001 PDB given to Bush before 9-11 warning that al-Qaeda was preparing to attack in the U.S. and was surveilling sky-scrappers in New York). The report also cites many instances where the intelligence community refuted the "facts" the administration was feeding to the American people and to Congress. This is absolute proof that the intelligence the administration was getting was not faulty, as the President and the Vice President has said continually. No, the intelligence was ignored and manipulated to paint Iraq as an imminent threat. The committee, made up of nine Republicans and eight Democrats, unanimously endorsed the reports findings. The American public doesn't know this because it didn't get the coverage it deserved.

The above report was only the first part. Phase two, which was to investigate how the administration used the Iraq intelligence, was due to be completed shortly afterward. Senator Pat Roberts (R-KS), the committee Chairman said of phase two, "It is a priority. I made my commitment and it will get done." Shortly afterward he reversed himself saying it wouldn't be fair to produce phase two so close to the November Presidential elections. After the elections, Roberts said what's the point, the elections are over. Roberts has stonewalled phase two for almost a year forcing Senate minority leader, Harry Reid (D-NV) to invoke a seldom used provision of the Senate rules to place the body in closed session to force the Republican leadership to complete the report. Phase one proved the intelligence was not faulty, but the administration can still fall back on the defense that they simply "got it wrong, however; phase two will prove they manipulated and fabricated the evidence against Iraq, and lied to Congress and the American people, and these are impeachable offenses. And there is the reason for the stonewalling of the investigation.

The evening news broadcasts covered the Republican leadership denouncing Reid's actions, but virtually nothing about the reason Reid took that action, which was a year of frustration trying to get phase two complete so the American people will know the truth.

It's not that these stories, and many more, don't get covered at all but that they are often on page A-18 or on television as a passing headline. There doesn't seem to be any follow through. In contrast we endure extensive coverage of a girl missing in Aruba and day in and day out coverage for a year of the Scott Peterson trial. Ask anyone about Brad Pitt and Jennifer Aniston and they'll tell you "oh no, Brad's with Angelina Jolie, I saw them on the news in Africa together." How many people know that Robert Blake was acquitted? Do the survey among your circle of friends and I'll bet it's 100%.

Very often both sides are simply quoted spinning the information. The "reporter" doesn't ask questions and if they do they simply print the answer without any fact checking. The "reporter" has done their job, giving each side equal time, but has done very little reporting.

Fred W. Friendly the pioneering television producer and onetime President of CBS News once said, "Because television can make so much money doing its worst, it often cannot afford to do its best."

Contrary to what most people believe, we don't hold the distinction of having the freest press in the world. In an annual survey released by Freedom House.org the United States is in 24th place out of 193 countries, tied with Barbados, Canada, Dominica, Estonia and Latvia. [21]

We have the most secretive administration in history with a President that does not answer questions from the media, or more accurately, does not talk to the American people. Question and answer forums are either scripted or heavily screened to allow only Bush supporters in. In October of 2004, on the campaign trail in Ohio, questions from the hand picked audience included, does the President like broccoli, what's your most important legacy to the American people and what can supporters do to ensure he win Ohio. Protestors at events like these across the country are relegated to fenced in "free speech zones" blocks from media cameras. At the end of his first term, Bush held 15 solo news conferences compared to Clinton's 42, his fathers 83, Jimmy Carter's 59 Lyndon Johnson's 88, Kennedy's 65 and Eisenhower's 94, at the same point in their presidencies.

This secretiveness and message control (or strategic communication) is designed to keep the American people in the dark on matters discussed in this book, such as the intertwining of corporate interest and the government, the real reason for the Iraq war and placing the executive branch above the law. In chapter 10, *Cheney's Play,* the question was asked, "What is the motive of this administration's attempt to create a presidency that is not accountable to Congress or the American people?" The neo-con agenda, as discussed in chapters three and four, of global domination that calls for military actions across the planet would require secrecy to the extreme and the removal of constitutional checks and balances by Congress over the executive branch. Cheney's own words have provided the clues to this point in that, as we've seen, he doesn't believe that a President's authority to wage war should be restricted by Congress. Their extreme ideological view of a corporate government and the transfer of virtually all government programs and agencies to the private sector would also require the executive branch be free from Congressional oversight. As Grover Norquist, a close advisor to the President and Karl Rove, once said, "My goal is to cut government in half in twenty five years to get it down to the size where we can drown it in the bathtub." Over the last twenty years he has been raking in huge amounts of corporate contributions for the extreme right wing of the Republican Party to do just that. We're watching the implementation of these policies right before our eyes over the last five years, many of which break not only U.S. law but international laws. The power needed to do this would require the executive to assume more authority than is granted under the Constitution and a legislative branch negligent in its duties of checking such overreaching. With the legislative and judicial branches firmly in control of the extreme right, in effect a one party form of government, this is exactly what we are witnessing. Also by assuming this authority they are insuring, in their view their ideology remains in power for generations to come.

Many see the corporate takeover of the government and accuse Bush and Cheney of selling the government to corporate interest. This is inaccurate because it implies that corporate interest has paid for it. While they have contributed record amounts to political campaigns the money they are receiving in return dwarfs the initial investment. The money to be made through the deregulation of their industries, perpetual wars, protection from lawsuits and the emptying of the countries treasury in the form of corporate tax breaks, or corporate welfare, means that we the tax payers have in effect paid them to take over the government. Bush and Cheney simply brokered the deal. And brokers always make a handsome commission, in this case a commission on billions of dollars.

The secrecy, militarism, attempting to control all forms of media through corporate allies and the corporatization of the government itself has lead to comparisons between the Bush administration and Fascist regimes throughout history. While enraging supporters of Bush and Cheney, the comparisons are there to be made.

On February 27, 1933 terrorists burned the Reichstag building in Berlin Germany, the equivalent of the Capitol building in Washington D.C. (Many historians believe the Nazi's themselves were responsible for the crime). When Hitler arrived on the scene with the media in tow, he declared war on the terrorists (he used the word terrorists) and their sponsors, reminiscent of Bush standing on the rubble of the World Trade Center with his bullhorn. The terrorists were identified as the Comintern (communists) and their ideological sponsors were of Middle Eastern decent, the Jews. Hitler persuaded President Hindenburg to sign the Reichstag Fire Decree which abolished many of the civil rights provisions of the 1919 Weimar Republic Constitution. The Fire Decree, formerly known as the *Decree of the Reich President for the Protection of People and State* is similar in many was to the USA Patriot Act. Both deny certain civil liberties with the express purpose of protecting the people, such as the right to habeas corpus, search and seizures without a warrant (under the Patriot Act, if homeland Security wants a warrant all they have to do is tell a judge that it involves a terrorist investigation, without presenting any evidence, and the judge cannot deny it), wire taps and the search of medical records and library records without notifying the suspect. It's impossible to know if these provisions of the Patriot Act are being abused because the person providing the records is prohibited by the law to acknowledge that they have been contacted by the FBI. Under the Patriot Act, the definition of a terrorist was broadened to such a point that groups exercising their constitutionally protected rights to protest could now be considered terrorist groups. Both were passed within weeks of a terrorist attack.

Hitler also merged the government with corporation by appointing former industry executives to high level government positions. Government contracts were exclusively given to Nazi Party loyalists in Hitler's Germany. The 1983 American Heritage Dictionary defined fascism as "A system of government that exercises a dictatorship of the extreme right, typically through the merging of state and business leadership, together with belligerent nationalism." Fascist governments place the rights of corporations above the rights of the individual. In 1935, in *The Doctrine of Fascism,* Benito Mussolini wrote, "The corporate State considers that private enterprise in the sphere of production is the most effective and useful instrument in the interest of the nation." The comparison of the Bush administration to a Fascist regime cannot be ignored when one considers actions like the suspension of the Davis-Bacon Act and chapters five through nine in this book.

Hitler's empire building began with the annexation of Austria, which was a pre-emptive war, in which he claimed he was liberating them from the terrorists, the communists and the Jew's. As in this country currently, dissenting voices that disagreed with the policies of the Nazi regime were labeled as anti-German and unpatriotic and often treasonous. Extreme nationalism was the theme of the day. Unquestioning loyalty to the government's decisions was the only acceptable course. This theme was repeated over and over by "journalists" paid to promote the agenda. All journalists in Nazi Germany were card carrying members of the Nazi Party. The simplistic slogans they used were very effective as predicted by Hitler. "The most brilliant propagandist technique will yield no success unless one fundamental principal is borne in mind constantly and with unflagging attention. It must confine itself to a few points and repeat them over and over." [22] As Attorney General John Ashcroft said, "You're either with us or you're with the terrorists" which we've heard over and over. Selling war to the German people was meticulously planed by Hitler's propaganda machine. In a conversation with allied intelligence officer and psychologist Gustave Gilbert on April 18th 1946, while on trial in Nuremberg, Hermann Goering discussed how it was accomplished. Gilbert said the average person doesn't want war to which Goering agreed but stated that, "after all, it is the leaders of the country who determine the policy." Gilbert pointed out that in a democracy "the people have some say in the matter through their elected officials and in the U.S. only Congress can declare wars." Goering replied, "That is well and good, but, voice or no voice, the people can always be brought to the bidding of the leaders. That is easy. All you have to do is tell them they're being attacked and denounce the pacifists for lack of patri-

otism and exposing the country to danger. It works the same way in any country." [23]

Hitler also portrayed himself as a Christian often ending his speeches in
prayer. His propaganda machine made him a messianic figure and encouraged
religious teaching and prayer in schools and promoted the idea of a "good versus
evil" dichotomy when it came to the Reich's enemies. The phrase, "Gott Mit
Uns"—God is with us—was everywhere, including on the uniforms of the military. Hitler and Goebbels recognized the benefit of convincing a basically Christian nation they had God on their side. Hitler once said, "Secular schools can
never be tolerated because such a school has no religious instruction and a general
moral instruction without a religious foundation is built on air; consequently, all
character training must be derived from faith." Does this sound familiar, like
faith based initiatives?

After rounding up and jailing all the communist members of parliament and
replacing them with Nazi's the Reichstag was effectively under the control of one
party, a rubber stamp for Hitler's policies. On March 23, 1933 they passed the
Enabling Act giving Hitler legislative powers and the power to suspend the constitution which gave him unlimited power (the dictatorship) to save the country
from its enemies. The only members to vote against it were the SPD (the Social
Democratic Party). With these newly established powers, Hitler outlawed the
KPD (the Communist Party) and the SPD and banned the formation of any new
parties.

Do these comparisons mean we are living in a Fascist state? That Bush and his
cronies are a gang of Nazi's? One thing is for certain; we are a lot closer to an
authoritarian form of government than we were just five years ago. By using their
current single party power to further suspend constitutional rights (I say further
because portions of the Constitution have already been suspended), and their
corporatization of everything from our free press to our voting process, their
attempts to silence protest by relegating dissenters to "free speech zones," and the
attacking and labeling of anyone who questions their policy as un-patriotic and
un-American, the only thing left for us to completely cross over that bridge is the
suspension of the Constitution altogether, the outlawing of the Democratic
Party, and the cancellation of elections. Simply because the current administration has not made these final steps does not mean the comparisons to Fascism are
not valid. It does not require zero opposition to be a Fascist tyrant. Hitler had
opposition during his rise to power. The point is that democracies can and have
failed throughout history. Germany was a democracy when Hitler came on the

scene. The comparisons should not be arrogantly dismissed as outlandish impossibility.

The most troubling comparison between 1930's Germany and early 21st century America is the complacency about where our government is taking us, the disconnect that is apparent when people simply accept bumper sticker slogans as fact. The disillusionment, or belief that "things will never change" and "what can I possibly do." After World War II the average German, when asked "how did this happen" replied in one of three ways:

1. We didn't think this could happen here

2. We didn't see it coming (or didn't want to see it coming) and

3. If you weren't doing anything wrong, you had nothing to worry about.

We hear this from average American's today. The phrase, "Those who don't learn from history are doomed to repeat it" is not a cliché. Nor is Ben Franklin's observation that "those who give up essential liberties to purchase a little temporary freedom deserve neither."

In his farewell address on January 17th, 1961, Dwight Eisenhower warned the American people of the consequences of corporate power dominating government. "In the councils of government, we must guard against the acquisition of unwarranted influence, whether sought or unsought, by the military-industrial complex. *The potential for the disastrous rise of misplaced power exists* and will persist.

"We must never let the weight of this combination endanger our liberties or Democratic processes. We should take nothing for granted. Only an alert and knowledgeable citizenry can compel the proper meshing of huge industrial and military machinery of defense with our peaceful methods and goals, so that security and liberty may prosper together." [24] The Republican Party of Theodore Roosevelt, Dwight Eisenhower and Barry Goldwater wouldn't recognize their party today.

Fascism is not the only comparison to be made to the Bush/Cheney administration.

An oligarchy is a regime in which all the political power rests with a small group of society, usually through wealth, military strength or political influence. In an oligarchy politicians don't represent the people that elected them; rather they represent their own interests and the interests of their cronies. There is certainly evidence of this in this country with the politicians of both parties under the control of their corporate contributors and special interest groups. The transformation to an oligarchy is usually the result of gradual accumulation of unchecked economic power. Oligarchs often rule behind the scenes exerting control through economic means. The apartheid regime in South Africa was an oligarchy based on racism. A small segment of society, the Afrikaans-speaking whites, controlled all access to education, the countries resources and trade and denied this to the black majority.

A plutocracy is simply an oligarchy of the wealthy. The word comes from the ancient Greek *ploutos* meaning wealth. A country whose government is run by an affluent wealthy class and derives its power by perpetuating a high degree of economic inequality and exerting its influence in the political process is considered a plutocracy. The comparison here to the Bush administration is pretty obvious. Wealthy entities writing legislation and influencing policy in return for enormous amounts of campaign contributions and tax cuts for corporations and the wealthiest 1% of Americans certainly doesn't benefit the average person. On the contrary, it goes a long way to perpetuating the economic inequality in this country. While there has been a push in recent years for campaign finance reform to reduce the influence corporate money has over candidates, any legislation addressing this would have to be passed by the politicians that benefit from the practice in the first place. Many are not willing to give up the cash cow that easily.

Political theorists suggest the natural progression of democracy occasionally leads to oligarchy and that both an oligarchy and a plutocracy often morph into a more authoritarian form of government.

Then there are the Straussians. Straussians are not a form of government but followers of Leo Strauss' political philosophies. Strauss (1899-1973) was a German Jew who left Germany in 1937 as the Nazis were coming to power. He was a political philosopher who was teaching at the University of Chicago at the time of his death. Strauss held an extreme esoteric view of philosophy and politics. He believed the ancient philosophers never said exactly what they meant and there were hidden meanings in their teachings that only a select few would grasp. They did this, he surmised, because they lived in a time when it was dangerous to speak contrary to the beliefs of the day. A belief such as the earth was not the center of the universe, for instance, could get one killed in those times. By deciphering these hidden meanings, Strauss and his followers believed there was an "essential truth" about society, politics and history that only select elite could fathom and therefore needed to be withheld from those without the capacity to understand.

Strauss and his followers despised the counter culture of the 1960's. As young people became more and more disillusioned with their government, the war in Vietnam and the opposition to the civil rights movement, they broke with "normal" society which affirmed the Straussian belief that a liberal democracy would ultimately lead to a destructive nihilism. Strauss blamed a similar structure of liberalism and tolerance during the Weimar Republic of Germany for allowing Hitler to rise to power.

In order to prevent future collapses in society, Strauss and his followers subscribe to the view that Niccolo Machiavelli was right; there is a natural hierocracy of people that are destined to lead the masses. Machiavelli was a 16th century political philosopher who advocated, in his book *The Prince* the theory that "what ever was expedient was necessary," the ends justify the means and "an understanding that apparent cruelties and vice may be essential to maintaining stability and power." Machiavelli also disregards any connection between ethics and politics. "The prince should endeavor to be *seen* as merciful, religious, honest, and ethical. But in reality, the duties of the Prince don't allow him to actually posses any of these properties." This is one of Strauss' "essential truths" that the masses would not be able to handle, that the elite destined to lead would recognize there is no morality.

Strauss' views would go a long way in explaining the Bush/Cheney administration's obsession with secrecy and message control, and the reason their rhetoric almost never balances with their actions. The people are only told what they can handle. Manipulating information, or lying (let us call it what it is), is not only seen as morally acceptable but as a necessity in maintaining control to, in their view, prevent the breakdown of society, and wage war. Deception is an integral part of politics in their view.

By all accounts Strauss was an atheist, or at the very least agnostic, however he advocated a merging of religion and government, which is another Machiavellian view that the leaders should *appear* religious. While not being religious himself, Strauss argued that a secular society was the worst possible thing because it would lead to individualism, liberalism and eventually nihilism which would result in dissent. Religion, he believed, was for the masses alone and should be used as a way to manipulate the masses by playing to their often sincere moral values, while the leaders, the manipulators, were not bound by such constraints. It's interesting to note that many of the people surrounding Bush are secular Jew's who have aligned themselves with the religious right in this country. Bush himself, while claiming to be a born again evangelical Christian does not attend church.

Another view held by the followers of Strauss is that people can only be united if there is an external threat and if one doesn't exist then, following the Machiavellian philosophy, a threat would have to be manufactured.

There are many Straussians in and around the Bush administration. The number two in the Pentagon and one of the architects of the Iraq war, Paul D. Wolfowitz received his doctorate in political science under the tutelage of Leo Strauss at the University of Chicago in 1972. Abram Shulsky, the director of the Pentagon Office of Special plans (PNAC member profiled in chapter three) also received his doctorate under Strauss. Other Straussians include most of the PNAC members profiled in chapter three, Elliot Abrams (currently serving on the National Security Council, NSC), Richard Perle, William Kristol, Kristol's father Irving Kristol, considered the godfather of the neo-conservative movement, Under Secretary of Defense for Intelligence (Pentagon) Stephen Cambone and many senior fellows at the American Enterprise Institute (AEI) which employs Lynn Cheney, wife of the Vice President.

It's a little more than coincidence that all of these people who have advocated for the overthrow of Saddam Hussein and for wars in the Middle East for more than a decade are followers of Leo Strauss whose philosophy is deception of the masses and perpetual war.

The question of this chapter is Where are we Going? That question is now less difficult to answer. While the comparisons to fascism, oligarchy, plutocracy, authoritarianism, and Straussianism are now clear, there is no one direction that is identifiable. The answer is that we are witnessing a form of government that has yet to be named, a sort of morphing of or combination of all of the above with an emphasis on corporatization of the government with an underlying hint of theocracy (as per the Straussians). Corporations will, under Bush's vision, be handling our retirement, they'll decide what doctors we can see and when. Under the Bush administration, they are already deciding policy that affects them and dismantling legislation designed to protect us and our environment and they are already deciding policies affecting labor rights.

The path the Bush administration is taking us down is definitely not where most of us want to go. Suffice it to say that American democracy, under this regime, is broken and while it has faced challenges before, such as the Civil War, World War II, the Cold War and Watergate, nothing like this has been seen. We must recognize the fact that the last five years have been an attack on democracy and we must fight it.

George W Bush should have been nothing more than a foot note in history as the son of a former President who once ran for President himself, but failed.

Instead he will be remembered as the worst President in American history, not only for his failed domestic policies that will continue to affect 250 million Americans for years, but his foreign policies that will affect every person on the planet for years to come. His legacy will be his failed policies on terrorism and an unprecedented pre-emptive war in the Middle East that had nothing to do with September 11th 2001, which has made the world a more dangerous place.

Bush supporters to this day, still say Clinton did this, and Clinton did that, or Kerry would have done this, or that and all politicians are the same. This is an unacceptable defense of the crimes of the Bush administration. George Bush is well into his second term. The lies and corruption, the stonewalling of investigations, the manipulation of the media, the theft of our rights, and the stealing and plundering of our commons, all should be laid squarely at the feet of George W. Bush.

2006 is our chance to at least restore the two party system of government and hold those responsible for the mess we're in accountable. It is crucial; we can't wait until 2008 and neither can the world.

Post Script

As I was nearing the end of this writing, Hurricane Katrina hit New Orleans and the Gulf Coast on August 29th, just two weeks before the fourth anniversary of the September 11th attacks. As it became apparent, during the first crucial 72 hours after the disaster, that our government was not responding, it occurred to me that I am not over 9-11. As 72 hours turned into five days, I realized why. It's painfully clear that, while we'll never know if 9-11 could have been prevented, although it is highly likely it could have, our government didn't do anything with all the evidence that was available beforehand, and their response has been to use the tragedy as a means to further their agenda. (Former Senator Bob Graham has identified 12 ways 9-11 could have been prevented in his book *Intelligence Matters*). We know this; I wrote about it in this book, but somewhere inside me, unconsciously, I hoped someone in the administration was doing something to protect this country. But Katrina has made it clear there is nothing more important than the political agenda with this administration. Katrina, an act of God, couldn't have been prevented, but the lack of response could have been. God help us if there is a terrorist attack without warning. After the worst natural disaster in American history, we find out the President's choice to head FEMA, Mike Brown, was a Republican advance man for the President's campaign with absolutely no experience in disaster management. He worked, for 11 years, for the Arabian Horse Association supervising horse shows. Bush's political appointments to people with little or no experience for the posts they are holding are the norm not the exception. If, after Katrina, we saw our government functioning to its capacity, responding quickly and efficiently, we could say, "wow, what a tragedy, but look how fast things are getting done," lessening the psychological impact, but we can't. Our government's actions have made the tragedy worse, not only for the victims, but for all of us.

This is why I'm not over 9-11. Katrina has blown the deception that we are safer as a country wide open. We are not safer. After the election, many people cited Bush's strength and his ability to protect the nation from terrorism as reason for their support of him. The Presidents "stay the course" mentality, while presiding over one failure after another, should no longer be confused with strength, but rather a pathetic attempt to appear strong. The dispersal of blame, usually directed at a Democratic opponent or a whistle blower, and the inability to take responsibility for his own actions, also, should no longer be confused with strength.

The Bush apologists are already blaming the Governor of Louisiana and the Mayor of New Orleans (both Democrats) for not being prepared. In 2001 Bush's budget cuts cut the funding for the upgrade and maintenance for the Louisiana levee project. In 2004, the Army Corps of Engineers, for the first time in 36 years, all but ceased work on the levees because of lack of funds. [1] Both the Governor of Louisiana and the Mayor of New Orleans begged to restore the funding. In July of 2005, Governor Blanco asked Bush to accompany her on an aerial tour of the coastal region and asked that the money be restored in the upcoming energy bill. Bush sent word through the Secretary of Energy, Sam Bodman that there would be no funds because it would be "too costly with the current deficits." [2]

After the tragedy, Bush apologists began with their talking points. They're easy to recognize. All the right wing talk show hosts on Fox and the right wing radio talk shows use the exact phrases almost immediately after a news event breaks. One can listen to Limbaugh in the morning, and then throughout the day listen to the "news" anchors on Fox, and then in the evening O'Reilly, Hannity and Scarborough and they all say exactly the same thing as if they "got the memo." Then the next day around the water cooler, you hear the Bush supporters repeating it like parrots. It's a very effective propaganda tool or simply misinformation if you will. A couple of days after the storm they started with the "fact" that Bush pleaded with the governor to declare a State of Emergency two days before the storm hit, but she did nothing. This is an out and out lie which the administration is allowing to stand. On August 27, 2005, two days before Katrina made landfall, Governor Blanco sent an official letter through FEMA to the President not only declaring a State of Emergency, but asking the President to declare a Federal Emergency, something she cannot do. A state official can't declare a federal anything. The Bush administration agreed at which point it became the Federal government's responsibility and thereby George W. Bush's responsibility to act accordingly.

Another twist on the truth occurred on September 6, about a week after Katrina hit. A *Washington Times* article by editor-in-chief Wesley Pruden stated that Mayor Nagin "kept the city's 2,000 school buses parked and locked in neat rows when there was still time to take the refugees to higher ground." Right wing blogs began linking Pruden's piece to their web-sites. That night Fox News' Sean Hannity said, "Two thousand buses sat; 2,000 school buses." The next day Fox news political analyst and former Republican Speaker of the House Newt Gingrich picked it up and ran with it when he said, "the fact is there was more than enough busses to, in a methodical way, orderly way, help *every poor person in New Orleans leave the city.*" Gingrich repeated the claim on September 11 on ABC's Sunday morning news show *This week with George Stephanopoulos* and even had Stephanopoulos agreeing with him.

But these are the real facts:

- The Orleans Parish school district, which operates all of New Orleans public schools, only owns 324 school buses. [3]

- The Louisiana Department of Transportation and Development shows that as of May 5, 2005 the New Orleans Regional Transit Authority (RTA) owns 364 public buses, for a total of 688 buses. [4]

- Approximately 70 of the 688 busses are under repair and not available leaving a total of just over 600 buses. [5]

- There are over 100,000 poor and elderly people stranded in New Orleans.

- In July of 2005, a *Times Picayune* article said that in the event of a hurricane "Even if the entire fleet [of RTA buses] was used they could carry only about 22,000 people out of the city-far short of the 134,000 people estimated to be without cars in a recent University of New Orleans study." [6]

- The *New York Times* reported many of the city's buses were in use as Katrina approached evacuating people to the Superdome. [7]

We have all, by now, seen the AP photograph of the school buses in a parking lot up to their windshields in water. If the right wing pundits had said there were over 300 school buses that could have been used to help in the evacuation effort and another 300 plus city buses, that would be a valid argument that brings up valid questions. Even if those buses were not nearly enough needed to do the job, why the ones that were available were not used is a valid question. But once again by using false figures and intentionally distorting and manipulating facts and attacking any and all administration critics, they have shown themselves to be nothing more than Bush administration apologists. They have had their hands full distorting facts and putting out misinformation for every failure of this administration for the last five years without any challenge from what they call the "liberal" media.

The day after Katrina hit, on Tuesday August 30th, the President flew from his vacation home in Crawford, Texas to San Diego to once again link Saddam Hussein to 9-11 in a speech at North Island NAS. He then flew back to Crawford for one more day of rest and relaxation. On Wednesday, he finally flew back to Washington D.C. ending the longest vacation of any President in 36 years. For almost three days, the only person in charge of the Federal relief effort was Mike Brown.

Also on Wednesday, our Secretary of State, Condoleezza Rice, was shopping at Farragamo's in New York City and later that same night, attending a Monty Python comedy. Meanwhile offers of help from governments around the world were coming in, including from Iran and Cuba, yes Cuba, who offered 1600 doctors to go into the Superdome in New Orleans. It wasn't until Friday September 2, Five days after Katrina hit and countless numbers of people died that Rice finally showed up in Washington to say, "We're evaluating the offers of help." Shouldn't the fucking Secretary of State have been doing that on Tuesday morning?

Also on Friday, Bush said, "No one could have predicted the breech of the levees." In a one week long special in the *New Orleans Times Picayune* in 2002, they discussed exactly that, as did a number of other articles over the last three years. The article's examined the effects of Bush's budget cuts on the levee system. They predicted that a category three or above hurricane could breech the levees, flooding New Orleans, killing thousands and trapping thousands more in their homes and the Superdome. [8]

Dick Cheney didn't surface from his fishing vacation in Wyoming until Thursday September 8th, a full ten days after the event.

Since Bush/Cheney *took* office in 2001, they have been systematically cutting the budgets to states with Democratic Governors and representatives, especially in red states with Democratic Governors and representatives. Case in point: While there are no funds for Louisiana's levees, in the recent Highway Bill Alaska's Republican Representative Don Young has secured almost $1 billion to build a couple of bridges. One of them will connect Ketchikan with Gravina Island that has a population of 50. The bridge is being called a bridge to nowhere and the 50 residents of Gravina Island don't even want it. The Island has a small private airport. The President of Citizens Against Government Waste, Tom Schatz said there was so much pork in the highway bill that the money for the bridge project "could just as well buy all the residents Lear Jets."

Another case in point: After hurricane Francis hit Florida in 2004, *by noon the following day*, according to the White House website:

- About 100 trucks of water and 280 trucks of ice are present or will arrive in the Jacksonville staging area today. 900,000 Meals-Ready-to-Eat [MRE's] are on site ready to be distributed.

- Over 7,000 cases of food (e.g., vegetables, fruits, cheese, ham, and turkey) are scheduled to arrive in Winter Haven today. Disaster Medical Assistance Teams (DMAT) are on the ground and setting up comfort stations. FEMA community relations personnel will coordinate with DMATs to assist victims.

- Urban Search and Rescue Teams are completing reconnaissance missions in coordination with state officials.

- FEMA is coordinating with the Department of Energy and the state to ensure that necessary fuel supplies can be distributed throughout the state, with a special focus on hospitals and other emergency facilities that are running on generators.

- The Army Corps of Engineers will soon begin its efforts to provide tarps to tens of thousands of owners of homes and public buildings that have seen damage to their roofs.

- The National Guard has called up 4,100 troops in Florida, as well as thousands in other nearby states to assist in the distribution of supplies and in preparation for any flooding.

- The Departments of health and Human Services, Veterans Affairs, and Defense together have organized 300 medical personnel to be on standby. Medical personnel will begin deployment to Florida tomorrow.

- FEMA is coordinating public information messages with Georgia, Tennessee, Alabama, and North Carolina so that evacuees from Florida can be informed when it is safe to return.

- In addition to Federal personnel already in place to respond to Hurricane Charlie, 1,000 additional community relations personnel are being deployed to Atlanta for training and further assignment to Florida. [9]

Why did New Orleans not get the same attention that Florida got in 2004? There is a method to this madness. Florida not only has a Republican Governor but a Republican Governor who happens to be the President's brother. This was also three months before the Presidential elections. They kinda needed Florida.

The end game here is strictly political. The Republican Party will run Republican candidates in 2006 and 2008 on a platform that says your (Democratic) representative or your (Democratic) governor has failed you. Vote for me and I will get things done. This is what people will hear over and over and over until it becomes "fact." There is no regard for the people, only political posturing. This has been a hallmark of the Bush administration for five years now.

A bill introduced into Congress by John Conyers (D-MI), Sheila Jackson Lee (D-TX), Mel Watt (D-NC) and Jerrold Nadler (D-NY) sought an exemption from the bankruptcy bill passed, in April and due to take effect in October, for the victims of Hurricane Katrina. The Representatives said in a released statement the bill would "prevent new bankruptcy provisions from having adverse and unintended consequences for the hundreds of thousands now facing financial catastrophe by providing needed flexibility for victims of natural disaster." F. James Sensebrenner (R-WI), chairman of the House Judiciary Committee, said he will not hold hearings on the new bill. He has single handedly blocked our representatives from even voting on it. Sensenbrenner has also voted against a massive relief package for Katrina victims. [10] The goal of the bankruptcy bill, according to its supporters, is to protect the industry from the "deadbeats" and "frauds" even though the studies show 90% of filers are victims of one or more catastrophic life event (chapter 9). Are victims of the worst natural disaster in U.S. history, that have literally lost everything from family members to their homes, businesses and jobs, now deadbeats and frauds?

Are we safer as a country? The President's non-leadership after Katrina and the failure of Homeland Security and FEMA, also the President's responsibility, screams NO. Are we as a people ready to accept this fact now, or do we need a non-natural disaster, another 9-11 to convince us? The response to a natural disaster like Katrina would be very similar to what we can expect if there is a terrorist attack. If we suffer another terrorist attack, we're really going to need these agencies and the Federal government. So far, all they've been able to show us is that they can't, or won't, help. Has anyone seen the President's bullhorn!

September, 2005/1,575

Notes

Chapter 1: Introduction

1. See the PIPA archives at www.pipa.org

2. Ibid.

3. Report by www.politicsandscience.org also www.washingtonpost.com/ac2/wp-dyn/A31318-2003Aug7?language=printer and http://Democrats.reform.house.gov/features/politics_and_science/index.htm

4. www.pipa.org

5. http://people-press.org/reports/print.php3?PageID=834

6. http://mediamatters.org/etc/about.html

7. The big ten. www.thenation.com/special/bigten.html also www.takebackthemedia.com/owners.html

Chapter: 2 How Did We End Up Here?

1. www.thehill.com/news/012903/hagel.aspx

2. www.blackboxvoting.org

3. www.lancastercountyDemocrats.org/matulka.htm

4. *Fox News* November 8, 2002

5. *The Daily Standard.* A Rupert Murdoch Publication

6. www.wexler.house.gov/pressrelease/062104.htm

7. www.cnn.com/2004/allpolitics/11/05/voting.problems.ap/index.html

8. *Cincinnati Enquirer* Article by staff writer Erica Solvig. www.enquirer.com/editions/2004/11/05/loc.warrenvote05.html Also see interview by Keith Olbermann on MSNBC.

9. http://boe.cuyahogacounty.us/BOE/results/currentresults1.htm. Explanation by Cuyahoga County Officials for the discrepancy of the num-

bers. The explanation appears shaky at best, so they should be investigated. Absentee ballots, provisional ballots etc…could easily have been line itemed, Therefore the original numbers were left in. http://pages.ivillage.com/americans4america/idzo.html

10. www.ericblumrich.com/gta.html www.gregpalast.com/detail.cfm?artid=29&row=1

11. http://ustogether.org/florida_election.htm

12. www.commondreams.org/headlines04/1106-30.htm From an article by Thom Hartman.

Chapter 3: The Real Reason for the War with Iraq

- The common western spelling is Osama bin Laden, however the intelligence community refers to him as Usama bin Laden or UBL. When quoting sources, I use their spelling.

1. First hand account, By Secretary of the Treasury Paul O'Neill, of the first Cabinet meeting, as told to Ron Suskind in *The Price of Loyalty, George W. Bush, the White House, and the Education of Paul O' Neill* Pages 71-72.

2. Ibid, page 76.

3. Ibid, page 86.

4. *Against All Enemies*, by Richard A. Clarke, pages 29-32. Clarke began Federal Service in 1973 in the Office of the Secretary of Defense, as an analyst on nuclear weapons and European security issues. During the Reagan administration, he was Deputy Assistant Secretary of State for Intelligence. During the first Bush administration, he served as the Assistant Secretary of State for Politico-Military Affairs. In 1998, was appointed by President Clinton, as the first National Coordinator for Security, Infrastructure Protection, and Counterterrorism. Dubbed by the press as the Counterterrorism Czar.

5. CNN's Inside Politics, April 30, 2001

6. www.washingtonpost.com article titled *Top Focus Before 9/11 Wasn't on Iraq*, by Robin Wright, Thursday, April 1, 2004

7. Since his resignation from the CIA in October 2004, Michael Scheuer has been identified as the author of *Imperial Hubris*. He was a senior analyst at CIA and the head of the CIA bin Laden unit until 1999.

8. The Price of Loyalty, pages 258-59

Chapter 4: Making the Case as per RAD

1. http://www.whitehouse.gov/nsc/nss.pdf

2. *The Presidents Real Goal in Iraq* by Jay Bookman published in The *Atlanta Journal-Constitution* 9/29/2002

3. www.cbsnews.com/stories/2004/05/21/60minutes/ printable618896.shtml Full transcript of interview with Gen. Zinni by Correspondent Steve Kroft.

4. Colin Powell's February 5, 2003 speech to the United Nations Security Council. www.whitehouse.gov/news/releases/2003/02/ 20030205-1.html

5. Video of Rumsfeld on Face the Nation www.moveon.org/censure/ caughtonvideo See the full transcript of the Schieffer interview with Rumsfeld at www.cbsnews.com/htdocs/pdf/face_031404.pdf

6. www.fandz.com

7. *Douglas Feith: Portrait of a Neoconservative* by Tom Barry http:// rightweb.irc-online.org/analysis/2004/0409feith.php

8. *A Pretext for War 9/11, Iraq, and the Abuse of America's Intelligence Agencies* by James Bamford pp 288-289

9. Ibid, page 290

10. See *L.A. Weekly* interview, *Soldier for the Truth, Exposing Bush's Talking Points War*, with Karen Kwiatkawski by Marc Cooper Feb. 20-26 2004 at www.laweekly.com/ink/04/13/news-cooper.php Karen Kwiatkowski worked in the Pentagon at OSP. She was appalled at what she saw going on. Deeply frustrated and alarmed, and still on active duty, she began to write an anonymous column of internal dissent that was posted on the internet by former Colonel David Hackworth, America's most deco-rated veteran. She realized the only way to resist what she terms the "expansionist, imperialist" policies of the neoconservatives was by retir-

ing and taking up a public fight against them. A lifelong conservative, after twenty years in the Air Force, she retired with the rank of Lieutenant Colonel the week the invasion of Iraq began. She now writes under her own name. Karen Kwiatkowski is this generations Daniel Ellsberg.

11. *A Pretext for War* pp 290-291

12. www.laweekly.com/ink/04/13/news-cooper.php

13. *The Price of Loyalty* page 130

14. October 2003 interview with Fox TV anchor Brit Hume

15. *The Price of Loyalty* pp 148-49

16. *The President of Good & Evil, The Ethics of George W.* Bush by Peter Singer pp 180-81

17. This paragraph adapted from January 2005 issue of *Newsweek*. Article by Michael Isikoff titled *2001 Memo Reveals Push for Broader Presidential Powers* www.msnbc.msn.com/id/6732484/site/newsweek also read the memo at www.usdoj.gov/olc/warpowers925.htm

18. http://pilger.carlton.com/print/124759

Other Sources for Chapters Three and Four

1. www.americanprogress.org

2. General Zinni's speech to the Center for Defense Information on May 22, 2004. www.cdi.org

3. The *Rebuilding America's Defenses* document can be read at www.newamericancentury.org/RebuildingAmericasDefenses.pdf

4. *A Clean Break: A New Strategy For Securing The Realm* can be read at www.israeleconomy.org/strat1.htm

Update to Chapters Three and Four

1. Bush Administration's First Memo on al-Qaeda Declassified, edited by Barbara Elias, February 10, 2005 www.gwu.edu/~nsarchiv/NSAEBB/NSAEBB147/index.htm There are links on this site to all three of Clarke's memos. The August 6th PDB is at www.onegoodmove.org/1gm/whitehouse.pdf

2. *Rumsfeld Seeks to Revive Burrowing Nuclear Bomb* by Walter Pincus, *Washington Post* February 1, 2005.

3. Center for Defense Information www.cdi.org/pdfs/doe-fy06.pdf

4. *Rumsfeld Seeks to Revive Burrowing Nuclear Bomb* by Walter Pincus, *Washington Post* February 1, 2005.

5. The Downing Street Memos can be found at http://www. timesonline.co.uk

6. *The Other Bomb Drops* by Jeremy Scahill, *The Nation*, June 1st 2005

Chapter 5: U.S.A., Inc.

1. For an in depth discussion on the Santa Clara County v. Southern Pacific Railroad case read Thom Hartmann's book *Unequal Protection: The Rise of Corporate Dominance and Theft of Human Rights*. Also *Everyman's Constitution* by Howard Jay Graham and The Conspiracy Theory of the fourteenth Amendment by Graham at *The Yale Law Journal,* Vol. 47:341, 1938

2. *The Confessions of a Reformer* by Frederic C. Howe pp. 154-55

3. See the transcript of Theodore Roosevelt's 1912 speech at www.ssa.gov/history/trspeech.html

4. Center for Responsive Politics www.opensecrets.org/industries/indus.asp?Ind=E01 Also see *Power Rangers* by Craig Aaron Nov 21, 2003 www.tompaine.com/scontent/9465.html

5. *A Year in the Life of Spencer Abraham* by Jeffrey St. Clair www.counterpunch.org/stclair0418.html

6. CBSNews.com September 26, 2003 www.cbsnews.com/stories/2003/09/26/poltics/printable575356.shtml

7. *U.S Coal Fired Electricity Plants among North America's Largest Polluters,* Study Shows by Phill Courvrette, *Associated Press* January 13, 2005 citing a study by the Commission for Environmental Cooperation. www.enn.com/today.html?id=6921

8. *New York Times* December 4, 2001

9. *Nominee's Interior Stress* by John D. Echeverria. *National Law Journal* January 22, 2001 www.law.georgetown.edu/gelpi/papers/norton.htm

10. Bush administration ties to (page 3) www.citizen.org/documents/ DominionCorpProfile04.pdf

11. *Appalachia is Paying Price for White House Rule Change.* By Joby Warrick, *Washington Post* August 17, 2004; Page A01 www.washingtonpost. com/ac2/wp-dyn/A6462-2004Aug16?language=printer

12. Ibid.

13. *The Price of Loyalty* by Ron Suskind page 146

14. Center for Responsive Politics

15. *A Year in the Life of Spencer Abraham* by Jeffrey St. Clair

16. Center for Responsive Politics

17. The 1972 Texas Clean Air Act exempted (grandfathered) plants built before 1971 from new stricter pollution controls. By the mid 90's however Cabot was to comply with curbs to pollution. See article by Jason Leopold titled *Bush's Choice for Energy Secretary Was One of Texas' Top Five Worst Polluters.* www.commondreams.org/cgi-bin/print.cgi?file=/ views05/0116-09.htm

18. Read the Federal Advisory Committee Act at www.epic.org/open_gov/ faca.html

19. *Worse than Watergate, The Secret Presidency of George W. Bush* by John W. Dean page 78.

20. *Crimes Against Nature* by Robert F. Kennedy Jr. in the December 11, 2003 issue of *Rolling Stone.* www.rollingstone.com/politics/story/_/id/ 5939345 see the chapter "Looting the Commons" in the article.

21. From the National Environmental Trust. www.net. org/proactive/newsroom/release.vtml?id=27498

22. National Resources Defense Counsel www.nrdc.org/bushrecord/ printArticles/health_mercury.asp

23. www.nwf.org/nationalwildlife/article.cfm?issueid=62&articleid+803

24. Ibid.

Chapter 6: Timber and Logging

1. Oregon Timber Industry Contributions to President and the Republican Party. Research by George Draffan. www.commoncause.org (The figure includes soft money contributions)

2. www.whitehouse.gov/infocus/healthyforests/

3. www.nrdc.org/land/forests/qroadless.asp

4. www.latimes.com/news/opinion/commentary/la-oe-clinton4aug04,1,5014437.story?coll=la-news-comment-opinions August 4th, 2004 commentary by President Bill Clinton

5. Oregon Timber Industry Contributions to President and the Republican Party. Research by George Draffan.

6. Ibid.

7. *Meet Mark Rey: The Fox in the Hen House* by Brock Evans. www.nativeforest.org/campaigns/public_lands/rey_5_30_02.htm

8. *SuperCar: The Taking of an American Dream* by Sam Roe, *Chicago Tribune* staff reporter. An excellent, in depth three part special report that ran in 2002. www.chicagotribune.com/news/specials/car/one/chi-startingup-special,0,7249692.special

9. www.house.gov and www.senate.gov Phone numbers: White House (202) 456-1111, U.S. Senate (202) 224-3121, U.S. Congress (202) 225-1904, Senate switchboard: 1-877-762-8762

10. The Center for Public Integrity. www.publicintegrity.org

Chapter 7: Big Pharmaceutical and the FDA

1. www.opensecrets.org/industries/list.asp

2. *Bush administration ordered Medicare plan cost estimates withheld.* By Tony Pugh, Thursday March 11, 2004. Night Ridder Newspapers.

3. *Medicare Drug Benefit May Cost $1.2 Trillion* by Ceci Connolly and Mike Allen. *Washington Post*, Feb. 9, 2005; Page A-1. www.washingtonpost.com

4. www.whitehouse.gov/news/releases/2005/02/print/20050209-13.html

5. *Pfizer Cracks Down on Drug Importation.* www.pbs.org/newshour/updates/pfizer_08-07-03.html August 7, 2003

6. From a letter from Representative Dan Burton (R-In.) to the Secretary of Health and Human Services Donna Shalala, M.D. www.vaccineinfo.net/issues/mercury/vaccine_with_Mercury_recall.shtml

7. Read the Protecting America in the War on Terror Act of 2005. www.senate.gov The bill is S.3.IS

8. www.pbs.org/wgbh/pages/frontline/shows/prescription/hazard/independent.html

9. www.findarticles.com/p/articles/mi_m0815/is_2002_April/ai_84312121/print also see the Center for Medical Consumers web site @ www.medicalconsumers.org

10. Reporter and author Katharine Greider writes about the skyrocketing prices of drugs and the drug industries soaring profits in her book *The Big Fix: How the Pharmaceutical Industry Rips of the American Consumer.*

11. www.edwatch.org

Chapter 8: Agri-Business, Corporate Farming and the USDA

1. Center for Responsive Politics www.opensecrets.org/industries/indus.asp?Ind=A&Format=Print

2. www.cbsnews.com/stories/2002/05/13/politics/printable508765.shtml

3. www.mccain.senate.gov/index.cfm?fuseaction=Newscenter.Viewpork&Content_id=508

4. Comments by Bush about free trade from *The President of Good and Evil*, by Peter Singer, pages 126-27. Also see Bush's remarks at the signing of the Trade Act of 2002 at www.whitehouse.gov/news/releases/2002/08/print/20020806-4.html

5. www.oxfam.org The report titled *Rigged Rules and Double Standards, Trade, Globalisation and the Fight Against Poverty* is at www.maketradefair.com

6. www.cid.harvard.edu/cidtrade/geneva/cotton.html

7. Google Chronic Wasting Disease

8. A simple Google search of "Mad Cow" results in about 3 million hits. One article referred to often in the mad cow discussion is by John E. Peck, Executive Director of Family Farm Defenders, titled *The Mad Cows finally come home*. www.familyfarmdefenders.org

9. www.nffc.net

10. Secretary   of   Agribusiness   www.thenation.com/thebeat/ index.mhtml?bid=1&pid=2052

11. Ibid.

12. www.creekstonefarmspremiumbeef.com also see www. cloemannatural.com There are others. I buy from Coleman because I can get it near where I live, rather than ordering on the internet. www.pennvalleyfarms.com is another

13. *Government does mad cow kowtow*, by Edward Lotterman. *St. Paul Pioneer Press* www.twincities.com

14. *U.S. Officials Confirm Second Mad Cow Case*, by Marc Kaufman, *Washington Post*, June 11, 2005; A02

15. www.pcrm.org

Chapter 9: Banking and the Credit Card Industry

1. February, 2005 Harvard Study http://content.healthaffairs. org/cgi/content/full/hlthaff.w5.63/DCI

Chapter 10: Cheney's Play

1. Stock charting was accomplished using Telechart® 2005 software by Worden brothers, Inc. www.worden.com Reliant Energy (RRI) went public on May 1, 2001 and Peabody Energy (BTU) went public on May 22, 2001 and therefore was tracked from those dates. All other companies in the example were tracked from January 22, 2001.

2. www.usinfo.state.gov/products/pubs/oecon/chap4.htm

3. *Top 200: The Rise of Corporate Global Power*, by Sarah Anderson and John Cavanagh, Institute for policy studies. December 4, 2000 www.corpwatch.org/print_article.php?&id=377

Chapter 11: Tax Cuts; It's Your Money Right?

1.   www.whitehouse.gov/news/releases/2001/02/print/20010220-5.html

2.   *The incredible shrinking budget surplus* by John King. CNN.com July 4, 2001 http://archives.cnn.com/2001/ALLPOLITICS/07/02/shrinking.surplus/

3.   Tax data from the Center on Budget and Policy Priorities. Report titled Studies Shed New Light on Effects of *Administration's Tax Cuts* by David Kamin and Isaac Shapiro. www.cbpp.org/8-25-04tax.htm

4.   The full effect of Bush's tax cuts compiled by the Citizens for Tax Justice www.ctj.org/html/gwb0602.htm

5.   Discussion on the estate tax and its effects from Estate Tax Repeal: *A Costly Windfall for the Wealthiest Americans* by Iris J. Lav and Joel Friedman. Revised May 25, 2002 www.cbpp.org/5-25-00tax.htm

6.   From the Economic Policy Institute www.epinet.org

7.   *The Price of Loyalty*, by Ron Suskind pages 40-42

8.   For numbers on cuts to domestic programs, see www.cbpp.org/2-7-05bud3.htm

9.   www.factcheck.org/article144.html

10. www.medicalnewstoday.com/printerfriendlynews.php?newsid=19982

11. Bush's budget cuts for the VA are often topics of discussion at Operation Truth and Paralyzed Veterans of America as well as other veteran's groups. Operation Truth www.optruth.org was founded in June of 2004 by Army Reserve 1st Lieutenant Paul Rieckhoff after a one year tour in Iraq. He has created a forum for soldiers to tell their side of the story. These men and women are liberal, conservative, independent and a-political. It's not about ideology on this site, it's about them. Also see www.pva.org/newsroom/PR2005/pr05004.htm

12. *The President of Good and Evil*, by Peter Singer, page 27. Singer cites the Luxembourg Income Study website at www.lisproject.org

Chapter 12: Social Security Crisis? A Solution in Search of a Problem

1.   From the Social Security Administration www.ssa.gov/OACT/STATS/table4a3.html

2.   From a report titled *Management's Discussion and Analysis* by the Social Security Administration, page 11 www.ssa.gov/finance/2004/MDA.pdf

3.   Ibid. page 9.

4.   Senator Harkin's speech on the Senate floor on January 31, 2005 www.nosscr.org/harkin.pdf

5.   Bush speaking at Montgomery Blair High School in Silver Spring, Maryland in June 2005. www.whitehouse.gov/news/releases/2005/06/print/20050623.html The administration no longer uses the word "crisis" because it didn't play well with their focus groups. In his short speech before the question and answer session with his hand picked audience, Bush used the word "problem" 24 times, at one point three times in one sentence.

6.   The 2042 estimate by the Social Security Administration is at www.ssa.gov/OACT/TRSUM/trsummary.html The 2052 estimate by the CBO is at www.cbo.gov/showdoc.cfm?index=5666&sequence=0

7.   From the Bureau of Labor Statistics

8.   President's speech at West Virginia University at Parkersburg in April 2005.   www.whitehouse.gov/news/releases/2005/04/print/20050405-4.html

9.   Bush speaking at Montgomery Blair High School in Silver Spring, Maryland in June 2005. www.whitehouse.gov/news/releases/2005/06/print/20050623.html

10.   www.washingtonpost.com/wp-dyn/content/article/2005/05/13/AR2005051301376_pf.html

11.   The report on the effects of Social Security benefits pegged to inflation is titled *Just the Facts on Retirement Issues* dated January 2005. www.bc.edu/centers/crr/facts/jtf_14.pdf

12.   From the report by the President's Commission to Strengthen Social Security revised in March 2002. www.csss.gov/reports/Final_report.pdf

13. www.whitehouse.gov/news/releases/2005/02/print/20050216-3.html

14. The life expectancy statistics are from two reports from the Center for Disease Control (CDC). The first is from the Estimated Life Expectancy at Birth in Years, by Race and Sex: Death-Registration States, 1900-28, and United States, 1929-2002 Table 12 www.cdc/nchs/data/dvs/nvsr53_06t12.pdf The second is from Life expectancy at Birth, at 65 Years of Age, and at 75 Years of Age, According to Race and Sex: United States, Selected Years 1900-2002 www.cdc.gov/nchs/data/hus/hus04trend.pdf#027 Also see www.ssa.gov/history/lifeexpect.html Table 1

15. www.cdc.gov/nchs/data/hus/hus04trend.pdf#027

16. For a more detailed discussion of the mechanics of Social Security see the report by the Center for Retirement Research at Boston College www.bc.edu/centers/crr/facts/jtf_14.pdf

17. From the Congressional Black Caucus Foundation, inc. titled *Protecting and Strengthening Social Security's Value for Vulnerable Populations*. Testimony before the Committee on Ways and Means Social Security Subcommittee U.S. House of Representatives, May 17, 2005 http://cbcfinc.org/pdf/waysandmeans2.pdf

18. Speech at Montgomery Blair High School in Silver Spring Maryland, June of 2005. www.whitehouse.gov/news/releases/2005/06/print/20050623.html

19. www.whitehouse.gov/news/releases/2005/02/20050210-6.html#3a

20. Wall Street lobbying is From an AFLCIO report titled *Wall Street Links to Groups Attacking Worker Retirement Security* www.aflcio.org/issues/retirementsecurity/socialsecurity/wallstreetgreed/wsg_retirement.cfm

21. Ibid.

22. http://msnbc.msn.com/id/6746628

23. Goolsbee's report is titled *The Fees of Private Accounts and the Impact of Social Security Privatization on Financial Managers*. http://gsbwww.uchicago.edu/fac/austan.goolsbee/research/ssecfees.pdf

24. *The Politics of Social Security* by Jonathan Weisman. *Washington Post*, September 22, 2004; Page A02

Chapter 13: The Morals of Compassionate Conservatism

1. BCCI was the target of a Senate investigation by Senator's John Kerry and Hank Brown in 1992. BCCI was found guilty of corruption, fraud, money laundering, support of terrorism, obstruction of Justice and many other crimes. http://www.fas.org/irp/Congress/1992_rpt/bcci/22legrec.htm

2. www.forbes.com/global/2002/0318/047.html

3. http://en.wikipedia.org/wiki/Khalid_bin_mahfouz

4. From Corp Watch, July 2002 www.corpwatch.org/print_article.php?id=2988

5. Boston Globe, July 12, 2002 www.commondreams.org/cgi-bin/print.cgi?file=/headlines02/0712-06.htm

6. House of Bush, House of Saud, by Craig Unger. Page 123.

7. Ibid., page 124

8. Washington Post, July 30 1999; page A1

9. Garrett Morris, Saturday Night Live

10. From the Texas Observer, May, 1997 www.mollyivins.com/showMiscForPrint.asp?FileName=970509_fl.htm

11. Ibid.

12. Ibid.

13. *The Book on Bush, How George W. (Mis)leads America* by Eric Alterman and Mark Green, page 62

14. The article *The Texas Clemency Memos* by Alan Berlow appeared in the July/August 2003 issue of *The Atlantic Monthly*. Alan Berlow is a freelance journalist who writes frequently about death penalty issues. www.niemanwatchdog.org/index.cfm?fuseaction=showcase.view&showcaseid=008

15. Ibid.

16. Ibid.

17. *The President of Good and Evil* by Peter Singer, page 49

18. From the Death Penalty Information Center www. deathpenaltyinfo.org/article.php?did=412&scid=6

19. Ibid.

20. From CNN.com www.cnn.com/2003/LAW/01/11/illinois.death.row

21. *The Federal Death Penalty system: A Statistical Survey!988-2000* www.deathpenaltyinfo.org/article.php?scid=29&did=196

22. *Capital Punishment Commentary* by Alan Berlow. *Washington Post* February 21, 2000.

23. See note 14 above

24. www.humanrightsfirst.org/us_law/etn/misc/factsheet.htm

25. Abuse of Captives More Widespread, Says Army Survey, by Douglas Jehl, Steven Myers and Eric Schmidt. May 26, 2004 www. refuseandresist.org/article-print.php?aid=1388

26. http://en.wikipedia.org/wiki/Bagram_torture_and_prisoner_abuse

27. Ibid.

28. From Human Rights Watch. http://hrw.org/english/docs/2005/05/20/ afghan10992_txt.htm

29. The January 25th memo from Gonzales to the President can be read at http://msnbc.msn.com/id/4999148/site/newsweek

30. The 50 page memo can be read at www.washingtonpost.com/wp-srv/ nation/documents/dojinterrogationmemo20020801.pdf Section 5 beginning on page 31 makes the case that the Commander-in-Chief does not have to abide by the War Crimes Act or international law, and in fact such laws may be unconstitutional.

31. The March 6, 2003 memo released by the *Wall Street Journal* can be read at http://antiwar.com/rep/military_0604.pdf

32. If you must see some of the photo's, you can view them at www. notinourname.net/war/torture-5may04.htm

33. From CNN.com article titled *Government: Evidence gained by torture allowed* www.cnn.com/2004/LAW/12/02/guantanamo.detainees

34. Ibid.

35. *One Huge U.S. Jail* from the Guardian, March 19, 2005 www.guardian.co.uk/afghanistan/story/0,1284,1440836,00.html

36. Results of study by Peter Bearman PhD, sociology department chair at Columbia University and Hannah Bruckner PhD of Yale University for the *Journal of Adolescent Health.* www.medicalnewstoday.com/printerfriendlynews.php?newsid=21606

37. Ibid.

38. *The Content of Federally Funded Abstinence-Only Education Programs* prepared for Rep. Henry A. Waxman www.Democrats.reform.house.gov/Documents/20041201102153-50247.pdf

39. From the Centers for Disease Control. www.cdc.gov/hiv/pubs/facts/transmission.htm

40. Ibid.

41. www.cdc.gov/pubs/facts/condoms.htm

42. *Why Abortion Rate is up in Bush Years* by Glen Stassen and Gary Krane. www.chron.com/cs/CDA/printstory.mpl/editorial/outlook/2851283

43. *Pro-Life? Look at the Fruits* by Dr. Glen Harold Stassen. www.sojo.net/index.cfm?action=sojomail.display&issue=041013

44. *The Biography of a Bad Statistic* May 25, 2005. www.factcheck.org/printerfriendly330.html

45. *Berkeley High: A sex Ed Success Story* by Laura Lambert. www.plannedparenthood.org/pp2/portal/files/portal/webzine/newspoliticsactivism/fean-050127-berkeley.xml

46. Ibid.

47. Ibid.

48. From the Sexuality Information and Education Council of the United States (SIECUS). SIECUS public policy office Fact Sheet. www.siecus.org/inter/exporting_us_foriegn_policy.pdf

Chapter 14: Where Are We Going?

1. The 111 page report can be read at www.acq.osd.mil/dsb/reports/2004-09-Strategic_Communication.pdf

2. Ibid., page 35

3. Ibid., page 40

4. Ibid., page 36

5. Ibid., page 40

6. Study by the Program on International Policy Attitudes (PIPA) www.pipa.org/OnlineReports/Iraq/IraqPresElect_Oct04/IraqPresElect_Oct04_rpt.pdf

7. *Buying of News by Bush's Aides is Ruled Illegal* by Robert Pear. *New York Times* October 1, 2005.

8. The 111 page report can be read at www.acq.osd.mil/dsb/reports/2004-09-Strategic_Communication.pdf Wolfowitz's memo is found in Appendix A beginning on page 87.

9. Ibid., page 58

10. Ibid., page 4

11. Ibid., page 29

12. From the Columbia Journalism Review. www.cjr.org/tools/owners/ge.asp

13. Ibid., www.cjr.org/tools/owners/newscorp.asp

14. Ibid., www.cjr.org/tools/owners/clearchannel.asp

15. From CNN. *RNC tells TV stations not to run anti-Bush ads* March 7, 2004 www.cnn.com/2004/ALLPOLITICS/03/07/moveon.ads

16. Transcript of Keith Olbermann discussing the Brit Hume distortion of Roosevelt's speech with the grandson of FDR, James Roosevelt on MSNBC's *Countdown with Keith Olbermann* http://mediamatters.org/items/printable/200502160003

17. www.mediamatters.org

18. *Don't use FDR to undermine Social Security* by James Roosevelt Jr. *Boston Globe* January 31, 2005. www.boston.com/news/globe/editorial_opinion/oped/articles/2005/01/31/dont_use_fdr_to_undermine_social_security

19. www.usatoday.com/news/washington/2005-05-10-ridge-alerts_x.htm

20. The full 524 page report is at www.gpoaccess.gov/serialset/creports/iraq.html

21. www.freedomhouse.org/media/pressrel/042804.htm

22. The quote is often mistakenly attributed to Hitler's propaganda minister Joseph Goebbels, however was actually written by Adolph Hitler in *Mein Kampf*. The quote can be found in Volume 1, chapter 6, page 184.

23. *Nuremberg Diary* by Gustave Gilbert published in 1947.

24. Eisenhower's speech was broadcast on television and radio and can be read at www.eisenhower.archives.gov/farewell.htm

Post Script

1. http://dc.indymedia.org/newswire/display_printable/129182/index.php

2. www.gov.state.la.us/New_Stories_detail.asp?id=50

3. http://mediamatters.org/items/printable/200509120005

4. www.dotd.state.la.us/intermodal/transit/resource/providers.asp?parish=36

5. http://mediamatters.org/items/printable/200509120005

6. Ibid.

7. Ibid.

8. www.timespicayune.com

9. www.whitehouse.gov/news/releases/2004/09/20040906-1.html

10. *No Bankruptcy Relief for Katrina Victims* by Martin H. Bosworth Consumer Affairs.Com   www.consumeraffairs.com/news04/2005/katrina_bankruptcy03.html

The following publications and websites are alternatives to the 90% of the mass media owned by the "big ten."

- www.pbs.org/newshour

- www.salon.com

- www.slate.com

- www.thenation.com

- www.harpers.org

- www.americanprogress.org

- www.vanityfair.com

- www.commondreams.org

- www.crp.org (Center for Responsive Politics)

- www.counterpunch.org

- www.nrdc.org (Natural Resources Defense Counsel)

- www.mediamatters.org

- www.guardian.co.uk

- www.bbc.co.uk

- www.npr.org (National Public Radio)

- http://thehill.com

- www.capitolhillblue.com

Index

D

978-0-595-37774-9
0-595-37774-2